Prosper

An Insider's Guide to Investing in Off-plan Property

by Ashley Osborne

Published by Clink Street Publishing 2021

Copyright © 2021

First edition.

ISBN:
978-1-914498-66-4 - paperback
978-1-914498-67-1 - ebook

Contents

Introduction

People all over the world are fascinated by property. Many dream of owning an investment property or even a property portfolio and living off its income. But how many achieve this goal and retire early to pursue their ambitions? My guess is not many.

When it comes to buying property off-plan, the deck is stacked against small investors. Information and timing are critical to generating wealth, but access to information is out of reach for all but the privileged few. Without this information, small investors can't make fully informed investment decisions.

Small investors are often bombarded with fake news about investment opportunities crafted by those who have the most to gain by selling them. Overwhelmed by inaccurate and misleading information, most small investors make poor property investment decisions and ultimately pay far more than they need. In doing so, they are lining the pockets of property agents and marketing companies who prey on their lack of knowledge. It is not until the property completes that they realise they didn't quite get what they had hoped to buy.

The current market reality

When buying off-plan, small investors currently have little choice but to endure an antiquated system. Access to investment property takes place via the high-pressure property exhibitions that regularly take place in the world's capital cities, particularly in Asia and the Middle East.

Property development marketing through property exhibitions was an effective way to generate awareness in the early-2000s, at a time when investors' understanding of property investment was generally low, so international investment experts' presentations were a necessity. Time has moved on, investors are savvier, but property agents have just kept on running the same property exhibitions.

In the early 2000s there weren't many property exhibitions, but now there are thousands, and as competition has grown so has the cost. Ultimately, someone must pay the bill, and it is always the investor. Marketing through property exhibitions adds between $US 25,000 to $US 50,000 to the purchase price!

Not only are investors paying for market access, but they are also making decisions based on highly biased information produced by so-called 'property experts.' These experts generate vast quantities of market information designed to create a frenzied demand for property. Whether or not the investor gets a good deal does not come into the equation - the sale is all that counts.

A massive industry has grown on the back of the promotion and sales of the off-plan property market. Other industries have seen tremendous technological advancements, which have improved their processes and created tangible benefits for purchasers. However, the property market has remained stagnant and stuck in its old ways. Why is that? It is because there is little incentive for those in the property market to drive change.

A better solution

Investing off-plan can be highly rewarding. However, there is no magic negotiation tactic or shortcut investors can use to win. As a small investor, you win by understanding the market, grasping how it works, and by leveraging this knowledge.

With second-hand property, a unique product is for sale to a high number of buyers. Investing in off-plan property is different - developers are selling a ubiquitous product to a smaller pool of buyers. For investors buying off-plan, the shoe is therefore on the other foot!

As an investor, if you can recognise this market reality and understand the risks and costs associated with developing, promoting, and selling new development property, you can win by reducing risk for developers and leveraging the unique role you play in funding new development to your advantage.

How do I know?

I used to work on the other side. I built one of Asia's largest international sales businesses at Colliers International. I have worked with some of the world's largest residential property developers, promoting property to interested buyers.

During that time, I have been responsible for the sale of billions of dollars of real estate. I have seen both sides of the coin. I have seen savvy investors make wise investments and build valuable portfolios. However, I have also often seen investors making poor decisions based on insufficient information and ultimately paying the price. Either way, as the agent, we made a lot of money!

The stark reality is that most small investors get pressured into buying property off-plan at inflated prices. The inflated costs cover the enormous amount of money demanded by the off-plan sales industry to cover the cost of excessive marketing budgets, property company overheads, and the massive fees required to motivate those selling property. It's not personal; those who have the most to gain in the industry don't want to rip buyers off. They want to sell a property at the highest possible price, and get paid their fee!

However, the reality for investors is that there are huge costs involved. The cost of marketing and promotion alone can cost between 10% to 20% of the purchase price. These costs don't include the additional fees and taxes investors must pay to buy the property.

Why have I written this book?

After years of working in the chaotic new-build sales business, I saw a better way. I am passionate about the residential development industry. I genuinely believe that off-plan investors make a dramatic difference to the development of communities, and that they provide excellent quality new housing to rent to those who want to make their way in the world. Rather than being to blame for the terrible state of housing markets, buy-to-let investors actually help solve housing problems by providing developers with the ability to access the funding required to commence construction.

However, the industry is broken and in need of innovation and change. I believe there is a better way. Change must start by empowering investors with the information and tools they need to make better-informed investment decisions.

Instead of spending millions of dollars trying to convince investors that our property was better than a property promoted by the agent next door, what if we invested the time and resources in educating people about how the market works?

Increasing knowledge and transparency can reduce market friction and create a market resembling the stock market, where **all** investors have equal access to information, rather than just a privileged few.

With their new knowledge, investors would have the confidence to make better, quicker, more fully informed decisions. Better information would change the requirement for marketing gimmicks and reduce the cost of promoting property, and everyone would win:

- **Investors** would pay a lot less, improving their yield and boosting their ability to meet their objectives more quickly;
- **Developers** would spend less on promoting property and would be willing to pass part of those savings on to investors; and
- **Communities** would not suffer from the massive property price inflation driven by excessive market costs, which ends up being blamed on investors.

At Colliers International, I was constantly asked questions by people within our company about how various elements of the new-build market worked. The more I thought about this, the more I realised a significant knowledge gap existed between what investors thought they knew and what they actually knew.

Perhaps surprisingly, with all the resources of a large property agency, even I found it challenging to get the correct information. More concerning was that most of the available information is either biased or covers small market elements.

The objectives of this book are to give you industry insights and an understanding of the basics of large-scale residential development; to show you how agents and developers determine marketing values and how marketing campaigns work; and to give you the tools and knowledge to create as much leverage as possible when negotiating to buy off-plan.

There are many books about real estate investment, but few focus on investment strategies in the off-plan market. Even fewer are written by those who have walked the walk. I am a successful portfolio investor and worked at the highest levels within the residential project marketing industry. I want to give you the insights, knowledge, and ability to make informed investment decisions. *My overall aim is to help you to Analyse, Invest, and Prosper.*

Successful investors

I have noticed several different things about the winners and the losers in the off-plan property market in my career.

It was **the losers** who always seemed to buy a property with the herd. They bought late in a marketing campaign or late in the market cycle. They paid 20% more for the property than the winners. They did not give deep thought to the market or what they were buying. They just followed a sense that values would always be going up.

These investors believed the 'research' produced by large property agencies. Have you ever noticed that this research always seems to suggest that now is an excellent time to buy? No matter how bleak things look in the economy, the research always seems to find hidden diamonds in the rough which will, it is claimed, buck the trend.

When these new buyers tried to let their new property, they soon found out that it would not rent for what they had been promised. Not only was there not a queue of merchant bankers and doctors wishing to rent their flat, but the rents were about 20% less than expected.

The **investment winners** were different. They were sceptical and had formed their own views. They always had a sense of reality and knew when the right time was to buy.

These investors had some key things in common:

- **Access to high-quality market information:** Large property agencies thrive on making market data challenging to obtain. But how can you make a sound investment decision if you don't understand what a good deal is?
- **An understanding of the fatal error of paying today for tomorrow's growth:** As an investor, you need to be cognisant of what today's reality is and what risk you are taking. Most importantly, you need to know how you will share in the risk/reward equation.

- **An uncanny sense of the cost of excessive marketing campaigns:** Market access costs are the enemy of both investors and developers. Expensive brochures and substantial marketing campaigns are excellent ways for large agencies to increase their profile and line the pockets of those in the media industry. However, they serve no real purpose. They simply increase the cost of the property and ultimately dilute returns for investors.

- **A well-thought-out plan for buying and when they would get the maximum purchasing power from their capital:** Most investors do not have a plan. They buy real estate simply because it seems like a sensible thing to do – and often it is. But why are they buying, and to what end? Is it a long-term investment, or is it part of a broader plan to develop a portfolio? Are they buying for yield or capital appreciation? How should the property be owned? At what point in the development and market cycles is the right time to buy? These are essential questions that you must have the answers to before signing on the dotted line.

- **Strong networks:** These successful investors were in the market, and people in the property market knew who they were. That does not mean they were constantly buying – just that they had their fingers on the pulse. They understood that the most cost-effective way to purchase real estate is not via the open market. And the only way that they could avoid the open market is if the people in the market selling property knew who they were and how to contact them. The agents knew that they could go to these people early in the sales and marketing campaign (when the best deals get done) and sell to these people quickly and quietly because they knew they would buy – at the right price!

- **Clever ways of buying a lot of property at once:** This is the most important factor. The investment winners got their friends and networks to pool together and leverage the economies of scale they could create. As a developer or as an agent, there is nothing better than de-risking your marketing expenses by doing early deals, especially if they are large, even if this means you need to agree a considerable discount.

I have developed these investor behaviours into **6 Investment Principles**, which all successful investors follow in their buying and market activities:

1. **Have a plan:** They have a clear plan for why they are purchasing a particular property and how it fits into their long-term strategy. This plan empowers them in negotiations as they understand the impact of a decision on their plan, and more importantly, when to say no to a deal.

2. **Get market information:** They have access to high-quality market data and make decisions based on economic reality rather than the highly biased property agency research reports.

3. **Have a network:** They have strong professional relationships and networks, they nurture them over many years, and they use them as a sounding board to sense check decisions.

4. **Understand mis-priced risk:** They have a detailed understanding of how the development cycle works, and more importantly, where the pain points are for developers; they leverage these to create win/win deals where they will have a better share in the risk and reward equation.

5. **Recognise excessive market access costs:** They understand the actual cost of overly expensive sales and marketing campaigns. They do not buy via these, because they realise who ultimately pays for them – the purchaser.

6. **Buy in bulk:** They find clever ways to leverage economies of scale created through buying in bulk. This may be easier to do than you first imagine.

How this book works

This book has five parts, each designed to take you through the off-plan property market and to help you develop your own property investment strategy. At the start of each part, I set out the key considerations. In order not to overwhelm you with information, each has its own chapter. At the end of each part, a recap crystallises the significant takeaways. The structure is as follows:

- **Part 1: New-build Market Fundamentals:** What are the fundamental principles behind the new-build property market? How does residential property development work?

- **Part 2: Purchase Price and Costs:** How are properties priced, and how do you get to the bottom of how to consider purchasing costs?

- **Part 3: Purchase and Operational Considerations:** What should you be thinking about when you purchase property, both today and from an operational perspective?

- **Part 4A: Financial Performance:** How do you measure and compare the potential financial performance of different investments?

- **Part 4B: Driving Financial Performance:** How do you improve the financial performance of your investment?

- **Part 5: Your Property Investment Strategy:** How do you bring all this information together to put together your investment strategy?

In the book, I have focused on the apartment market rather than houses. The simple reason for this is that my opinion, buying apartments makes more sense for most first-time investors.

Throughout this book, I have referenced the following fictional example, based on real life, to give you a true sense of how the market operates.

Location: Metropolis

Metropolis is a real town, but for obvious reasons I have changed some of the details. I have referred to Metropolis throughout the book to put different scenarios into context.

After many years of being seen as a bad part of London, Metropolis is currently undergoing urban renewal. The catalyst for this was the economic growth experienced by many of its neighbouring suburbs. Metropolis has not experienced as much regeneration as its neighbours because it had a run-down housing estate (Metropolis Estate), which has always been considered rough. Recently, a prominent developer has purchased the Metropolis Estate with a plan to redevelop it.

Metropolis is five miles northwest of Oxford Street. It has a busy local high street as well as a London Underground Station. Adjacent to the Metropolis Estate is a parcel of land available for a new residential property, Kingsley Tower. I have used Kingsley Tower as an example throughout the book.

Developers

I have used two developers to highlight how different developers view different scenarios.

Ashley's Homes

Ashley's Homes is a private developer run by two brothers, Kingsley and Alfred. Ashley's Homes are local in Metropolis and typically build complex buildings of up to 250 units. They have a small management team and some key staff. They always act as developer, and outsource most of their work - including planning, construction, and sales.

Alfred and Kingsley use their own capital to purchase land and then use construction finance to fund the development. When they do not have enough money to buy land, they can call upon a group of investment partners to invest in their development projects.

Osborne Corporation

Osborne Corporation is a prominent, listed developer; it employs 5,000 staff across the United Kingdom. Osborne Corporation comprises 30 business units, each with its own independent management team led by a managing director. Osborne Corporation is listed on the London Stock Exchange, and it develops 20,000 homes a year across the UK. Osborne Corporation has its own construction staff; in some scenarios it self-builds with these in-house staff, while in others it appoints a main contractor to build the development.

Osborne Corporation uses its shareholder funds and debt to fund its business and developments. Capital for development is allocated to managing directors on a project-specific basis. When a managing director wants to undertake a project, they submit a standard pro forma document to the Board of directors. The CEO and CFO decide which development projects they would like to proceed with, and allocate the required level of capital to the managing director.

Potential buyers

I have presented a potential purchase in Kingsley Tower from the perspective of two buyers: one investing onshore, and one offshore:

- **Buyer 1:** An investor in the UK who earns £50,000 per year and is buying an investment property to rent out; and
- **Buyer 2:** An investor who does not live in the United Kingdom and generates no other income in the United Kingdom from any additional investment(s).

I have explained what the cash flow and tax implications are from owning an investment property.

I have also set out how that investment would change if Kingsley Tower were in Australia or New Zealand. I have adjusted the currencies to make similar comparisons, so the investment can be compared across different tax brackets.

I have used Australia, New Zealand, and the United Kingdom in my comparison, for multiple reasons:

- **Income tax rates:** The income tax rates and the effective tax rates for someone earning £50,000 p.a. or the equivalents in Australia and New Zealand are similar.

Table 1.1: Effective income tax rates

	Australia	New Zealand	United Kingdom
Annual Salary	$AUD 100,000	$NZD 100,000	£50,000
Income Tax	$AUD 22,967	$NZD 23,920	£12,366*
Net Take Home Pay	$AUD 77,033	$NZD 76,080	£37,634
Effective Tax Rate	22.97%	23.92%	24.72%

* includes National Insurance

- **Residential real estate markets:** The market dynamics of the three countries' real estate markets are similar. They all have established rental markets, and similar laws.

Table 1.2: Residential real estate markets

	Australia	New Zealand	United Kingdom
Levels of Home Ownership	65.5%	63.2%	63.5%
Gross Rental (Major Capital City)	3.97%	3.86%	2 – 6%
Estimated Annual New Housing Requirement (Major Capital City)	41,200 p.a.	10,000 p.a.	66,000 p.a.

- **Real estate taxes:** Australia, New Zealand, and the UK differ significantly in their taxes for real estate investment and ownership. They therefore provide a great example of how tax treatment affects the net returns derived from an investment, and how this can inform your investment strategy.

Table 1.3: Real estate taxes

	Domestic Investors	International Investors
Australia	Low cost for ownership and long-term hold	High purchase taxes and lower taxes for long-term investment
New Zealand	Low cost	Low cost
United Kingdom	Moderate cost for purchase, average tax costs to sell, and expensive to hold from an income tax perspective	Moderate cost to purchase, average tax costs to sell, and can be expensive to hold from an income tax perspective

Whether a country has low or high real estate taxes for a specific market function is not necessarily an issue in itself. However, it is crucial to understand what real estate taxes are in order to design your investment strategy with them in mind.

Throughout this book, I go through each of the different real estate taxes as they relate to property investment in a market context, and give you strategies to deal with different scenarios.

Further information

Alongside this book, I provide online content. I maintain a series of country and investment guides that provide information on more than just Australia, New Zealand, and the UK, the countries which form the focus of this book. These guides are FREE, and are available in my investor library alongside my regular blogs at: **www.proptechpioneer.com**

PART 1

New-Build Market Fundamentals

You cannot make an informed investment decision without a fundamental understanding of the new-build market. Therefore, your journey must start with what the real estate market is, how it works, and what drives it.

Most people have a specific idea of what the residential real estate market is. However, very few give a much thought to real estate and what drives its value. What is it which gives one property a higher value than another?

To successfully invest in new-build property, you must understand what drives value, and how the residential development process works. Therefore, Part 1 of this book covers the basics:

- **Real estate market:** What is the real estate market, and how does it work in practice?
- **Residential development:** What is residential development, what is the process, and how does it work? Why do you need to understand this? Because you cannot effectively negotiate with a developer unless you know what risks they face. You negotiate the best deal by overcoming and reducing these risks.

These fundamental concepts are the foundation for your overall understanding of how you can prosper through the purchasing and investment process as an off-plan investor.

CHAPTER 1

The Real Estate Market

When people talk about real estate, they are typically talking about its characteristics. These are physical, institutional, and economic characteristics. People trade real estate in the abstract; they trade based on what it can provide from a combination of these characteristics, rather than the physical thing.

Physical characteristics

Many of the physical characteristics of real estate are immediately evident. However, others are less so.

- **Land:** Its location, size, the views it provides, exposure to sunlight, and other environmental features are usually evident from a simple visual inspection of the land. However, land also has other, equally important features. The load-bearing capability of the soil impacts its value, but is not known without investigation. Other factors such as soil contamination from harmful elements also affect land value, but cannot be understood without expert investigation. The value of a parcel of land depends on the costs involved in making the land productive, and whether it is profitable to do so. Additionally, the value is impacted by whether other parcels of land could deliver the same reward at lower cost.
- **Improvements:** To realise the full economic benefit from land, improvements need to be made on or to it. Some of these improvements will be obvious, such as buildings and structures. However, others will be less obvious, like drainage, filling, clearing, levelling, and other modifications which will help to improve its future economic utilisation.

Institutional characteristics

Land also has institutional characteristics - these are the rights that run with it, how local laws affect how it may be used, and how it is taxed.

In most European countries, the institutional characteristics flow from the tenurial system in which landed property is held. The tenurial system stems from feudal law. Feudalism was a combination of legal, economic, military, and cultural customs that existed in medieval Europe. Feudal law is a political system that placed a country's inhabitants under a hierarchical structure, which granted superior rights to lords and vassals (a person regarded as having a mutual obligation to a lord or monarch). A principal feature of this system was its way of structuring society around relationships derived from the holding of land in exchange for service or labour. The right to all land was vested in the sovereign.

A transaction in land does not deal so much with the physical thing itself; it is more about the legal rights that run with it. This system is known as the tenurial system. In common law, land tenure is the legal regime under which land is owned by an individual, who is said to 'hold' the land. The land tenure defines how access is granted to it, the rights to use it, control it, and transfer it, as well as other associated responsibilities imposed through its ownership. This system determines who can use the land, for how long, and under what conditions.

Land tenure is typically categorised into:

- **Private:** The assignment of rights to a private party who may be an individual, a married couple, a group of people, or a corporate body such as a company;
- **Communal:** A right may exist within a community where each member of the community has a right to use the holdings of the community independently;
- **Open access:** Specific rights are not assigned to anyone, and no one can be excluded; or
- **State:** Property rights are assigned to an authority in the public sector.

The highest form of ownership under which real estate can be held under common law is a "Fee Simple Absolute" in relation to an estate in land. If you think of the individual rights that could be granted to a parcel of land as a bundle of sticks and each of the sticks represents a separate right, then a Fee Simple Absolute represents land ownership as a bundle containing all of the sticks. The Fee Simple Absolute is often referred to more simply as freehold ownership.

To keep things simple from now on, I will refer to 'fee simple absolute' as a *freehold* interest in the land. This freehold interest infers a series of rights and powers, such as:

- **Use rights:** Rights to use the land for a series of purposes;
- **Control rights:** Rights to make decisions on how the land should be used;
- **Transfer rights:** Rights to sell or mortgage the land, to convey the land to others, to transmit the land to heirs through inheritance, and to reallocate use and control rights.

It is through exercising these rights that developers and investors create various inferior interests granted to other parties, through which they can drive economic value. Importantly, the absence of some of these rights will mean either that value can be impacted, or some type of development cannot take place, which is why a lawyer (conveyancer) is needed to act on your behalf when you purchase a property. Some of these rights and obligations are obvious; however, others are not. It is the job of the conveyancer to undertake detailed investigations into the property to ensure that the interests being inferred to you as an investor are what you had envisaged.

Economic characteristics

In addition to its physical and institutional characteristics, land has economic characteristics.

Immobile

Real estate is immobile, in that it cannot be moved. This has several implications:

- **Users:** The pool of users for it come from a small and defined geographic location. The property cannot be moved to a market where there is greater demand from users, or where users are more affluent.

- **Inhomogeneity:** No two parcels of real estate are the same. Even if all other characteristics of two parcels of land are identical in all respects, their location is not.
- **Income:** This is derived from a fixed location. A user of real estate will only pay for the benefit it provides in a specific location.

The immobile nature of real estate has several consequences. First, there is a thin trading market for property. It is difficult to obtain a significant amount of data from sales transactions to determine value. Therefore, it is difficult to create an index for trading property which is similar to a stock exchange. By comparison, if you trade two separate parcels of 1,000 shares in a company on a stock exchange, those two parcels are identical.

Because real estate is immovable, its value is driven by its position relative to other things which drive value. For example, suppose you take two identical properties, one adjacent to the sea front and one several streets away. In that case, all other things being equal, the one adjacent to the sea front will have greater value than the other, because the 'nearness' of the property to an amenity is what drives its value.

You will have no doubt heard the saying "Location, location, location"; it comes from a quote:

> *Since value depends on economic rent, and rent on location*
> *and location on convenience, and convenience on nearness,*
> *we may eliminate the intermediate steps and say value*
> *depends on nearness. The next question is, nearness to what?*

Richard M. Hurd

It is this 'nearness' that drives value rather than location specifically.

Large economic units

The purchase of real estate entails the outlay of large sums of money. In a study undertaken in the UK by the Office for National Statistics (ONS) in 2018, the average cost of buying a home was 7.77 times the average gross annual income. Australia and New Zealand have similar rates, of 7 and 8.5 times respectively. This limits the market not only to those with the desire to buy - but, equally importantly, those who can raise the funds to do so.

Durability

Land is regarded as indestructible. When the value of buildings on it declines for whatever reason, the land always remains. This is referred to as its *residual value*. For this reason, an insurance valuation for a property only considers the replacement value of the buildings rather than the value of the buildings with the land. This is because no matter what happens to the building, the *land will always remain*.

Scarcity

Land is a finite resource, in that its physical supply is limited. Because land is scarce, there is generally competition for it. Its scarcity and the competition for it determines its value.

Land by itself is unproductive

For land to be productive, the application of labour, capital, and management to it is required. These factors of production need to be combined in the property if its most profitable use is to be realised.

The real estate market

The purpose of a market is to arrange for the production and exchange of goods and services. A market acts to enable producers and suppliers to determine the level of production. Price is the mechanism within a market that determines how much a given producer is willing to supply, and how much a consumer is willing to demand.

As prices vary in a market, their level sends signals to buyers and sellers, who modify their behaviour accordingly. *Both buyers and sellers will always act in a self-interested way.*

A perfect market

If a market is thought to be a 'perfect market' then it has several features, which include:

- Many buyers and sellers.
- High levels of transactions.

- Both buyers and sellers being in possession of sound technical knowledge of the goods or services they are trading.
- Both buyers and sellers being able to enter or leave the market at will.
- Pricing determined by competitive bidding.
- No cost to move goods and services to and from the market.
- All transactional information freely available to those who wish to participate in the market.

Under these market conditions, all market participants are only ever likely to agree on one price for a given good or service. If a good or service were to be bought and sold at a different price, then this would be considered a non-market price or an 'outlier'. There would likely have been other reasons why the buyer and seller bargained at a different price.

Many people compare the concept of a 'perfect market' to the stock market. A stock market is a highly organised market with rules, regulations, and procedures which are rigidly enforced. The reason these rules and regulations are so tightly enforced is to create a deep secondary market. Investors are willing to purchase shares after they have been issued to the initial buyer because their value is maintained. A stock market exists so that shares can be created by corporations to raise finance, and these interests can be traded.

Shares are traded on an exchange, which bridges the distance between buyers and sellers. Documenting a sale is a simple process, which can be done quickly. One of the primary objectives of the stock exchange is to provide a high level of information and research to investors. This helps to create confidence in the market.

Many of the differences between the stock market and the real estate market are obvious. In the real estate market:

- The market is far less organised than the stock market.
- Buyers and sellers are physically separated, and real estate agents have evolved to facilitate transactions.
- Information relating to historic transactions is difficult and costly to obtain, making it hard to study historic market trends.
- Buyers typically trade infrequently, and are therefore relatively uninformed.
- The transfer of ownership following a transaction is a complex and expensive process.

- The price is harder to determine and is typically a range of values based on assumptions, because the market involves the trade of multiple inhomogeneous products by participants who are not fully informed.

New-build property market cycle

Like all markets, the new-build property market moves in cycles. A combination of the demand and supply for property and the market inefficiencies and performance of the broader economy drives the new-build residential real estate.

The new-build property market cycle can be broadly categorised into four market phases. The point in the cycle dictates how much a participant is willing to buy or sell a new-build property for.

Figure 1.1: New-build market cycle

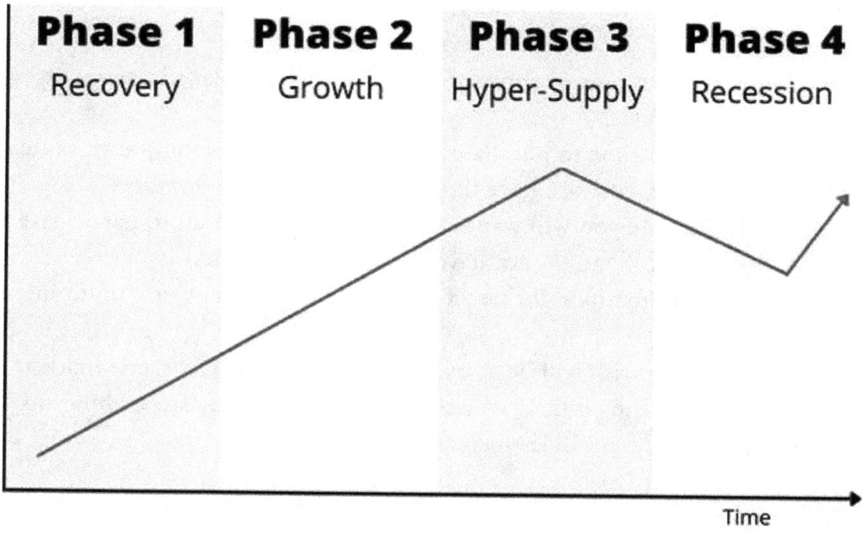

| **Phase 1** | **Phase 2** | **Phase 3** | **Phase 4** |
| Recovery | Growth | Hyper-Supply | Recession |

Time

Phase 1: Recovery

The recovery phase is the first phase of the market cycle, and it follows a recession. During this point in the cycle the demand for housing is low, and there may be significant amounts of vacant housing. At this point, residential real estate prices are low.

The important point to recognise is there is no magical switch that can be turned on as the market moves from recession to recovery. It is a gradual process, driven by economic sentiment. Some people may feel the economy is recovering, while others still feel the economy is in recession.

Indicators you should look for:

- Home sales and letting rates will still be low;
- Housebuilding will be at low levels as developers will be unwilling to create an oversupply of new housing which will impact the price at which they can sell;
- Interest rates will be low;
- Media coverage will be largely negative and will forecast future declines in pricing;
- Developers will be pursuing long-term land (sites that require planning permission to develop).

Opportunities for you to consider:

- This is typically a great time for you to borrow to take advantage of low-interest rates.
- This is a good time to purchase a property that offers long-term value - as an investor, you will have the greatest negotiation leverage.
- This is the time you will want to be liquid; it is difficult to participate in the market if you do not have the cash to purchase.
- 'New-build premium' for new housing will be at the lowest point in the cycle.
- Purchase price risk will be at its lowest point in the real estate market cycle - this is the point at which you will have your greatest ability to recover from 'poor' investment decisions.

There are also some risks you need to be aware of:

- Vacancy rates for property will be high.
- Tenants will have a lot of choice and rents will be at their lowest point in the cycle, so you need to be conscious of your ability to pay your mortgage from rental income.
- It will be more difficult for you to obtain a mortgage, and banks will require a higher deposit to arrange one.

Phase 2: Growth

The market will start showing signs of growth. The broader economy will be growing at this point, the number of jobs will be growing, and incomes may also be growing as the economy recovers and new jobs are created. Economic growth will increase demand for housing, which will increase tenant demand, thus putting pressure on the small pool of rental properties available. This is the point in the cycle at which the construction of new housing increases. At this point in the cycle, investor activity will be high.

Indicators you should look for:

- Home sales and leasing activity will increase.
- House prices and rents will increase as demand increases and supply remains relatively low.
- Construction activity will accelerate.
- 'Trading' in the secondary market (second-hand property) will be high.
- There will be a general feeling of optimism within the economy and a general confidence of better times ahead.
- Developers will be buying development sites that are 'oven ready' which they can develop quickly and bring to market for immediate sale to take advantage of market conditions.
- The 'new-build premium' will expand.

Opportunities for you to consider:

- Interest rates will remain low and lending terms will begin to loosen.
- If you have an existing property, this is a good time to re-finance as the equity in your portfolio will have increased and you can lock in at lower interest rates.
- There are likely to be opportunities for new development, re-development, or acquiring properties where you can add value.

Risks you need to be aware of:

- Overpaying for property, as at this point in the cycle investors can easily get carried away with unrealistic growth expectations.

- Over-extending with leverage, as many investors will take on too much debt at this point in the cycle.
- New property will be sold based on 'future price growth' prospects.

Phase 3: Hyper-supply

At this stage in the cycle there will be a tipping point from a balanced supply to an oversupply of housing. In other words, the residential property on the market outstrips demand. This will have a moderating impact on prices, and house price growth will slow down.

At this point, new construction begins to slow. However, there is already a significant amount of 'committed work' which will flow through the system and further increase supply. Prices will typically peak at this point in the cycle, before seeing a decline.

Indicators you need to look for:

- In the development market, there will be a significant number of development sites which are on the market but are not yet sold, as the gap between landowner aspiration and developer risk appetite grows.
- There is an oversupply of housing – where supply exceeds demand, and prices stop growing and may decline.
- Rents remain high, but demand for rental property declines.
- There tends to be overconfidence in what the market is delivering, and developers are typically unwilling to discount on asking prices.

Opportunities for you to consider:

- If you are thinking of selling a property, now is the best time to do so.

Risks you need to be aware of:

- This is a bad time to buy, as there will still be a significant amount of confidence in the market. Good investors will recognise the warning signs.
- The 'new-build premium' will be at its highest point in the cycle.

Phase 4: Recession

During a recession, businesses may close and unemployment rates will rise. Ultimately, the property market will hit the bottom of its pricing at this phase in the cycle. Some investors will become financially stressed, and some will go under at this point in the cycle, because of over-exposure to debt.

Indicators you should look for:

- House prices decline as will rental rates.
- Demand for housing will decline.
- Some businesses will close down.
- Spending will slow as people lose economic confidence.

Opportunities for you to consider:

- This is a good opportunity for you to purchase from distressed sellers.
- When people sell at this point in the cycle, they typically do so because they need cash.

Risks you should be aware of:

- Not having sufficient liquidity or capital reserves could be your downfall if you are overextended.

Length of the market cycle

You will often hear people refer to the length of the market cycle. People will talk about the market moving in a 7-year cycle or an 18-year cycle. The reality is that there is little evidence to support any definitive time period; it is simply true to say that the market moves in cycles, and that those cycles have the characteristics set out above.

The easiest way for me to demonstrate this to you is to show you the average house prices in the UK for new-build property between 1960 and 2020.

Figure 1.2: UK Nationwide House Price Index 1960–2020

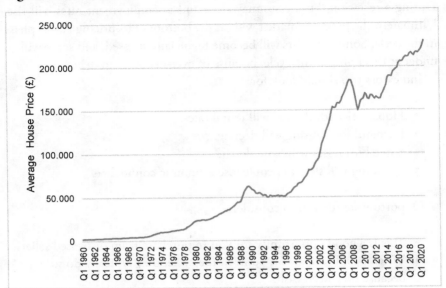

Now, let's look at what happened. How long did it take for UK house prices to double?

Table 1.1: UK average time for house prices to double

Quarter	Q1, 1960	Q1, 1970	Q2, 1973	Q1, 1979	Q1, 1986	Q2, 1999	Q1, 2005	Q4, 2020
Price (£)	2,189	4,378	8,832	17,793	35,647	70,010	140,225	N/A
Quarters	-	40	12	22	27	52	18	67
Years	-	10	3	6	7	13	5	17

Over the past 60 years in the UK, it has taken between three years and 17+ years for house prices to double. There is little to show in terms of a pattern in time in which the market moves.

And guess what? It does not matter how long the market cycle is. You are never going to identify the absolute bottom of the property market cycle. And even if you could, would you wait for years to buy a property just because you wanted to buy at the bottom of the cycle?

The most important thing is to understand that the market moves in cycles, and to recognise what point of the cycle you are in, and bear this in mind when you are buying.

New-build premium

I have referred to a 'new-build premium'. New homes typically sell at a premium compared to second-hand properties. There are several reasons for this, including:

- They are more modern and have newer features, such as freshly installed bathrooms and kitchens, while second-hand properties tend to be more dated and generally require capital to be spent on them to bring them up to date;
- New homes are more efficient and have lower running costs;
- New homes have insurance that protects buyers against defects;
- Some new-build properties have amenities such as gyms and other facilities which owner-occupiers are willing to pay more for; and
- There is less risk regarding major defects which may occur over time, such as subsidence or termites, etc.

Market factors

Many countries have schemes specifically designed to help first-time buyers get on to the housing ladder. This means that first-time buyers have more capacity to pay more for new-build property, as they can borrow more money.

How does it work?

The new-build premium is not a fixed amount; it is simply a premium that shifts with the market cycle:

- As the **economy expands**, demand for property increases. As demand increases, prices increase, and so does the new-build premium.
- As **demand decreases** and the market contracts, developers must either lower their prices to sell property or build less property in order not to create a glut of new property in the market. However, it is not possible for developers to simply turn off the supply. So, they must reduce their prices to sell. As prices reduce, so does the new-build premium.

The easiest way to demonstrate the new-build premium is to use the UK Nationwide House Price Index – it tracks average prices for both new and second-hand properties. Over the past 60 years in the UK, the average new-build premium has fluctuated from between 32.8% in 1982 to virtually zero (0.22%) in 2010.

Figure 1.3: UK Nationwide House Price Index, new homes and second-hand, 1960–2020

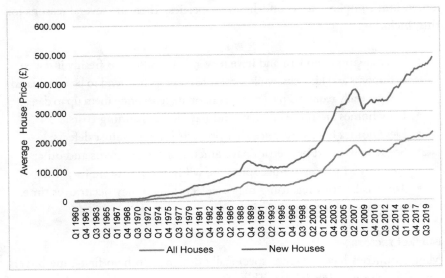

Figure 1.4: UK Nationwide House Price Index, new-build premium, 1960–2020

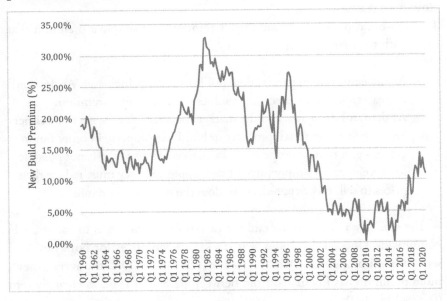

Highest and best use

Because of the characteristics of real estate and market inefficiencies, real estate will not always be employed at its optimal economic value, giving rise to the concept of Highest and Best Use.

Highest and best use is a term generally used in property valuation. It is defined as:

> *The reasonable, probable, and legal use of vacant land or an improved property, which is physically possible, appropriately supported, financially feasible, and that results in the highest value for an estate.*

All real estate will theoretically be employed at its highest and best use. However, it does not always necessarily follow that this happens immediately. Several things may prevent this from happening:

- **Existing user:** The most common example is that a tenant is in situ and has an unexpired lease term for the property. In some cases, this may be for a long time. Therefore, a developer cannot simply gain 'vacant possession' of the land to re-develop it.
- **Rights granted to a third party:** Sometimes rights are granted to a third party, restricting the re-development of the site. Commonly, these are in the form of restrictive covenants, rights of way, easements, or rights of access.
- **Not economically viable:** In some cases, the total cost of buying the land, obtaining the necessary building consents, demolishing the existing improvements, and building a new building is greater than the income which will be generated through the sale of the new development.
- **Planning and building consents:** It takes a considerable amount of time and capital to obtain consent for a new building, and it is not necessarily obvious in advance what will be permitted on a parcel of land. Developers must therefore invest time and money in designing schemes in association with various professionals to come up with a scheme acceptable to the relevant local planning authority.

- **Land is not large enough:** Sometimes a parcel of land is simply not large enough to accommodate a large enough building. Therefore, a 'site assembly' may be required to create a large enough parcel of land to cope with the footprint of the building which maximises value. In this situation, a developer needs to purchase adjacent parcels of land in order to create one larger parcel of land to develop.
- **Lack of infrastructure:** Not having mains water, power drainage, access, and/or links to roads or transport means that it may simply not be cost-effective to develop a scheme.
- **Unwilling seller:** There is no requirement for the owner of a parcel of land to do anything with it. Just because a profit could be generated by developing it, this does not mean that it must be done. Development sites often float in and out of the market through many market cycles before eventually being sold and developed.

Real estate lifecycle

Except for very few cases, built improvements on the land have a lifespan. Ultimately, the improvements on the land are wasted, either economically, physically, or functionally. When this happens, the land will be redeveloped. Theoretically, it will be redeveloped into its Highest and Best Use.

This process is described as the *Real Estate Lifecycle*.

Figure 1.5: Real estate lifecycle

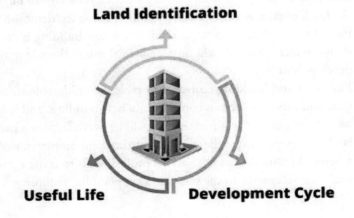

Land identification

All residential development has one thing in common, land. You cannot build a building without having somewhere to put it! The first stage of development is to identify a parcel of land.

Rather than starting with a vacant parcel of land, most development involves taking a parcel of land with existing improvements such as an office building or industrial building, then demolishing it and developing a new building on the land. Typically, developers will look for existing buildings where the land is not being utilised at its Highest and Best Use.

Development cycle

The developer assembles a team of development professionals to plan what type of development is to be delivered. This consists of several core activities:

- **Planning permission and/or relevant development consent:** A developer must develop detailed development drawings and make a formal application to the relevant authorities for the rights required to develop the land.
- **Construction:** The new buildings and improvements must be physically constructed.
- **Sales and marketing cycle:** The new building will be promoted and sold to its new owners.

Useful life

The building will perform the function for which it is designed. The longer that this process can be extended, the greater the return relative to the initial cost. Eventually the improvements on the land will become obsolete; this could occur for several reasons, including:

- **Changes in taste:** People simply no longer wish to use the site for its intended purpose; for example, if the main employer in the town closes down, people may not want to live there anymore because of the limited employment opportunities.
- **Dilapidation, wear, and tear:** Buildings age due to several factors, including the environment, movement to the soil, the weight of the structure itself, changes in materials and laws (asbestos and cladding), new technologies, external environmental factors, and general wear and tear through use

- **Changes to planning laws:** As cities expand and grow, zoning and intended uses can change.
- **Retail:** With the rise of internet shopping, how retail space is used is changing fast. This has led to large areas of vacant shops on urban high streets, as they are simply no longer economically viable due to reduced footfall.

For whatever reason, other than in some unique circumstances, this process will take place and the development cycle will begin again.

Who's who in the new-build market

Many players operate within the new-build market. Who are they, and what are their roles in the development of new residential housing?

Landowners

Landowners are the initial building block of any new development. No new development can take place without land. People and companies own land for a variety of reasons, the most common of which are:

- **Self-use occupiers:** Parties who own a parcel of land to use it themselves, whether to operate a business or have their home on the land.
- **Governments, utilities & public bodies:** These are large owners and occupiers of land. Some of this land is utilised to its full capacity, while other parcels of land may not be being used, or may be significantly underutilised.
- **Investors:** They own potential residential development sites, because they believe there is long-term value in speculating on what may be developed on the land in the future.
- **Developers:** They own land which they intend to develop in the short term. However, many also have significant land holdings, known as *land banks,* which they hold to have a supply of land which can be developed in the longer term.

Regulatory bodies

Most regulatory bodies relating to real estate investment are either government bodies or have their powers granted by central governments:

- **Governments** set laws and regulations relating to real estate, including ownership and the operation of land rights, as well as laws relating to how construction work should be procured and delivered.
- **Planning authorities** set guidelines for residential development, and assess and preside over applications for new developments.
- **Central tax authorities** impose taxes on land and its transfer, as well as taxes on the newly developed asset.

Developers

When people use the term 'development', they generally mean constructing a new building. In practice, development covers a much broader area of improvements, from obtaining permission for development, to building a scheme or undertaking a refurbishment program.

Purchasers

Numerous parties purchase property throughout the development cycle. They can generally be categorised into the following groups:

- **Owner occupiers:** One of the key characteristics of owner-occupiers is that they will generally be more willing to pay the highest amount for the property being developed. This is because they usually consider its perceived use as having greater value to them.
- **Government & social housing providers:** In most developed economies, governments have an obligation to provide housing to their most vulnerable citizens. Many do this through social housing providers; these social landlords buy new housing and provide this accommodation to their residents.
- **Institutional landlords:** Often referred to as being part of the 'multifamily' or build-to-rent market, institutional landlords are large investors such as pension funds, who invest capital on behalf of their shareholders to generate income from the long-term ownership of residential property. These investors own the whole asset, and assume

responsibility for managing the asset and generating income from rentals and providing additional services to their tenants.

- **Professional landlords, family offices:** A professional landlord is distinct from an institutional landlord in that they rarely own or control the whole building.
- **Buy-to-let investors:** A buy-to-let investor purchases residential property to generate a return, whether for capital appreciation or to generate income, or a combination of both.
- **Underwriters:** Underwriters are a group of purchasers who are rarely discussed or understood by the mainstream market. Underwriters sit between the developers of residential assets and purchasers. They purchase large allocations of residential property from a developer, thereby accepting the developer's sales risk, and then sell the property at an increased price.

CHAPTER 2

Residential Development

As an investor, you need to understand the development process. By doing so, you will gain insight into how you can leverage your position to get the best deal when purchasing.

What is residential development?

It is important to have a broad definition of what development is, as this will give you a much better idea of what drives value in the residential development process.

Development is not simply just the process of building something. You need to think of development as improving a parcel of land so it can be better utilised for residential use. This is an important distinction, because many companies obtain planning consent for residential development but do not physically build anything. These developers simply sell the parcel of land with the benefit of this work having been undertaken.

The reason it is important to think of this as 'residential development' is that value has been created through this process, and the developer will realise a profit for these activities. The value of the house or apartment being built has not changed, and therefore neither has the total available 'profit' which is achievable through the development process. In simple terms, the profit is being split between this developer and the next developer who physically undertakes the construction works.

I define development as:

> *The process by which an individual or company undertakes improvements to a parcel of land to generate profit from residential users who will utilise the improvements which have been made to the land.*

45

What is a developer?

You need to think of a developer as a company that produces something for sale. Like any other company, they simply create products, like Toyota makes cars or Apple makes computers. They take assets, land, and building materials, and employ human resources to build a building, which they then market to potential buyers and sell at the highest price possible. In this process, they seek to minimise their costs and maximise the sale price to increase their profits.

Think of development in terms of Figure 2.1.

Figure 2.1: Commercial considerations for developers

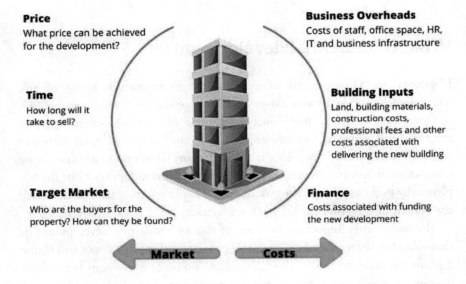

Price
What price can be achieved for the development?

Business Overheads
Costs of staff, office space, HR, IT and business infrastructure

Time
How long will it take to sell?

Building Inputs
Land, building materials, construction costs, professional fees and other costs associated with delivering the new building

Target Market
Who are the buyers for the property? How can they be found?

Finance
Costs associated with funding the new development

Market **Costs**

Types of residential developers

It is important to understand who the different types of developers are, and what each of them does, to help you to develop your buying strategy when negotiating with them. If you understand what drives them, you will understand what is important to them - and what is not.

Developers are categorised by the role they undertake, the type of product they develop, and the scale of development they undertake:

- **Land promoters** take large parcels of land through the planning process to get the locations considered for residential development. They do not build on the land; instead, they sell it with the added benefit of planning consent.
- **Estate developers** purchase large parcels of land and sub-divide them into more manageable parcels of land. They sell these smaller serviced parcels of land to other developers.
- **Institutional developers** undertake large-scale developments, usually in city centres or large urban areas. Generally, they develop tall and complex buildings which have multiple uses, not just residential.
- **Residential developers** develop sites within inner cities and prime central locations. They generally do not develop other types of property, focusing solely on residential development. Residential developers typically outsource construction work. I characterise a residential developer as a company that produces more than 2,000 properties p.a.
- **Small and medium sized developers** are nimble and will generally try to offer clever deal structures to landowners to encourage them to sell to them rather than another developer. These may include joint venture arrangements, or a share in the profit generated by the development. Small to medium developers ordinarily build more than 500 but less than 2,000 properties annually.
- **Housebuilders** build houses as their primary function. They may build other forms of development, but most of their income is derived from the sale and development of houses. Housebuilders build high volumes of housing, and derive their competitive advantage by developing large parcels of land, using a limited number of different designs, and creating economies of scale through the volume of housing they develop.
- **Small builders** typically have specific types of development which they specialise in. These are generally focused on small geographic areas. Small builders generally build developments themselves, rather than sub-contracting construction. Small builders do not have the capital or internal resources to undertake multiple developments at once.
- **Housing authorities & not for profit developers** are specific types of developers who receive their authority from the government. They go by a variety of different names; however, regardless of their name, they all exist for the same purpose, which is to provide low-cost housing

to residents and act as a form of 'wealth sharing' across economies. To occupy, rent, or own this type of property, residents need to meet specific requirements which vary from country to country.

- **Development managers** (DMs) are not strictly developers as such. DMs facilitate development on behalf of their client. A DM is a company or person with specific skills and knowledge of development which they will employ on behalf of their client to undertake development. A DM is employed either by a landowner or an investor to facilitate a new project for them.
- **Build to Rent (BtR)/multifamily developers:** BtR is relatively new in many cities around the world, but has existed for many years in the United States, where it is called multifamily housing. The difference between BtR and other residential investment properties is that they are owned by a single investor. Some developers build for the BtR market and sell developments to investors, while others develop property specifically for their use.

Basic financial model of a development project

Below, I have set out a basic residential development in terms of the cash flow it generates. I have simplified the cash flow to make it easier to understand. However, from an accounting perspective, the model below is not realistic because there are differences in terms of when costs are recognised from a cash and an accounting perspective.

Kingsley Tower consists of 100 apartments. Let's assume the following:

- Development time - 3 years
- Average Sale Price - £500,000
- Land Costs - £15 million
- Construction Costs - £15 million
- Construction - paid in three annual instalments of £5 million each
- Sales - 50 p.a. in years 2 & 3

In this simple example, I have not taken into account any financing costs, or any other costs associated with the development. Nor have I considered any timing differences from a collection of cash perspective.

Table 2.1: Kingsley Tower, simple development model

		Year 1	Year 2	Year 3
	Income			
	No. of units sold		50	50
Line 1	Gross Sales Revenue		25,000,000	25,000,000
	Costs			
	Land	(15,000,000)		
	Construction Costs	(5,000,000)	(5,000,000)	(5,000,000)
Line 2	Total Costs	(20,000,000)	(5,000,000)	(5,000,000)
Line 3	**Development Profit** *(before tax)*	**(20,000,000)**	**20,000,000**	**20,000,000**

The project generates a net income of £20,000,000 that is calculated by subtracting land and construction costs of £30,000,000 from a gross income of £50,000,000. Therefore, the development has generated a development profit of £20,000,000.

When thinking about development and undertaking financial modelling, developers will refer to a Gross Development Value, or a project's GDV. The GDV is simply the total income realised in Line 1 of the model above, i.e., the forecast gross income of the sum of all the apartments, together with any other items sold such as car parks or commercial space produced by the development.

Development projects

First, you need to know that there are different financial considerations for a developer and a development project:

- **Developer:** A business in its own right; it has costs and overheads just like any other business, and it seeks to generate income greater than its costs to generate a profit. It does this by undertaking development projects.
- **Development project:** A financial entity. You should view it as a financial project – it is a series of costs and incomes over time that generates a profit by developing a specific parcel of land.

How a developer manages the financial interplay between their costs and revenues, depends on the type of development they do, the level of risk involved, and their sources of capital.

A development project is a separate legal entity created to develop a parcel of land into a new residential development. This legal entity will ultimately be broken up into a series of smaller legal entities which will be sold (i.e., the new homes or apartments).

Developers generate returns by managing their costs. Among these costs are the overheads to run their business. The profit, referred to as *development profit*, is the return a developer seeks to:

- Account for the capital they have put 'at risk' to employ staff and operate premises, etc.;
- Pay overheads to purchase land; and
- Cover their finance costs, the costs of building materials, and professional costs associated with building and selling the development.

Development profit and the profits of a developer are not the same thing. The profit a developer generates is the income less costs they achieve from undertaking a series of different developments – which all generate an individual development profit. The development profit is an outcome of the development itself, so while it can be assumed or 'guesstimated', it will not be known until the end of the project.

Development is a series of risks

Development is more complex than the simple model outlined above. Development is a series of risks. The developer manages these risks to deliver the development profit.

The developer's development profit is the 'GDV' less the cost of the risks associated with developing and selling the development. Think of it like this:

Gross Development Value, *less*

- **Land risk:** Cost of buying the land
- **Planning risk:** Cost of obtaining consent
- **Construction risk:** Cost of any demolition works and building a new building

- **Sales risk:** Cost of marketing and selling the development
- **Finance risk:** Cost of the capital employed for the development

= Development Profit

So, the model can then be re-adjusted to that shown in the following table:

Table 2.2: Kingsley Tower, development cash flow

		Year 1	Year 2	Year 3
	Income			
	No. of units sold		50	50
	Gross Sales Revenue		25,000,000	25,000,000
	Less			
	Marketing Costs (5%)		(1,250,000)	(1,250,000)
	Sales Costs (3%)		(750,000)	(750,000)
Line 1	**Gross Income**	0	23,000,000	23,000,000
	Costs			
	Land	(15,00,000)		
	Planning Costs (2% of Construction Costs)	(300,000)		
	Construction & Overhead Costs	(5,000,000)	(5,000,000)	(5,000,000)
Line 3	**Gross Costs**	**(20,300,000)**	**(5,000,000)**	**(5,000,000)**
	Cumulative Debt (50% of Total Capital Employed) *	10,150,000	12,650,000	15,150,000
	Finance Costs (5% of Capital Borrowed)	(507,500)	(632,500)	(757,500)
Line 4	**Development Profit** (before tax)	**(20,807,500)**	**17,367,500**	**17,242,500**

* For simplicity, I have assumed that none of the debt is extinguished until the end of the development.

You will notice that with the addition of all these costs, the developer's income has fallen from £20,000,0000 to £13,802,500.

This is a simple model to illustrate the process, but of course the reality is far more complex and would also consider the following:

- **Accounting differences:** From an accounting perspective, the income would not be recognised at the same time the cash was spent;
- **Debt:** Would be extinguished throughout the development process.

Developers constantly battle to acquire land and take it through the planning process, build the development, and sell it as quickly as possible at the highest price possible to generate the highest possible profit. In going through these steps, the developer manages a series of risks to achieve their profit. So, therefore:

- The more a developer underestimates those risks, the more it will cost to build the development and the lower their total profit will be.
- The better a developer can manage those risks, the lower their costs, and therefore the higher their total profit will be.

So, how do these risks work? It is important to understand that there are risks associated with the project itself, and then there are also all the other risks companies have to manage in owning and operating their business.

Land risk
Buying land for development incorporates several elements which need to be considered and managed.

Existing landowners
Land which is likely to be developed for residential use is generally held by companies or individuals for specific purposes, and many of these are not residential uses. When negotiating to purchase land, developers need to consider the needs of the existing owners.

Alternative locations
Many landowners use their land for the operation of a commercial enterprise. If they sell their land and plan to continue trading, they will have to find an alternative location. Often, a developer will have to assist the owner to find an alternative location to relocate to.

Major asset

For many landowners, the land is one of their largest assets. Understandably, they want to ensure that they are maximising its value when they come to sell it. Many owners watch several market cycles before they sell their land to a developer, so that they can be confident they are getting the best possible deal.

Many developers and agents track land sites for many years, staying in regular contact with the landowner to maintain a relationship with them. They do this to be there at exactly the right time when the landowner decides to sell.

Site assembly

Many parcels of land are small, and do not easily lend themselves to residential development on their own. In this scenario, a developer will need to undertake what is referred to as a 'land assembly' by linking two or more parcels of land together to create a greater density of development from one larger parcel of land.

Planning status

Land can be purchased with three specific different types of planning status:

- A site not allocated for residential development;
- A site without specific planning consent;
- A site with specific planning consent.

From a development perspective, there is a risk attached to taking a site through the residential planning process. Just because a developer wishes to develop a certain type of building on a parcel of land, it does not necessarily follow that the local planning authority will grant that application.

Planning authorities and residents may typically respond negatively to a development because of the following arguments:

- It causes disruption.
- It changes the local area.
- New residents moving to a location will have an impact.
- Additional stress and strain will be put on the local infrastructure. In many cities and countries, the public infrastructure is already under tremendous strain.

Site risk

Most developers will tell you that most of the risk associated with development is under the surface of the ground. This is because it is difficult to know what is below the surface until they start digging (groundworks). Some of the issues which may arise from groundworks are:

- **Site contamination:** The land is contaminated, and remedial works are required before construction can take place. In many situations, the extent of the remedial works will not be known, and until this is known it is difficult to determine what the cost will be.
- **Soil substructure:** The load-bearing capacity of the soil will be a major factor in the depth of piling, foundations, and works required for basements, all of which will have a significant impact on the cost of construction. Whilst it is possible for a developer to undertake soil tests, it is virtually impossible for them to effectively cover the whole site.
- **Archaeological issues:** It is not uncommon for groundworks to uncover various archaeological issues. Dealing with these issues in the soil can add both significant time and cost to construction projects.

Market competition

Competition is another consideration and thus another form of risk for developers. Land is a scarce resource, so when parcels of land are available for sale which lend themselves to residential development, competition from other developers is highly likely.

It is not uncommon for developers to find themselves in a bidding war with other developers to purchase land. Developers can purchase land via various methods, including:

- **Unconditional purchase:** Simply buying the property outright and accepting all the risk associated with the land;
- **Option:** Agreeing an option to purchase the land subject to several things happening, the most common being obtaining a planning consent or undertaking a land assembly;
- **Subject to planning:** Agreeing to purchase a site subject to obtaining a planning consent; or
- **Purchasing with planning consent:** Purchasing a site with an existing planning consent which has been achieved by the landowner.

There are costs associated with bidding on a parcel of land, and a significant amount of work is required in bidding to purchase a site. Developers typically need to go through several rounds of bidding and interviews to purchase land. It may therefore take several months to go through the bidding process.

In determining to bid on a development site, developers need to consider how much work will be required to formulate a bid, and estimate the likelihood of being successful. In undertaking this work, the developer will undertake a residual land value calculation, which involves determining what they believe they can build on the land, and the collective sale price of its components. This is referred to as its **Gross Development Value** (GDV), and they will then make their best estimates of the following:

- Cost to get planning permission
- Cost to demolish any existing improvements
- Cost to build a new building
- Cost to market and sell
- Cost of finance
- Their expected profit from the development

The net result will be the Residual Land Value, which is therefore how much the developer can pay for a site – assuming their assumptions are correct. The lower they pay for the land, the more profit they will make (all other things being equal), and likewise the more they pay for the land above the residual value, the lower their profit will be.

There is a significant risk for developers that if miscalculate the sales prices for different parts of the development or the costs involved in the development, they could pay far too much for the land. If this happens, the development may generate a loss rather than a profit.

Planning risk
The content of a planning application varies between countries; however, their purpose is the same everywhere: to obtain the consent required to construct a new residential development.

Most planning applications broadly have the same content, and the intention is to provide as much detail as possible about what is proposed to be developed and how the new development will impact the local economy, infrastructure, and environment.

I have set out an overview of the English planning process to give you an understanding of the process a developer needs to go through to obtain planning consent. The English process is one of the most complex planning processes in the world, so in other countries, it is usually either similar or less complex.

National Planning Policy Framework

A National Planning Policy Framework (NPPF) sets out the government's planning policies for England and how these are expected to be applied. The NPPF states that:

> *The planning system should be plan-led. Succinct and up-to-date plans should provide a positive vision for the future of each area and a framework for addressing housing needs and other economic, social, and environmental priorities.*

Local Plans are prepared by the Local Planning Authority (LPA), which in practice is usually the council or the National Park authority for the area. Once the LPA has prepared a local plan, it must be submitted to the Secretary of State, who will appoint an inspector to carry out an independent examination. This process is dealt with by the planning inspectorate.

Local Plans set out the strategic priorities for the development of an area. They set out policies that cover housing, commercial, public, and private development, including transport infrastructure, together with protection for the local environment. They comprise a series of documents that should clarify what development will and will not be permitted in a specific area.

The objective of the Local Plan is to plan for the development and infrastructure communities need, setting out the strategic priorities for the area. This should include priorities to deliver housing (including affordable homes), as well as other key infrastructure to meet local demands.

Land will be designated as one of the following:

- For residential development;
- For mixed-use (including residential) or *sui generis* (Latin for "of its/his/her/their own kind, in a class by itself", therefore unique);

- For an alternative form of development, such as industrial, retail, or commercial; or
- Not designated for any specific use.

For parcels of land already designated for residential development, the developer will simply make a planning application for residential development. However, for land which either has consent for an alternative form of development or has no development consent at all, the developer needs to apply for a change of use to the Local Planning Authority (LPA). This process can be extraordinarily complex, and can take many years.

Planning applications

Planning applications for residential development can be achieved through two forms of application: either a Full Planning Application or an Outline Planning Application.

Full planning application

A Full Planning Application, often referred to as a detailed planning application, allows a developer to start construction once it has been granted. Essentially, the developer can implement everything that was agreed in the full application unless there are conditions that need to be meet (discharged) as part of the grant of consent.

Full planning applications must include full detail of what is to be built, including access, the layout of the site, siting of the buildings with full plans, and elevations of all buildings. Highways and drainage details are also required. Full planning applications are always required for developments situated within a Conservation Area.

If the principle of development is unlikely to be an issue, it is more cost-effective and saves time for the developer to submit a full planning application. However, when development is more controversial, or the development will take several years to complete, or it will be constructed in several phases, it will be more difficult to justify the expense of a full planning application.

The following is the process with a full planning application:

1. **Formal planning application:** A formal planning application is submitted to the LPA with relevant information for consideration.

2. **LPA validate application:** The LPA will validate the application confirming its receipt of the application and relevant information required.
3. **LPA consultation:** The LPA will consult with various stakeholders including the Environment Agency (EA), the Police, etc., to understand the impact of the proposed development on the surrounding environment and economy.
4. **Determination:** The LPA then has a 13-week period in which to review and determine the planning application and either reject or approve it.

Planning applications can be determined by either of the following:

- The Planning Officer – under specifically designated powers; or more often, by
- The Planning Committee.

Once approval has been determined, the developer receives a Resolution to Grant Planning Approval. This is not a formal planning approval; it is merely an intention to grant a Planning Consent. Generally, this will be subject to several conditions being satisfied, referred to as 'Planning Gain'. Planning gain is the amenity that is provided to the local council in exchange for giving the developer consent to develop the property. It can typically include social housing, new infrastructure, and taxes and levies. These are all costs incurred by the developer which will reduce their overall development profit.

Outline planning application

Outline Planning Applications are typically used for larger, more complex developments, where the scheme is likely to be developed over a longer period, or where the developer is looking to establish whether residential development will be granted for a site.

Outline planning applications must include enough detail for the LPA to evaluate the proposals, including the scale and nature of the proposed development. An outline consent allows the developer to gain assurance that development will be accepted in principle. However, an outline consent is not permission to build; it is simply the establishment of an outline for the broad parameters of a residential scheme on the land. Essentially, the outline permission has established the principle of residential development on the land.

An outline planning application allows fewer details about the proposal to be submitted. Once outline permission has been granted, the developer will need to obtain specific approval of the details ("reserved matters") before they can start work on site. These details will be the subject of a "reserved matters" application at a later stage.

Where outline permission has been granted, a developer has three years from the outline approval to make an application for the outstanding reserved matters, i.e., to provide the information excluded from the initial outline planning application. This will typically include information about the layout, access, scale, and appearance of the development.

Risks associated with obtaining a planning consent

Developers must weigh up a series of risks in order to determine the best course to obtain planning approval. Local Planning Authorities are seen as highly inconsistent in the way they respond to planning applications, and rarely meet their own proposed timelines to process planning applications.

The primary risks associated with the planning process are in the following areas:

- **Determining what to build:** What the planning authority is likely to accept in terms of a building; how big, how much of the site is covered (the footprint of the building), and its height all impact how much new space can be built, and therefore the income it will generate. It is up to the developer to design a building that maximises the site, is financially feasible to build, and will be liked both by the planners and the local community.

- **Time:** Planning can take a long time to achieve, even though the guidance sets out that the LPA will determine a planning application within 13 weeks. The reality is that they rarely meet this timeline. Various reports have been published on housing delivery in the UK to speed the process up, but for all these pages of research, little has been achieved. Effectively, the time required to obtain planning permission for a new development has increased. The following were noted regarding the time required to obtain planning permission for developments with more than 20 homes:
  - **The Callcutt Review:** Between 1.8 to 2.6 years.

- **Molior:** The average time taken to achieve planning consent in London is 497 days, with the longest recent application recorded taking 1,612 days.

- **Rejection:** Making a planning application carries no guarantee that it will be successful, and that development can take place. Many applications are unsuccessful, which presents a developer with three options:
  - Go through a costly and lengthy appeal process which may or may not be successful.
  - Amend the proposed development scheme, most likely to reduce the size of the development and therefore the volume of houses it can provide. This will reduce the GDV which can be generated, which means that without reducing the land cost (or other costs) the profit will be lower.
  - Abandon the application altogether.

- **Cost:** The planning process can require many experts and some level of control over a parcel of land. This can be a highly costly process, and is subject to many risks.

Construction risk

How construction works around the world is similar. The primary difference between countries is the terminology used to describe various processes and building methodologies.

The process of residential development construction incorporates three core phases, which I now explain.

Phase 1: Construction design

Planning permission will set the parameters for the external envelope of the building, its height, and size, how it looks, and what external materials it is constructed from. However, it does not include detailed technical drawings of how the building will be physically constructed.

Construction documents (blueprints) are drafted to provide contractors with a series of detailed and technical documents which act as a set of instructions to construct the building that has been designed. These construction documents also include the selection of interior finishes, plumbing fixtures, appliances, and light fittings. This phase is where an architect and consultants work through the technical aspects of development.

By the end of the construction design phase, a complete set of technical documents will have been created to provide detailed instructions for contractors on how to carry out their work. These will include:

- **Site plan:** A drawing that sets out the location of the building(s) on the site.
- **Floor plans:** Drawings of each floor showing the size and location of various rooms and fixtures.
- **Elevation drawings:** Drawings that detail buildings sides to convey conceptual design detail.
- **Key details:** Large-scale drawings of specific elements within the project.
- **Key sections:** Building cut-through drawings depicting the heights and relationships of the various floors and roofs.
- **Outline specification:** A written description of the project's major systems and its materials.
- **Interior elevations:** Drawings setting out the materials of the interiors.
- **Reflected ceiling plans:** Drawings of the ceilings, highlighting the locations of lighting and equipment.
- **Interior schedules:** A list of the type and location of interior finishes.
- **Consultants' drawings:** Including structural, civil, and mechanical drawings setting out the locations of building services, such as the locations of drains, electrical supply, water, and telecommunication services.

Phase 2: Site preparation and groundworks

To get a site ready for construction, demolition and site enabling works need to take place as well as groundworks:

- **Site preparation: demolition and site enabling works:** These works include the demolition of any existing buildings located on-site, together with site enabling work such as the diversion or disconnection of site services, geotechnical and decontamination work, as well as excavating any obstructions.

- **Groundworks:** Groundworks are the work done to the land to prepare it for construction. Groundworks are generally the first stage of a construction project, and may include:
  - **Ground investigation:** Ground investigation of the land is generally carried out to help identify past land uses, stability, and potential problems. These investigations allow data to be accumulated and used for design as well as to deal with any potential issues, such as ground contamination or other issues in the ground. A ground investigation typically includes geology, hydrology, hydrogeology, soil condition, and contaminated land issues.
  - **Site clearance:** As part of the initial preparatory works, the land will need to be cleared and the topsoil taken up from the area below the footprint of the new structure. The depth will depend on the 'lay of the land' – if the site slopes, the ground may also need to be levelled. Retaining walls may be required to create level development platforms to build upon.
  - **Substructure and ground stabilisation:** The substructure is all the work below the underside of the concrete floor, and significant work can be required to the land to stabilise it in order to give it the load-bearing capacity to cope with the new building.

- **Services:** Site services may include drainage and other utility connections. Complex sites may require specialist tunnelling or shaft sinking solutions to enable service ducts and cabling to be installed. Existing services such as water and electricity cables may also need to be altered.

- **Landscape:** Earthworks may be undertaken to remodel the site, including the creation of hard landscapes such as asphalt.

Phase 3: Constructing the building

Once the land has been cleared and made ready for construction, the building needs to be physically delivered. This is a process referred to as construction procurement.

How the three construction phases are brought together is largely down to how the construction works are procured, in what is referred to as a Procurement System. The Procurement System is an organisational system that assigns responsibilities and authority to different people and companies. It also defines the different elements of the project.

Procurement Systems are typically categorised into three core systems:

- Traditional;
- Design & Build; or
- Management Contract.

Essentially, the type of system which is used will allocate how much risk is borne by the developer, relative to how much is passed on to contractors. The level of risk which is outsourced will impact the cost of the construction.

Traditional procurement

In the traditional procurement process, the design and construction work are separated out. Consultants are appointed to work on design and cost control, and a contractor is responsible for carrying out construction work; this responsibility extends to all workmanship and materials, and includes work by subcontractors. The contractor is typically appointed by a competitive tendering process based on complete information.

One of the major drawbacks of the traditional process is that it can take a long time to deliver a building. This is because the process uses a two-stage tendering process whereby the construction contract cannot be tendered until the design work has been tendered and completed, as the tender documents are required for the contractor to tender their bid.

Design and build procurement

With a design and build contract, the contractor accepts responsibility for the design of the new building, accepts liability, and vouches for their fitness for the purpose intended. In the tender process, the developer's requirements will be provided in a detailed document setting out the required specifications. Generally, the contractor's input will be restricted to the developer's scheme design.

One of the major advantages of the design and build methodology is that it is possible to quickly start work on site. And, because the contractor is responsible for both design and construction, they can generally create programming efficiencies. However, a drawback of this process is that making changes to the program once it has been agreed can be costly.

Management contract

Several forms of management procurement exist - which include management contracting, construction management, and design and management. There are subtle differences between these procurement methods. In the case of management contracting, the contractor has direct contractual links with all the works contractors, and is responsible for all construction work. In construction management, a contractor is paid a fee to professionally develop and manage a program, and to coordinate the design and construction activities.

Factors influencing the procurement strategy

The type of procurement strategy a developer uses will be influenced by several factors, including:

- The in-house resources the developer has;
- The size of the project;
- How likely they will need to make changes during the design; and
- The time required to deliver the project.

Risks associated with construction

Many things could potentially go wrong throughout the construction process, from issues found in the soil, the escalating cost of building materials, to individual contractors going bust.

Developers need to evaluate and weigh up all of these risks while they are looking at sites to determine what can be built, how much it will cost, and what it can be sold for.

Sales risk

This is the risk over which you as a purchaser will have the greatest influence, and which will ultimately form part of your buying strategy. I go into considerable detail about these risks in Chapter 5: Sales and Marketing Campaigns. However, below, I explain sales risk from a developer's perspective.

Price risk

From a sales and marketing perspective, the greatest risk that a developer faces is price risk. Real estate is an inhomogeneous product, and the market is highly inefficient. There is no set market price for each apartment, and the developer will have to make an informed decision on pricing based on market evidence.

Because the product which they are selling does not yet exist, a developer can only look at other comparable properties in the market to see how much these properties have sold for, and then draw comparisons between their proposed development and past sales to conclude what their development units might sell for - or more realistically, what range of prices they should sell for.

However, this is more challenging than you may think, as it is difficult to get information about sales values in the new-build space. This is because there is a long lag between the time a sale takes place (exchange of contracts) and the time that this sale is registered with the relevant authority, due to the timing involved in construction. Most new-build property is sold off-plan; typically it takes 18 – 24 months to build a property, and then there is usually a lag between practical completion and registering the sale.

Additionally, prices are 'headline prices' rather than net pricing. That is to say that the sale recorded with the relevant authority will register the time of the sale and the sale price itself. However, it will not take into account any incentives offered to the purchaser to entice them to buy. These may be contributions towards stamp duty, costs paid towards legal fees, and other items such as furniture packs that will not be registered against the transaction.

A developer relies on the following sources when developing their pricing strategy:

- **Cost basis:** This is the most straightforward way a developer can develop a pricing strategy, by which they simply develop a package with the known cost of the inputs, land, construction, and sales costs, then add their anticipated margin (development profit) which will deliver them a net cost (book value). They will then add a dealing margin for negotiations.

- **Direct comparison:** By reviewing real estate sales data, a developer will be able to build a picture of historical sales and use this information together with their interpretation of market movements (up, down, or stable) to extrapolate where their pricing should be.

- **Competition:** By reviewing their competition, developers will typically look at all of the competition in the market to review competing schemes and how they compare. Generally, product types are very similar, i.e. number of bedrooms, size, and features (most bathrooms and kitchens are virtually identical across all new-build stock within a given product category). So, they will most likely draw a comparison between different attributes, such as:

- Quality of specification – how does the specification compare to a competitor?
- Property Features – balconies, car parking, outside space, etc.
- Building amenities – gyms, concierge, clubhouses, etc.
- Distance to amenities relative to competitors
- Distance to public transport relative to competitors
- Distance to transport infrastructure relative to competitors

In reviewing these attributes, the developer will conclude what their pricing should be.

- **Market view:** Developers will also consult with property agents to determine their view of the value of the development in the open market. Developers will typically speak with many domestic, large, and small property agents who are active in that market to get their view of pricing. This will typically involve the developer sending a package of imagery and design plans to property agents and requesting their advice on how these units may be promoted, and in what price range.

However, the issue is that there is an opportunity here. The agent will be looking to be appointed by the developer to market the development. So, they are likely to overprice the development rather than talk it down.

Product risk

The building itself consists of a certain volume of apartments, accommodation types, specifications, accommodation amenities, and building amenities. If you break this down to each of the specific elements, these are not necessarily all within the overall control of the developer.

- **Unit mix:** A developer will decide what to develop, which will usually include a mix of one, two, three, and four-bedroom units, together with affordable housing (if required). In some markets the unit mix will be down to the developer, and they will simply take this market risk. However, in other markets such as the UK, the local authority will dictate what the unit mix will be. Before going to the market, it is virtually impossible to precisely determine how deep a market may be for a certain type of product.

- **Specification:** One of the easiest ways for a developer to differentiate their product in a crowded market is through specification. The specification refers to the quality of internal fittings within the building, such as the quality of tiling and sanitaryware in bathrooms, the type and quality of kitchen equipment, heating and cooling, floor coverings, window treatments, wardrobes, and more recently, the technology. There is a risk that the developer creates a specification which the market will not be willing to pay more money for, which would create obvious cost implications.

- **Amenities:** Amenities are used by developers to differentiate their development in a crowded market. These include accommodation-specific items such as balconies and outside space, and development-specific items such as gyms, cinema/media rooms, pools, concierges, etc. Working within the relevant development guidelines, the developer will make a series of judgments about the balance of development features and amenities required, and at what price point.

Marketing campaign risk

From a specific development perspective, the risk to the developer occurs in several different areas:

- **Incorrect price and product risk:** Regardless of their sales and marketing campaign quality, if a developer cannot get buyers to believe in its pricing, then the only effective way they will have to achieve sales is to discount to meet the market.
  Additionally, the developer may simply not have their product mix correct relative to the size and depth of the market. For example, a developer builds a project with an extremely high level of studio apartments, but there are simply not enough buyers for studio apartments in the market at that time. Again, the options available to the developer will become limited as they attempt to drive and achieve sales.

- **Getting the market wrong:** With the changing nature of global markets, developers will typically plan out detailed sales and marketing campaigns that involve releasing their project to multiple markets. In doing so, they will make assumptions about what customers in these markets are looking to purchase. In some scenarios, the developer may simply find that buyers in that market may not like the location of its project.

- **Materials don't attract the right type of buyer:** Developers invest a significant amount of capital in marketing materials and sales campaigns. A common theme has been for marketing material to feature glossy images of downtown locations and amenities, which in reality are miles away from the actual location of the development, or indeed have nothing at all to do with the location of the scheme.

- **Pre-sales risk:** In most scenarios, the developer will need to achieve a certain pre-sales target to commence construction of the building. These targets will generally be set by lenders, and will be a pre-condition to draw down the funding used to pay contractors. Or, in the case of larger developers, they may simply need to meet internal sales targets in order to take the risk required to build.

- **Timing of sales:** In many scenarios, particularly for larger developers, the timing of sales will be very important. Larger listed companies will be concerned with their financial reporting, in terms of the company reports they deliver on quarterly days, their half financial year, and their end of financial year. The impact of these key metrics is important to their overall financial reports, and therefore their share price. If they cannot report positive sales results, this will impact the market perception of their financial performance.

- **Campaign costs:** Sales and marketing campaigns are extremely expensive (as is covered in the next section). Developers typically spend hundreds of thousands of dollars on marketing campaigns, and this can reach millions of dollars if the campaign includes international sales. If a developer spends a significant amount of money on a marketing campaign and does not achieve enough sales, this will significantly impact the overall cost of selling the development.

Market risks

Several risks also exist for developers during the sales and completion period.

- **Economic risk:** Sales and marketing campaigns extend over a long period, typically 12 – 18 months; larger schemes will be even longer. With the coronavirus pandemic, the UK's Brexit referendum, the Global Financial Crisis, and other key economic events it is easy to see that significant risks can unexpectedly change the economic conditions for residential property. This may mean that developers simply have to change their marketing strategy by focusing on investors rather than owner-occupiers, or vice versa. Or, it may mean that there is no market for the product at all, in which case the developer may need to completely re-think their approach.

- **Political risk:** Political risk has been a major risk for developers over the past ten years. The political battle for housing has raged over this time, and investors have often been blamed for house price inflation. In response to growing calls from their constituents to respond to international and buy-to-let investors, governments have changed taxation laws several times. In the UK, the government has changed laws and introduced measures every year since 2015. This makes it very difficult to develop a long-term sales and marketing strategy.

- **Completion risk:** Even though purchasers are legally bound to a contract, and therefore legally obliged to complete, there is still a risk that completion will not take place. This could be for several reasons, including:
  - Simply changing their mind
  - Change in personal circumstances
  - Change in laws
  - Change in market conditions
  - Inability to get a mortgage

- **Customer satisfaction:** This is a newly emerging and increasing risk, driven by a growing culture of Corporate Social Responsibility, consumer protection, and social media use. Development is an expensive endeavour, and accordingly, consumers are generally difficult to win over and keep happy. Developers are therefore highly protective of both their brand and perception in the market. Therefore, most large developers now have customer care teams in place to deal with and manage the risk of negative publicity, which nowadays can be amplified via the power of social media when things go wrong.

Financial risk

When you think about financial risk, two considerations drive risk and therefore, behaviour:

- Corporate Structure – how a developer's company is structured will impact their decision making.
- Developer Funding – at a project level, how debt will drive specific behaviour.

Corporate structure

From a corporate structure perspective, developers fall into two broad categories:

- Listed Developers
- Private Developers

The distinction between the two is how they raise and use capital for development and to run their company, which impacts the pressure they face when they deploy and use that capital.

How listed developers fund developments

Listed developers are listed on a stock exchange, which means that they are regulated and have specific requirements over and above those of private developers. Many of these relate to transparency about their activities and the need to report their business activities and financial results.

It is much easier for these listed developers to raise capital, and their primary form of capital comes from the shareholders who own their shares via a publicly traded market. These companies are restricted in the sort of activities they can undertake, as their shareholders have purchased their shares because they want to have financial exposure to a specific sector or part of the economy.

Generally, these companies fund their developments through a central treasury function. The role of a central treasury is to raise capital for the company's use from a variety of sources, which include:

- Shareholder Equity – Stocks and Shares;
- Corporate Bonds – long term loans; and
- Senior Debt Facilities – sometimes referred to as a revolving credit facility.

Listed developers generally do not raise capital for each specific development they are engaged in. They simply use their centrally generated capital to deploy within their business for development projects. This capital is deployed to different business units to use when they identify development projects which they anticipate will generate profits in line with their expectations.

These developers' target rate of return is linked to how much income their capital (shareholders and debt) expects to receive based on the given risk they are taking. Their primary consideration is their weighted cost of capital (WACC).

When creditors and owners invest in a business, they incur an opportunity cost that is equal to the returns they could have earned from alternative, similar-risk investments. Together, these opportunity costs define the minimum rate of return which the company must earn to meet the expectations of its capital providers. This is the firm's cost of capital.

The WACC is its weighted average cost of capital – it is a way of measuring its return expectations for all its capital, rather than just its debt (i.e., of considering the return expectations of its shareholders).

How private developers fund developments

Private developers raise and allocate capital differently from listed developers. Unlike listed developers, which have the luxury of being able to easily raise capital from their shareholders and other lower costs of debt, they are not able to allocate capital to different business units to 'draw down' as and when it is required.

Instead, they raise and deploy capital on a project-by-project basis. Every time they source a project for potential development, they have to seek equity (or use their own) together with debt to fund the development.

Why does it matter how the developer is funded?

It is important to understand the differences between the two operational models, as they have significant implications for the way the respective types of developer track their financial performance, and more importantly, the way they behave. Let me explain why.

Listed developers

Listed developers do not have as many issues concerning raising capital to employ in projects. They will look at their business as a company that is simply making a product and taking it to market. Whilst there is no doubt they will be interested in specific projects' financial performance, they will generally have a significant amount of work in progress (WIP) across several schemes or larger projects.

They will be most concerned about how their shareholders and the share market view their financial performance. Their issues will be balancing the capital they have employed to purchase various assets and the return they can generate. The metrics they will primarily be concerned about will be as follows:

Average Selling Price (ASP)
This is the average selling price of each property. This will be a function of market prices, but will also be impacted by the mix of product they sell, and the locations of the properties they sell.

Cost of land
A key determinant of profit, as in downturns developers seek to build their land bank of property without planning permission (i.e., land banking) because the costs of buying land are much lower.

Build costs & overheads
The cost of both wages and materials employed by the company in development.

Number of properties sold
How many properties they are producing and selling over a given period.

Return on Capital Employed (ROCE)

ROCE is a common measure of financial performance for listed entities. It is a financial ratio that determines a company's profitability and the efficiency of the capital (debt & shareholder equity) in their core activities. ROCE is expressed as a percentage, and is calculated as follows:

Operating Profit / Total Equity + Non-Current Liabilities x 100

ROCE is used as a key measure for several reasons:

- It is an easy way to evaluate the overall financial performance of a business.
- It is an easy way to benchmark a company against its competitors (i.e., if you compare two companies in the same industry and one has a ROCE of 22% and the other has a ROCE of 15%, then that means the first company is generating a greater return than the second, and is more efficiently using its capital).
- ROCE is therefore a good measure for companies to use when evaluating whether or not to take on individual development - they know if a project generates a return that is lower than their ROCE, it will weaken their financial performance.
- ROCE is commonly used because it is an easy calculation for listed companies to make. The information required to undertake the calculation is published in a company's financial statements. This is an important factor, because this data is a 'snapshot' of the company's financial performance on a given day (i.e., the day its financial statements are produced). Therefore, companies which track ROCE will be very interested in achieving sales on and before key dates – these will be the quarter days and at the end of their financial year (more on this point in Part 5: Your property investment strategy).

Operating profit (headline margin)

Operating profit or earnings before interest and tax (EBIT) margin is a key measure for companies, as the percentage of turnover turned into profit.

Private developers

Private developers' decision-making is different. These companies place far greater importance on the specific financial performance of each individual project, because most do not raise capital to fund their business operations. Instead, they raise capital for deployment on specific projects.

For these companies, the structure of their debt for projects is likely to be far more complex (i.e., several 'layers of debt'), with a series of different obligations and requirements to the providers of the debt. These companies will be far more focused on paying off specific debt obligations and driving their financial performance by clever management of debt and specific equity provisions such as preferred equity.

Internal rate of return

A final common measure of project performance likely to be used by developers is the project's internal rate of return (IRR). The IRR is a metric used to estimate the profitability of potential investments. The internal rate of return is a discount rate which makes the net present value (NPV) of all cash flows from a particular project equal to zero.

Typically, the higher the project's IRR, the more desirable it is for the developer to undertake it. If the IRR is negative or below their target return, then this implies that the developer was losing money, because the rate of return from the project is apparently less than the cost of the capital used to undertake the development.

A developer will then assess the quality of a particular development opportunity by how much return it generates as a percentage. Therefore, for a listed company, if the IRR is greater than its WACC, the difference is profit. Meanwhile, for a private developer, if their IRR is greater than their cost of debt and any preferred equity, the difference is profit.

Developer funding

Funding is the oxygen which allows a development to take place. In most scenarios, developers will need to use a significant amount of debt to fund construction, and potentially also to purchase the land upon which the development is to be built.

Debt is a double-edged sword: it creates the funding required to bring a development to life, but it also creates an obligation to a third party to which interest is paid, as well as the capital borrowed in the first place. In addition to the cost pressure debt creates is the time pressure it creates. By accepting debt, developers create a pressure to rapidly deliver income through sales in order to begin to repay the debt.

The two principles of debt

Whilst the way different developers behave will vary depending on how they are structured, the way they use their capital structure within developments is similar. All developers have the same fundamental objective: to employ capital to purchase land, deliver a 'development', and derive a development profit from selling the newly-developed housing.

When you think of capital funding, specifically debt, you just need to remember two basic principles:

1. Debt has a cost associated with time; and
2. Debt has a cost relative to its specific risk (the 'Risk Premium').

It does not matter how complex someone tries to make debt sound - these are the two principles that drive the behaviour of debt.

The time cost of debt

When you think of this capital, you need to think of it in the same way as any other resource. Take for example an employee, who comes to work, undertakes activities, and are paid a wage for the work they do. The more productive a company can make an employee, the less time they will need to spend doing an activity, and thus, the lower the wages the company will need to pay if the price of the product remains the same. Then, the company will derive the same income from a lower input of costs and their profits will increase.

Capital has the same qualities. Equity and debt providers provide capital to developers so they can undertake developments, and for this they receive compensation in the form of dividends (equity providers) or interest (debt providers). Therefore, the less time a developer needs to use debt, the lower their interest payments because they are not using the funds for as long.

Risk premium attached to debt

The interest that a lender charges is related to the risk they are taking. All interest rates are comprised of three elements:

- **Risk-free rate:** The theoretical rate of return an investor will expect to receive from a risk-free investment over a specific period.
- **Inflation premium:** The compensation for the declining purchasing power of their capital (i.e., the rate of inflation).
- **Risk premium:** How much compensation the investor expects to receive from this specific investment (sometimes referred to as systematic risk).

The risk-free rate and inflation premium are relatively static, so it is only really the third component, the risk premium, which the provider of the debt will have any real input over. And for this provider, the risk they are taking will be related to several factors:

- How long will the project take?
- How much risk is there in that specific market?
- How much protection do they have in the situation of default? This is referred to as debt priority, i.e., where do they rank in terms of being paid back if the developer defaults?

By applying these concepts, a developer will use debt to fund their construction. However, because debt providers do not typically want to take the full risk for a particular development, they will take different levels of risk depending on their risk appetite and how much return they seek for that risk (the risk premium).

Types of debt
Debt is provided in three principal forms:

Senior debt
Senior debt is the cheapest form of financing of both debt and equity. Interest rates and terms vary for senior debt, but will generally be in the mid-single-digit range. While this type of debt is cheap, it also comes with some stipulations:

- For **non-listed developers**, this will typically be some form of collateral, such as a personal guarantee from the owner. Likewise, for private developers, senior debt will be more expensive than for listed developers because the risk is higher.

- For **listed developers**, stipulations are likely to be linked to their key financial metrics and share price. If these key financial metrics fall below pre-agreed levels, then they will be in breach of the covenants of their debt and will be required to resolve these issues. Otherwise, there will be mechanisms either to call the debt in, or more likely increase the cost of the debt to account for the increased risk.

Mezzanine debt

Many smaller developerswill not be able to raise enough debt to meet their funding requirements from senior debt alone. For these developers, mezzanine debt will be an option to 'bridge' their debt requirements, often referred to as a bridging loan. Mezzanine debt is an expensive form of debt, usually with an interest rate in the low to mid-teens. The reason mezzanine debt is more expensive is because the lender does not have as much security as a senior debt provider.

Preferred equity

Preferred equity is quasi-debt, sometimes referred to as a hybrid because it has qualities of both debt and equity. Raising debt is generally tied to how much collateral (equity) the developer is putting at risk, and in some scenarios the developer will not have the ability to raise enough equity by themselves and will therefore use preferred equity.

This preferred equity will be secured to invest in the development; it is generally considered cheap debt because there is no immediate requirement to repay it. However, in the long-term, equity is the most expensive option because the developer will have to give away a substantial amount of their profit in return for it. At the end of the development, the preferred equity will take its return after all debt has been extinguished, but before the developer receives their profit.

Common equity

Common equity is the amount that all shareholders have invested in a company. This includes the value of the shares themselves.

Capital stack

The different forms of debt and equity sit in what is referred to as a *Capital Stack*, representing the combinations of the different sources of debt and equity employed by the business.

Figure 2.2: Typical capital stack

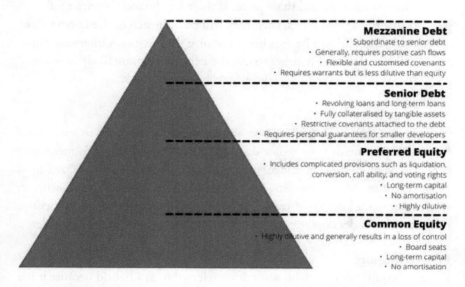

For a developer to generate the greatest possible profit, they need to use the cheapest forms of capital available, and to deploy them for the shortest period.

What this means is that a developer will evaluate a project in the form of a financial cash flow, to set out all the cash flows they anticipate being associated with the project. These will include:

- **Revenue:** Income from sales less sales costs;
- **Costs:** Land, materials, and labour.

This will generate a capital requirement to fund the difference between the revenue and costs. This cash requirement will need to be funded by the capital stack.

From a financial perspective, a developer can best manage their Capital Stack by:

- Using as much debt as possible – because debt is cheaper than equity;
- Using as much long-term debt as possible – senior debt is cheaper than mezzanine debt; and
- Avoiding outside sources of equity.

Practical application of debt and equity

Turning attention back to the two development companies I introduced earlier, Ashley's Homes and Osborne Corporation, and looking now at their respective approaches to the development of Kingsley Tower from a funding perspective, each will have different objectives.

Osborne Corporation

Osborne Corporation are centrally funded. The capital employed for development is likely to be a small part of a much larger pool of capital. Their primary sources of funding are likely to be:

- Shareholder Equity – expensive capital;
- Revolving Long-Term Debt (Senior Debt) – the lowest cost capital.

They are not likely to be under significant pressure from their providers of debt, and the cost of that debt will be low relative to Ashley's Homes. Their principal concerns with Kingsley Tower from a funding perspective will be:

- What is the anticipated return and what impact will it have on its ROCE?
- How much capital will be tied up from the debt facility and where could it have been used elsewhere?
- How long will it take to get the capital back?
- How much is the Average Selling Price, and what impact will it have on the overall metric?
- How will owning the land impact the Balance Sheet? If it is a significant cost relative to their overall assets on the balance sheet, what impact might this have on the cost of debt?

From a sales perspective, their sales pressures will most likely be:

- How many sales do they need to achieve to hit their initial pre-sale target?
- Beyond selling these initial pre-sales, there may be more pressure on maintaining prices rather than discounting in order to simply sell the remaining apartments.

Where their sales pressures are likely to exist will be:

- Recording sales before key financial dates such as quarterly, half-year, and full-year reporting dates – in order to be able to report sales positions in their financial accounts.
- Once projects are complete, ensuring all apartments are sold to ensure that they can record sales, and collect and recognise their revenue.

Osborne Corporation is likely to look at Kingsley Tower from the perspective of the development in the context of their broader company and operations, rather than focusing specifically on the development as a standalone development.

Ashley Homes

For Ashley's Homes, the situation is quite different. They raise capital specifically for each development, and their funding is more likely to come from the following sources:

- Their own equity;
- Senior debt – likely at a higher cost than Osborne Corporation.

Additionally, where they cannot raise enough capital to fund projects from these sources, they are likely to use higher-cost capital from the following sources:

- **Preferred equity:** Additional capital providers, these private funding sources will not invest in Ashley's Homes, but will provide equity in the development itself. This will mean that Ashley's Homes can take on larger projects, but to do so, they will have to pay a third party out of the profits from the development before they pay themselves.

- **Mezzanine debt:** As this is an expensive form of short-term debt, the risk to Ashley's Homes arises if the costs of using this debt outweigh the benefits. For example, if the debt is only needed for a short time it will most likely be cheaper than using preferred equity, and therefore, they will be able to keep more profit to themselves. However, if they end up needing that debt for longer than anticipated, then they may simply run out of money.

Ashley's Homes are unlikely to be concerned about how the development of Kingsley Tower impacts their average selling price. They are likely to be far more interested in the specific return of the project and how quickly they can get capital in from sales and reduce their debt requirements.

The clever management of their debt will be one of the key factors which determine their profitability, rather than specific sales rates. Ashley's Homes will most likely be driven by two specific sales milestones:

- Undertake enough pre-sales to meet initial debt requirements; and then
- Continue selling as quickly as possible to ensure that they can recoup capital as quickly as possible.

Risks associated with development funding

There are several risks associated with development funding, most of which are relatively obvious:

- **Interest costs:** The cost of debt is essentially a ticking clock. For a developer, if their interest costs are too high then there is a risk that the cost of interest will simply erode the return generated by the development.

- **Additional costs due to time over run:** Construction delays or delays in selling and completing the sales that have been exchanged will extend the project's life. This will also extend the time debt required, thereby increasing their finance costs and reducing their profit.

- **Not meeting sales targets and inability to draw down debt:** If a developer cannot sell enough property at the early stages of their development, then they will not be able to access their debt and commence construction.

- **Failed completions:** If sales fail to complete, this will add additional time to re-sell those properties, and will mean the developer needs to utilise their debt for a longer period. This will increase their costs of funding and reduce their returns.

- **Cost escalations:** Increases in costs in areas such as marketing, sales, planning, and construction will all require additional capital, increasing the cost of debt and reducing returns.

- **Change in market conditions impacting debt covenants:** If market conditions deteriorate, a developer's land value will reduce, as will the anticipated return for unsold properties. This can potentially trigger a breach of covenant conditions – increasing the risk to debt providers, and increasing debt costs.

Part 1 Recap

Let's recap Part 1, which has presented the fundamentals of the residential real estate and development market. I have introduced several key concepts in the part, many of which you will already be familiar with.

Real estate

Real estate is often traded in the abstract - the land is where most of the value is stored; similarly, it is the value of the land which increases. However, land is unproductive by itself, and it is the improvements to the land that generate utilisation value. All real estate has three key characteristics - physical, institutional, and economic - and it is the combination of these characteristics which drives value.

Real estate market

The real estate market is not a perfect market. It is characterised by a small number of transactions where buyers and sellers are not equally informed. In the market, buyers are uninformed by a lack of experience (or regularity in transacting), and there is a lack of transparent information. The real estate market moves in four key cycles: recovery, growth, hyper-supply, and recession.

Highest and best use

The highest and best use is the reasonable, probable, and legal use of vacant land or an improved property, which is physically possible, appropriately supported, and financially feasible. It results in the highest value for an estate. There are many reasons why a parcel of land is not employed at its highest and best use.

Real estate lifecycle

Real estate, or more specifically improvements to real estate, have a life cycle driven by outside factors. These are broadly categorised as:

- Useful Life
- Land Identification
- Development Phase

Residential development

Residential development is essentially a series of risks:

- Land Costs
- Consent Costs
- Construction Costs
- Sales and Marketing Costs
- Finance Costs

Developers generate their profits through the effective management of these risks.

Building your property investment strategy

As a property investor, you should be asking yourself the following questions:

1. Where am I thinking about investing?
2. What are the characteristics of the land and its improvements which drive value?
3. At what point in the market cycle is the market in?
4. At what point in the property life cycle is a property in the location? If there is a lot of obsolete property in the location, this may mean that a significant amount of new development will take place, driving demand for land.
5. Who are the developers in the location, and what drives their thinking?

Understanding the market for residential development will help you to identify the key risks for the developer. You maximise your negotiating power by your ability to reduce these risks.

PART 2

Purchase Price and Costs

You will never be able to make back any of the *unnecessary costs* that you incurred at the time of purchase. Likewise, if you got your sums wrong and simply paid too much for the property itself, that will hurt you as well. This cost will be attached to your investment forever.

Think about it like this:

> *You can purchase a very average property and it can generate a strong yield and have fantastic long-term growth, simply by getting the right price. However, if you pay too much for a fantastic property, it is not possible to create the same return.*

As you build a portfolio, making sound decisions will impact upon your portfolio's performance. If you buy a property that generates a return at a lower rate than your existing portfolio, it will dilute your portfolio's performance.

Purchase an investment property poorly, and the sobering reality is that even as the market moves and capital values and rents increase, because of the costs involved in purchasing property, it will take *several years* to recover your initial purchase costs.

When it comes to buying property off-plan, the key to successfully investing at the right price will be driven by several critical factors. It is all about understanding what the costs involved in purchasing off-plan are, and being able to minimise them as much as possible. To do this, you need to understand three core aspects:

- **Price:** What is price, and how is it determined? Understanding the difference between the cost of developing the property and the asking price is the path to recognising where savings can be created.

- **Sales and marketing campaign costs:** "The developer pays these, so why do I need to worry about them?" Wrong - you may think the developer covers these costs, but ultimately they are baked into the price. So, how do you recognise these costs and minimise them?

- **Other purchase costs:** There are a whole host of other additional costs which you need to be aware of when investing in off-plan. Some of these are obvious; however, many are not. How do you recognise these costs and determine which make sense and which do not?

CHAPTER 3

Price

Understanding the nuances of price is key to developing your purchase strategy. *The costs associated with buying a property are the principal determinant of the financial performance of your investment.*

The price you pay is everything. Buying well is critical to the performance of your investment.

What is the price?

This is an interesting question. The price of the property means different things to different people. We have already discussed the mechanics of the property market. The real estate market is imperfect - there is no specific market price for property set by the market function. More realistically, price is simply a range of likely values.

Many market participants have a different version of what price is. Let's use an apartment in Kingsley Tower to see what they are.

Note: People working in new-build property refer to apartments as 'plots', so I am simply going to refer to apartment 1 as *'Plot 1 Kingsley Tower'*.

Table 3.1: Plot 1, Kingsley Tower

Plot No#	Floor	N# of Bedrooms	Area (m²)	Area (ft²)	External Space	Aspect
1	1	Studio	39.0	419.8	None	North

Open market value

You can think of the open market value as the closest 'price' to the true value if there was a perfect market. Many professional real estate bodies such as the Australian Property Institute (API) and the Royal Institute of Chartered Surveyors (RICS) have definitions of what this is. The RICS definition is:

> *Open Market Value – means the best price at which an interest in a property might be reasonably expected to be sold unconditionally for cash consideration on the date of valuation, assuming:*

- *a willing seller;*
- *that, prior to the date of valuation, there had been a reasonable period (having regard to the nature of the property and the state of the market) for the marketing of the interest, for the agreement of price and terms for the completion of the sale;*
- *that the state of the market, level of values, and other circumstances were, on any earlier assumed date of sale, the same on the date of valuation; and*
- *that no account is taken of any additional bid by a purchaser with a special interest.*

You will typically see the open market value assessed by a valuer when they act for a bank to arrange a mortgage, or for insurance purposes when an owner is looking to obtain building insurance.

For plot 1 Kingsley Tower, the open market value is determined by a valuer. This value is their view of how much the property would sell for between a willing seller and a willing buyer. This is assuming the property had been marketed for an appropriate period, and that no other special circumstances mean that either party was too eager to buy or sell. In determining the open market value, the chartered surveyor will have recourse to previous transaction records.

Book value

The book value is another version of 'price'. The book value is the value that a developer attaches to a property considering the cost of building the property together with their profit expectations. This is an easy figure to calculate, and is simply a combination of all the inputs. Therefore:

Book Value =
Cost of Land + Cost of Obtaining Consent + Cost of Construction +
Sales and Marketing Costs + Financing Costs + Development Profit

To put this into context for plot 1 Kingsley Tower, the book value would be defined as the price which a developer would theoretically be willing to accept from a purchaser. I have set out how this could be determined below.

First, we need to understand what proportion plot 1 comprises in relation to the whole development. This is relatively straightforward for Kingsley Tower because it *only* consists of residential apartments.

Kingsley Towers is a 100-apartment building with a total area of 6,232 m² and Plot 1 is a ground floor studio apartment with a gross area of 39.0 m². If you divide the area of plot 1 into the total building, this calculation will give you the percentage of the building it represents:

$$39.0 / 6,232 = 0.63$$

Therefore, Plot 1 represents 0.063% of the total building.

The book value can then be determined by allocating the percentage of the development that plot 1 makes up to each input's relative cost, as shown in Table 3.2.

Table 3.2: Plot 1, Kingsley Tower calculation of book value

Input	Cost	% Relative to Plot 1	Total Amount
Land	15,000,000	0.63	94,500
Planning Costs	300,000	0.63	1,890
Construction Costs	15,000,000	0.63	94,500
Sales & Marketing Costs	4,000,000	0.63	25,200
Finance Costs	1,897,500	0.63	11,954
Developers Profit	13,802,500	0.63	86,956
Total	50,000,000		315,000

Therefore, the book value of Plot 1 Kingsley Tower would be £315,000.

It is important to note that the book value is not a static amount, as it moves over time. For example, if the costs of construction were to fall, the developer's book value would decrease. Likewise, if the value of the land (an asset on the company's balance sheet) were to rise, the book value would also increase.

Asking price

The asking price is another different version of the price. The asking price is the price at which a developer promotes a property for sale. As with anyone selling something, developers assume a certain amount of negotiation will take place with a potential purchaser. A developer will not expect to receive their full asking price; they will usually accept a price below the asking price. This difference between the asking price and the purchase price is referred to as a *dealing margin*.

In determining what the asking price should be, the developer will look at other property that is available for sale in the market with similar characteristics. No two properties will have identical characteristics; therefore, the developer will need to make a judgment call as to how buyers in the market will value and therefore be willing to pay for these different characteristics.

Purchase price

The purchase price is the price most people think of. It is simply the price agreed between the seller and purchaser.

Total purchase price

Finally, there is the total purchase price. Many investors will simply look at the purchase price or even the asking price, and work their figures based on this number. This will improve returns on paper and will make the investor feel great! But, this is not an accurate representation of what you are paying.

In fact, when you buy property there are many other costs involved with the purchase, including:

- **Stamp Duty:** This has different names in different countries. It is a tax levied on property purchases by the relevant government tax authority.
- **Registration and transfer fees:** These are costs associated with physically transferring ownership of the property into your name.
- **Mortgage arrangement fees:** For many mortgages, there will be a cost associated with obtaining the mortgage.
- **Valuation fees:** Mortgage providers typically require a valuation at the time that a property is purchased so that they can confirm the value of a property relative to the agreed purchase price.
- **Legal fees:** You will need to pay a lawyer or conveyancer to act on your behalf to register the sale and your interest in the property.

You need to account for these costs in your calculations, particularly when you are comparing properties from different countries, as the costs differ significantly depending on how you purchase, where the property is, and the price you have paid.

In some scenarios, this cost could be up to 20% on top of the purchase price, so it is a material consideration. Additionally, it is difficult to borrow this money in your mortgage – so you will need to come up with the funds on top of any equity deposit required by your bank for a mortgage.

There are two reasons why using the total purchase price is so important:

- **Accurate cost:** It gives you an accurate picture of the total cost of the investment allowing you to determine your return from the income you generate. Likewise, if you are thinking about selling, it gives you a real figure to work with so you can determine what your total gain will be if you sell.
- **Comparison:** It allows you to compare apples with apples. You cannot accurately make a judgement between two investment properties without comparing two items: (1) the total purchase price, and (2) the net operating income.

What is price?

So, if you ask the question again, maybe your thinking has changed? *There is no universal truth for what price or value is, there are simply a series of different possible answers:*

- Open Market Value;
- Book Value;
- Asking Price;
- Purchase Price; and
- Total Purchase Price.

Your view of the price will no doubt depend on which side of the fence you sit. It is unlikely that these numbers will all be the same, even at the same point in time.

The one exception to this is that at the point a property is being valued by a valuer, they will often equate the purchase price to the open market value, because the assumption is made that the open market value test set out above was met at point the sale was agreed.

Figure 3.1: Five versions of price for new-build development

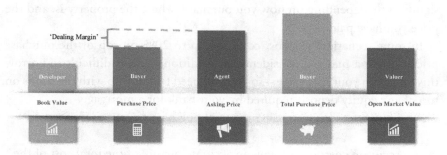

Determining the asking price: Comparable evidence

Now that we have looked at what the different versions of price are, let's look at how developers and property agents arrive at an asking price. There is no secret recipe that is followed, or absolute truth which produces the asking price. Like pricing any other product, the asking price is simply a reflection of what someone making a product thinks the market will pay for their product.

I have been through this process thousands of times; this is how I do it. Other agents and developers will have their own processes. However, the starting point is looking for comparable evidence.

A 'comparable' is a property that has been transacted in the open market, which has broadly similar characteristics (economic, physical, and institutional) to the subject property. Details of the sale are recorded together with the sale price, the timing of the sale, and any other information that may have impacted the price paid by the purchaser.

Comparable evidence comprises a series of comparable transactions, where the information from these transactions is pooled together as 'comparable evidence'. Property agents use this comparable evidence to form a view on pricing in the market and develop a schedule of pricing for the proposed development.

Where does the comparable evidence come from?

Property agents have access to powerful databases containing vast amounts of data, which they use to formulate their views on the market. This includes:

- Their internal transaction records;
- Land registration/Land Title office records;
- Large commercial databases which track sales records;
- Databases that track new planning applications and records;
- Credit and financial databases such as Experian; and
- Databases that track land sales data.

These databases are expensive to access, and therefore have a limited number of users such as property agents, developers, banks and mortgage providers, and other companies involved in the property industry.

In coming to a view on potential price, a property agency will consider the following:

- Sales of competing new-build projects, both recently sold and currently for sale;
- Recent sales in the secondary market;
- New-build projects that are scheduled to come to the market during the period in which the subject development will be marketed,
- Prevailing market conditions;
- The socio-economic conditions in the specific sub-market;
- The specification and layout of the apartments; and
- Amenities within the development and surrounding area.

Schedule of accommodation

To develop a detailed plan of pricing, the property agent will draft a schedule of accommodation for the various apartments within the development, setting out the various relevant physical characteristics of each of the apartments. The property agent will highlight those characteristics that it believes will impact how much purchasers will be willing to pay for properties in that sub-market.

These characteristics are typically:

- Floor – if it is a multi-storey building;
- Number of bedrooms;
- Area of the internal space;
- Any external space the property has such as a balcony, terrace, or yard; and
- Aspect – of the property.

Table 3.3: Typical schedule of accommodation

Plot N#	Floor	N# of Bedrooms	Area (m²)	Area (ft²)	External Space	Aspect

Comparable evidence in practice

To show comparable evidence in practice, I have set out a schedule of comparable evidence for Metropolis.

Table 3.4: Metropolis general market information

Median Age	Median Monthly Income	Population	Area Leverage	Credit Score
34	£3,923	151,332	44.9%	823

Table 3.5: Metropolis secondary sales

	£ per ft² Paid	Average Price £	Average Discount	Average Gross Yield	Supply	Transactions
Studios	869.30	314,900	4.2 %	5.9 %	128	10
Flats	842.00	695,300	5.9 %	3.5 %	4,446	1,529
Terraced Houses	896.20	1,200,000	4.9 %	3.0 %	1,037	209
Semi-Detached Houses	899.50	1,500,000	8.6 %	3.2 %	69	25

Table 3.6: Metropolis average monthly rental information

	1 Bedroom	2 Bedroom	3 Bedroom	4 Bedroom
Apartments	£1,500	£2,000	£2,900	£2,900

Figure 3.2: Metropolis new-build developments

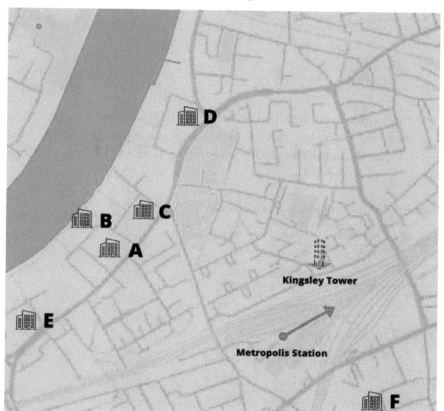

Comparable A

Table 3.7: Comparable A: Summary of development scheme

A six storey building with 52 residential apartments. The development includes a 360 m² ground floor retail shop currently let to a Marks & Spencer's convenience store.	
Total Units	51
Private Units	39
Social (Intermediate Units)	12

The private apartments are divided according to the unit mix set out below.

Table 3.8: Comparable A: Summary of accommodation

N# of Bedrooms	Quantity
1	13
2	24
3	2

The development was launched in October 2017. When the property was launched, the price list showed one-bedroom apartments starting from £482,500, and two bedroom apartments starting from £655,000 at a blended average of £830 per ft^2.

Table 3.9: Accommodation information

	Minimum	Average	Maximum
Price	£482,500	£596,300	£700,000
£ per ft^2	£780	£819	£859
Area ft^2	562	731	875

Table 3.10: Asking price ranges

	Minimum	Average	Maximum
1 Bedroom	£482,500	£514,800	£546,500
2 Bedroom	£659,500	£677,800	£700,000

Pricing Commentary:

- 1 bedroom apartments - prices range from £482,500 (562 ft^2 / £859 per ft^2) for a first floor apartment to £546,500 (636 ft^2 / £859 per ft^2) for a fourth-floor apartment.

- 2 bedroom apartments - prices range from £659,500 (822 ft^2 / £802 per ft^2) for a third-floor apartment to £700,000 (875 ft^2/ £800 per ft^2) for a second floor apartment.

Comparable B

Table 3.11: Comparable B: Summary of development scheme

A mixed used development built in 2008. Comparable B was originally used as office accommodation. However, after many years of vacancy, the developer converted the office accommodation into residential accommodation.	
Total Units	11
Car Parking Spaces	11

The private apartments are divided according to the unit mix set out below.

Table 3.12: Comparable B: Summary of accommodation

N# of Bedrooms	Quantity
1	3
2	5
3	3

This development scheme was launched in November 2015, and at the end of Q4 2017, four units remained unsold. At the time of pricing the scheme, the price list showed 2-beds starting from £695,000 at a blended average of £1,000 per ft². Refurbishment construction began in August 2015 and ran through until June 2016.

Table 3.13: Accommodation information

	Minimum	Average	Maximum
Price	£460,000	£815,348	£1,185,000
£ per ft²	£804	£973	£1,171
Area ft²	475	839	1,404

Table 3.14: Asking price ranges

	Minimum	Average	Maximum
1 Bedroom	£460,000	£555,833	£625,000
2 Bedrooms	£640,000	£832,000	£1,150,000
3 Bedrooms	£899,000	£1,086,800	£1,185,000

Pricing Commentary:

- 1 bedroom apartments - prices range from £460,000 (475 ft² / £968 per ft²) for a first floor apartment to £625,000 (607 ft² / £1,030 per ft²) for a second floor apartment.

- 2 bed prices range from £640,000 (731 ft² / £876 per ft²) for a second floor apartment to £1,150,00 (1,060 ft² / £1,085 per ft²) also for a second floor apartment.

- 3 bed prices range from £899,000 (969 ft² / £918 per ft²) for a first floor apartment to £1,185,000 (1,404 ft² / £844 per ft²) for a ground floor apartment.

Comparable C

Table 3.15: Comparable C: Summary of development scheme

New residential development to be constructed by Developer C. The proposed development incorporates the erection of a podium building with three residential buildings of 8, 11, and 24 storeys.
The development provides 299 new residential apartments, together with approximately 6,000 m² of education space, as well as a 550 m² café.

Number of storeys	8, 11 & 24
Total Units	299
Private Units	249
Social (Intermediate Units)	50

This scheme was due to launch in January 2019. Construction began in November 2017 and was due to complete in December 2019. At the time of preparing the analysis, no pricing information was available on the scheme.

Comparable D

Table 3.16: Comparable D: Summary of development scheme

A mixed-use residential 17 storey building with a car showroom and workshop on the ground floor. The development's residential component will provide 173 new residential units comprising both private and affordable housing, with access to a landscaped amenity deck. A basement car park will provide residents with 87 vehicle and 184 cycle parking spaces. Within the ground floor will be 29 parking spaces for customers.	
Total Units	173
Private Units	130
Social (Intermediate Units)	43

The private apartments are divided according to the unit mix set out below.

Table 3.17: Comparable D: Summary of accommodation

N# of Bedrooms	Quantity
1	23
2	98
3	9

The scheme launched in November 2017 and by the end of 2017, only three apartments had been sold. Prices started at £499,950 for one bedroom apartments, £599,950 for two bedroom apartments, and £929,000 for three bedroom apartments.

Table 3.18: Accommodation information

	Minimum	Average	Maximum
Price	£499,950	£733,649	£1,199,950
£ per ft²	£723	£834	£1,068
Area ft²	538	718	916

Table 3.19: Asking price ranges

	Minimum	Average	Maximum
1 Bedroom	£499,950	£522,303	£594,950
2 Bedroom	£599,950	£716,405	£824,950
3 Bedroom	£929,000	£1,109,190	£1,199,950

Comparable E

Table 3.20: Comparable E: Summary of development scheme

A landmark development in a location popular in both local and international markets. The development is two additional phases of the existing estate. Those additional phases are Building 1 and Building 2		
	Building 1	**Building 2**
Total Units	74	56
Private Units	74	36
Social (Intermediate Units)	0	20

The private apartments are divided according to the unit mix set out below.

Table 3.21: Comparable E summary of accommodation

N# of Bedrooms	Building 1	Building 2
1	34	-
2	34	16
3	6	20

Multiple phases of the estate have been released since October 2010. At the end of 2017:

- Building 1 launched in September 2017 and 24 apartments were sold by the end of Q4 2017. The current pricelist shows one-bedroom apartments from £565,000, 2 bedroom apartments from £815,000, and 3 bedroom apartments from £1,350,000, at a blended average of £1,100 per ft². Construction was completed in 2019.

- Building 2 launched in February 2017, and by the end of Q4 2017 11 units had sold. The current pricelist shows 3 bedroom apartments ranging from £1,875,000 to £1,925,000.

Table 3.22: Accommodation information

	Minimum	Average	Maximum
Price	£575,000	£1,006,316	£3,300,000
£ per ft²	£1,084	£1,191	£1,913
Area ft²	565	845	2,427

Table 3.23: Asking price ranges

	Minimum	Average	Maximum
1 Bedroom	£498,750	£685,857	£765,000
2 Bedroom	£790,000	£955,302	£1,270,000
3 Bedroom	£1,325,000	£1,901,875	£2,950,000

Pricing Commentary:

- 1 bedroom apartments range from £498,750 (482 ft² / £1,035 per ft²) for a third floor apartment to £765,000 (578 ft²/ £1,324 per ft²) for an eighth floor apartment.

- 2 bedroom apartments range from £790,000 (744 ft² / £1,062 per ft²) for a first floor apartment to £1,270,000 (1,032 ft²/ £1,231 per ft²) for an eighth floor apartment .

- 3 bedroom apartments range from £1,325,000 (1,109 ft²/ £1,195 per ft²) for a fifth floor apartment to £2,950,000 (2,120 ft²/ £1,392 per ft²) for a ninth or tenth floor penthouse apartment.

Comparable F

Table 3.24: Comparable F: Summary of development scheme

Five buildings of 12, 8, 7, 7, and 6 storeys to provide 527 apartments, together with approximately 78,000 ft² of private, communal, and public space.	
Total Units	599
Private Units	284
Social (Social Rent)	243
Social (Intermediate Units)	78

The private apartments are divided according to the unit mix set out below.

Table 3.25: Comparable F: Summary of accommodation

N# of Bedrooms	Quantity
1	70
2	142
3	58
4	14

The scheme launched in March 2015, and by the end of 2017, Phase 1 with 73 apartments has been completed and has sold out.

Table 3.26: Accommodation information

	Minimum	Average	Maximum
Price	£490,000	£764,229	£1,025,000
£ per ft²	£787	£899	£1,013
Area ft²	538	835	1,528

Table 3.27: Asking price ranges

	Minimum	Average	Maximum
1 Bedroom	£490,000	£500,000	£690,000
2 Bedroom	£580,000	£744,333	£910,000
3 Bedroom	£850,000	£934,000	£1,025,000

Pricing Commentary:

- 1 bedroom apartments range from £490,000 (549 ft²/ £893 per ft²) for a second-floor apartment to £690,000 (787 ft²/ £877 per ft²) for a third-floor apartment.

- 2 bedroom apartments range from £580,000 (674 ft²/ £861 per ft²) for a second-floor apartment to £910,000 (1,009 ft²/ £902 per ft²) for a fifth-floor apartment.

- 3 bedroom apartments range from £850,000 (1,012 ft²/ £840 per ft²) for a second floor apartment, to £1,025,000 (1,302 ft²/ £787 per ft²) for a house.

Discussion of comparable evidence

We have now created a picture of the market. We have been able to generate the following information:

- **Secondary sales market:** We have a view of the prices properties have traded for in the market historically, the average time it has taken to sell an individual apartment, how much it sold for, the average rents achieved, and the gross yields achieved.

- **New-build (off plan) sales:** We know what new developments are for sale in the market, how many are being developed, the rate at which they are selling, and how much is being achieved for each unit (some of these sales will be known information, and some will be educated guesses).

Although we have built a good view of the market, there are still some things we do not know, such as:

- How many people in the market are looking to buy.
- The budgets of buyers in the market and their purchasing intentions.
- Exactly what every apartment has sold for individually - we have a good idea of sales for new-build developments, but we only know their asking prices.

Although we do not know everything there is to know about a property, we will have to come up with a view of pricing based on the information we know, and form a view about the things we do not know.

Forming a view of pricing will depend on the amount of comparable evidence we have. In this situation, the development is for sale in Metropolis, for which we have quite a lot of information. In coming to a view on pricing, there are two things we could do:

- **Option 1 (all comparable evidence):** Average the information about all the sales in the market; or
- **Option 2 (specific comparable evidence):** Pick the most comparable properties and focus on those.

The optimal method is Option 2, which focuses on specific comparable properties, because these are properties that share more of the same characteristics. Including other property sales would simply skew the pricing, because we would introduce pricing for characteristics that are not relevant to Kingsley Tower.

In this circumstances, because so much evidence is available, Option 2 is the best method to use. However, there are scenarios where a developer or agent simply will not have as much information, and the only option they have will be to go with Option 1.

Comparing properties

The most comparable properties to Kingsley Tower are A, E, and F. These properties have the following attributes:

Comparable	Location	Features	Quality
A	Located closer to Metropolis River and is in a more established residential location. However, it is situated on a busy road, and does not have river views.	A smaller development, there is little in the way of amenity in the building. Additionally, it is a low-rise development, and its apartments do not have the same views as the higher floors in Kingsley Tower.	The development has a relatively basic specification, and is built by a less well-regarded developer.
E	Located on the Metropolis River, and is close to local public transport.	A large multi-phase scheme with high-quality amenities, including a fitness club and spa, and other resident facilities.	A quality prestigious development built by a very reputable developer.
F	Located on the opposite side to Metropolis station and near to the railway line, in a similar location to Kingsley Tower. However, it is probably considered a lower quality location.	The development is a large one, which is predominantly low rise. It has little in the way of resident amenity, and a significant proportion of the development is affordable housing (53%).	The development is a mid-range quality development.

For Kingsley Tower, several comparisons need to be considered:

- **Location:** The development is located immediately north of the station which connects into London in 8 mins.
- **Specification:** It was anticipated that either Osborne Corporation or Ashley's Homes would develop Kingsley Tower to a similar level to Comparable E.
- **Amenities:** The site is located close to a variety of local amenities in Metropolis and within walking distance to shops and restaurants. Very little was proposed in Kingsley Tower other than a concierge.

The following sections provide further comparisons of Kingsley Tower and properties A, B, E, and F.

Size of apartment

Studio apartments

There were no studio apartments in any of the comparable properties. However, we know that in the second-hand market, 128 studio apartments were for sale over the past 12 months - only ten of them were sold. Of those ten apartments, the average price paid was £314,900, which works out at £869.30 per ft^2.

Table 3.28: Summary of studio apartments

	£ per ft^2 Paid	Average Price £	Average Discount	Average Gross Yield	Supply	Transactions
Studios	869.30	314,900	4.2 %	5.9 %	128	10

1 bedroom apartments

For one bedroom apartments, we know the following sales were recorded in developments A, B, E, and F.

Table 3.29: Summary of one-bedroom apartments

Comparable	A (£ per ft^2)	B (£ per ft^2)	E (£ per ft^2)	F (£ per ft^2)
First Floor	968	968		
Second Floor	1,030	1,030	893	893
Third Floor			877	877

2 bedroom apartments

For two bedroom apartments, we know the following sales were recorded in developments A, B, E, and F.

Table 3.30: Summary of two bedroom apartments

Comparable	A (£ per ft²)	B (£ per ft²)	E (£ per ft²)	F (£ per ft²)
First Floor	802		1,062	
Second Floor	800	876 & 1,085		861
Third Floor	760			
Fifth Floor				902
Eighth Floor			1,231	

Base level pricing

Based on the comparable evidence, we can surmise that the prices for the different units in Kingsley Tower should be:

- Studios - £900 per ft²
- 1 bedroom apartments - £800 per ft²
- 2 bedroom apartments - £750 per ft²

Table 3.31: Summary of base pricing for Kingsley Tower

Unit Type	Number	Total Area (ft²)	Price £ per ft²	GDV (£)
Studio	10	4,198	900	3,778,164
1 Bed	20	11,518	800	9,213,898
2 Bed	70	51,366	750	38,577,818
Total	100	67,081		51,569,845

To summarise, we have priced the building and we know that based on the above, the blended average price of all the units is £768.77 per ft². This was calculated by dividing the GDV of £51,569,845 by the total area of 67,081 ft².

However, this makes little sense when you compare two two-bedroom units, plots 4 and 71.

Table 3.32: Comparison between Plots 4 and 71

Plot No.	Floor	No# of Bedrooms	Area (m²)	Area (ft²)	Baseline £ per ft²	Price £
4	1	2 bedrooms	73	786	750	589,324
71	15	2 bedrooms	73	786	750	589,324

It makes little sense because the two units are on completely different floors but are the same price. Plot 4 is on the first floor, and is close to a train line and a busy street, whereas plot 71 is on the 15th floor, does not suffer from street noise, and additionally, will have views over the city. A buyer will therefore pay more for plot 71 than for plot 4.

We need to adjust the prices to allow for the key physical characteristics of the property.

Adjustments

The agent or developer is going to have to give some regard to the defining characteristics of Kingsley Tower, allocate some type of value to them, then adjust the pricing to allow for these differentials.

Balconies

Only some of the properties have a balcony. Not only do they provide additional space to residents, they also create additional amenity. Having reviewed the schedule of comparable properties it appears that a balcony adds £5,000 to the purchase price. All the units in the building from the 12th floor up have a balcony, so I have made that adjustment to the pricing.

Floor

The floor of the building on which the apartment is situated will have an impact on it because:

- There is a busy train line close by, which has a significant impact on the ground, first, and second floors due to the noise created by passing trains.
- The higher up the building, the better the access to light and views from each apartment.

Regarding other comparable sales, I have concluded that every additional floor increases the price by approximately £7,500 per floor. I have therefore made those adjustments to the schedule for the third floor upwards.

Aspect

The building has great views. These are the assumed premiums for apartments compared to those that face due west:

- North: 2.5%
- East: 2.5%
- South/East: 2.5%
- South/West: 1.5%

Dealing margin

In addition to the adjustments for physical characteristics, I am also adding dealing margins to negotiate with buyers of:

- Studios - 3%
- 1 bedroom apartments - 5%
- 2 bedrooms apartments - 7%

Summary of final pricing

Having made all the adjustments, I now have the following figures, based on asking prices:

- GDV £64,020,000
- Average £954 per ft^2

Table 3.33: Comparison between Plots 4 and 71

Plot No.	Floor	No# of Bedrooms	Area m^2	Area ft^2	Baseline Price £	Adjusted Price £
4	1	2 bedrooms	73	786	589,324	640,000
71	15	2 bedrooms	73	786	589,324	750,000

Commentary on pricing

For you as the investor, it is important to understand the process which has taken place. Hopefully, it highlights that there is no magic formula. Yes, there is some logic attached to the process - but it is simply a subjective view.

Let's assume that we change our assumptions to:

- Balcony Premium - £2,500
- Floor Premium - £3,000
- Dealing Margin Studio - 1%
- Dealing Margin 1 bedroom - 3%
- Dealing Margin 2 bedroom - 4%

This produces a different set of asking prices, giving us the following:

- GDV £57,335,000
- Average £855 per ft²

Table 3.34: New comparison between Plots 4 and 71

Plot No.	Floor	No# of Bedrooms	Area m²	Area ft²	Baseline Price £	Adjusted Price £
4	1	2 bedrooms	73	786	589,324	630,000
71	15	2 bedrooms	73	786	589,324	670,000

You can download a copy of the full pricing schedule at **www.proptechpioneer.com/ prosper** and adjust the parameters to see the impact on pricing.

The point I am trying to illustrate here is that *there is no universal truth for pricing*. It is just a number based on the quantity and quality of information available, and taking a view as to:

- What the important characteristics are to buyers of a property; and
- How much they are prepared to pay.

Additionally, you should also be aware that throughout this exercise, nothing has occurred which has changed the developer's book value.

The example also highlights how quickly the developers' profits can move:

- If asking prices in the market **increase rapidly,** so will land prices. However, because the developer has already purchased the land, their land cost will remain the same. If all other costs remain the same, then their profits can grow rapidly. This is why large regeneration projects can be very profitable for developers - because if they take many years to develop the land and prices increase in the interim, then so do their profits.

- If prices **decline,** the land price will not go down as they have already purchased, and therefore their profits will reduce if they cannot reduce construction or other costs.

CHAPTER 4

Cost not Price

Because of the different versions of price in the new-build market for property, you need to think of price differently. Indeed, instead of thinking about the price, you should be thinking about the *cost*. This is because you are not purchasing an existing asset in the secondary market; you are buying a property from a company that produces that product for sale, and as we have demonstrated, there is no universal truth on what price is.

Think instead of the cost for a developer to produce the property, and how much you should be willing to pay relative to their risk. If the combination of these costs is less than similar prices for similar properties, then this is an investment you should consider. This understanding is fundamentally the difference between a good investor and a poor investor.

Most purchasers I have talked with did not think of property investment in this way. They had little to no plan as to what they were looking to achieve, or why. Consequently, they were all ultimately buying at the whim of the property cycle. Most of these investors paid too much; it was just a question of how much!

Developer's costs

The obvious next question is: what are the developer's costs? How can I help them to reduce these costs, and therefore reduce the cost to me, the investor?

As we have discussed in Chapter 2, development brings five key costs/risks:

- Land Costs
- Consent Costs
- Construction Costs
- Sales and Marketing Costs
- Finance Costs

Quite obviously, sales and marketing costs are one cost you can influence, but what others can you influence? The other costs you can help a developer to reduce are:

Construction costs

By reducing the specification of what you are purchasing, you can reduce their costs and therefore improve their potential for greater profit.

Finance costs

By helping to de-risk their sales and marketing campaign, you can reduce their sales costs and sales risk, thereby reducing their requirement for financing and thus their financing cost.

Think about new-build pricing and what you are paying as an investor, i.e. your total purchase price. You need to think in terms of *cost* rather than *price*. Think of these as the three costs that form the overall asking price of a new-build property:

- **Absolute costs:** These are items that have already been spent by the time the property is on the market. The best way to describe these is that they are all items that the property would not exist without. These components are:
  - Land
  - Planning costs
  - Construction (the building)

  If the developer sold the property for less than the sum of these costs, they would lose money. So, unless the developer is simply desperate to sell, they are not going to sell at a price below their absolute costs.

- **Variable costs:** These are items that are direct costs to the developer, but they will change depending on several controllable variables. These costs can broadly be considered as:
  - Construction – internal fit-out
  - Sales and marketing costs
  - Finance costs
  - Developer's profit

- **Dealing costs:** The sum of the absolute costs and variable costs is the developer's book value, and any amount above that is simply 'dealing margin', or dealing costs.

How does it look to you?

As an investor, your version of 'price' is different - it is the 'total purchase price', which has more components. Your 'potential' costs are:

- Developer's absolute costs
- Developer's variable costs
- Dealing costs
- Facilitation and completion costs (purchase costs)

As an investor, if buying at the best possible price is the best way of ensuring financial performance, then your job is to know and understand how these costs work, what they look like, and how you can reduce them.

> *The lower your 'potential costs' the lower the total purchase price; the lower your total purchase price, the better your return, assuming rent and capital growth are the same.*

When you talk about costs and reducing them, they fall into two categories:

- **Cost savings:** Any action that results in a tangible financial benefit that lowers current spending, investment, or debt levels; and
- **Cost avoidance:** Any action that avoids having to incur costs.

You are buying an asset that you want to hold for a long period. So, you are going to have to pay something for it. The key to this process is understanding what the costs are involved in purchasing your property and identifying what can be avoided and what can be saved.

Many people will think they understand all the costs and hidden costs here. But, I can guarantee they do not. Your ability to influence your purchase costs when buying an investment property will fall into several broad categories:

- **Developers' variable costs:**
  - **Sales and marketing campaigns:** These costs are huge, and of all the costs involved in the development, they are ones which you have the greatest control over. These costs are what I call zero-gain costs - they

are just costs that help potential purchasers to understand an investment opportunity. The developer does not get the cost of sales and marketing in their bottom line, likewise you as an investor do not get any financial benefit from these costs. A tenant will not pay more rent because of the amazing brochure which was produced.

- **Specification:** A key cost that is often overlooked. The key to specification is getting the right balance between an attractive, durable property that tenants want to live in, against not paying for unnecessary gimmicks or an over-specified property which simply does not impact the rent.

- **Agency costs:** Who is acting as agent is an important consideration, and what they are being paid might surprise you! There are certain costs which can be avoided in this area (these are covered later in Chapter 6: Other purchase costs).

- **Facilitation and completion costs (purchase costs):**
  - **Taxes and legal costs:** You will have to pay taxes and legal costs when you buy. However, knowing precisely what you are paying will be very important. With the top rate of Stamp Duty Land Tax in the UK now an eyewatering 17% and anticipated growth rates in London at less than 3%, it is easy to see why having a long-term plan is important, and why understanding the relationship between growth and the total purchase price is critical.
  - **FX rates (purchase costs):** Currency is a great way to enhance returns and reduce purchase costs. For many investors, particularly in Asia and the Middle East, the strength of the USD (to which most Asian currencies are pegged) against the AUD, NZD, and GBP has been a key growth driver. However, what you are paying to purchase currency is a key consideration: this one is a no-brainer for offshore investors.
  - **Furniture & fittings:** In some markets, buying furniture and fittings are key to getting a tenant. Understanding what these costs are and driving them down will also impact your ability to improve financial performance.

- **Dealing costs:** These refer to the amount above the book value which you would otherwise pay. You do not want to pay these costs *under any circumstances*.

CHAPTER 5

Sales and Marketing Campaigns

The sales and marketing campaign is where the rubber hits the road for most investors, it is your first interaction with a company which is selling real estate for investment. That company may be a property agency, a developer directly, or some other third party such as a financial adviser.

As an investor, the sales and marketing campaign is where you have the greatest influence on the key risks of a developer. Pragmatically dealing with these risks can save you a huge amount of money and significantly enhance your overall return.

To fully appreciate how you can impact the developer's risks, you first need to understand how a sales and marketing campaign works. At Colliers International, I marketed about 100 new development projects a year for more than ten years. I have seen first-hand the financial waste incurred in sales and marketing campaigns.

As you read through this chapter, I suggest that you keep in the back of your mind that all sales and marketing campaigns have three core objectives:

- To achieve the highest price possible for the development by selling each of the individual properties for as much as possible;
- To create the largest possible audience to promote the development to;
- To sell all the properties before completion.

The ways in which different developers and property agencies construct their sales and marketing campaigns vary. Here, I have set out the principal considerations most developers and property agents will go through in developing and executing a sale and marketing campaign.

SWOT analysis

Some type of high-level analysis, such as a SWOT analysis, is typically the starting point for anyone determining what their sales and marketing campaign should look like. Some of this work will have been done by the developer when they purchased the land and decided to develop it. They would not have purchased the land if they did not already see the value in developing it.

However, this is a useful exercise as it helps drive thinking about the key selling points for potential purchasers (in terms of strengths and opportunities). These will be the areas where the development offers advantages or opportunities, or characteristics which might be valuable to potential purchasers. I provide an overview here, together with some thoughts about what the concerns about buying will be from the same group of people (i.e., weaknesses and threats).

It is this SWOT analysis that will form the key value proposition which the developer and agent are trying to convey to potential purchasers.

Table 5.1 is a SWOT analysis of Kingsley Tower. The comparable properties to which I refer are outlined in Chapter 3.

Table 5.1: Kingsley Tower, SWOT analysis

Strengths	Weaknesses
Kingsley Tower is in London Underground Zone 2, an area very popular for commuters. Metropolis is a popular residential location; there is great local amenity including a vibrant local high street with banks, supermarkets, cafes, and popular restaurants. There are highly rated local schools and colleges nearby.	There are currently many residential development schemes for sale in the market, including Comparable(s) A, E, and F. Several historic and new-build re-sales in the Metropolis area are being marketed by local property agents. The uncertainty of Brexit means that some residents are concerned about their jobs and may delay purchasing decisions.
Opportunities	**Threats**
Values have already been established by Comparable(s) A, E, and F, which have successfully been sold in recent years. The area is well regarded as an area of urban renewal, and is likely to experience rising demand as this regeneration takes place. Areas around Metropolis have recently experienced significant price growth. As prices continue to rise, many residents may be priced out of nearby locations and will choose to relocate to Metropolis. Brexit: the uncertainty created has weakened the pound relative to many international currencies, thus enticing many international investors.	New capital gains taxes have been introduced for international buyers, which may deter some from purchasing. New stamp duties have been introduced for buy-to-let and second home buyers. The uncertainty of Brexit means that some residents are concerned about their jobs and may delay purchasing decisions.

Determining the potential sales profile

The Global Financial Crisis (GFC) in 2007-8 has completely changed how developers sell their development projects.

Before the GFC, developers were happy to slowly sell through their development projects in the knowledge that after the development there would be some remaining apartments which they would sell as 'completed stock'.

However, the impact of the GFC was to pull all the available credit (debt) out of the market, meaning that it was difficult for developers to borrow money for developments, and that purchasers had huge difficulties in obtaining mortgages. The net impact was that residential property markets stalled, and many developers went bankrupt.

The adage that the property market would always go up went out of the window. The banks funding the developers now demand that they sell a significant amount of their developments off-plan before they will lend them the money for construction. This may sound like an insignificant change; I can assure you it was not, and as an investor, *this is where all your negotiation power comes from.*

As an off-plan investor, your sale helps the developer to achieve their sales targets, which they need to do to obtain the funding to develop the building. Without you and investors like you, the development will not happen, period.

Sales and marketing campaign milestones

When property agents and developers plan sales and marketing campaigns, they have three specific *sales milestones* in mind.

- **Sales milestone 1 – pre-sales:** All developers have a pre-sales target which they must achieve to trigger funding for development and commence construction. This varies across developers, but it is typically 30% – 50% of the total number of apartments for sale in the development or phase.

- **Sales milestone 2 – sales rate:** Once they have commenced construction on site, developers have a set sales rate that they need to maintain to sell through the site. This is typically a weekly sales rate. For example, if a developer needs to sell 40 apartments in a year, they need to achieve a monthly sales rate of 3.33, or 0.77 weekly.

- **Sales milestone 3 – no stock units:** Developers target to have completely sold out of all the apartments in their development before the completion of the development. Having unsold apartments after completion means that they must keep sales centres open and have costs for financing, which hits their bottom line.

To hit all three of these key sales milestones, developers and agents need to give some thought to who the likely buyers are and what their characteristics are. Not all buyers are the same; they have a wide range of different purchase objectives and financial capacities. This diversity impacts the timing in terms of when they are likely to purchase.

Purchaser characteristics

If you exclude social housing, which the general public cannot purchase, buyers fall into four key groups:

- Institutional Investors
- Large Buyers and Underwriters
- Retail investors
- Owner Occupiers

By understanding these four buyer groups, agents and developers can determine what their sales profile will look like and plan a sales and marketing campaign to ensure that their sales milestones are reached.

Institutional investors

Large institutional investors are typically pension funds and long-term investors. They have access to huge amounts of capital which they obtain at low cost because they are highly risk adverse. They buy high-quality residential assets on the basis of huge amounts of research on the demographics of the local market and the quality of potential future rental income.

These institutional investors purchase residential investments to hold for a long period of time, and they seek to generate a return over and above the cost of their capital.

Most of these investors now fall into a group of investors called the Private Rented Sector (PRS). These investors typically purchase whole developments, in order to generate economies of scale in the management of these properties.

Because institutional investors buy a significant volume of apartments in a single transaction, they have a huge amount of bargaining power when it comes to negotiating with a developer. Institutional investors purchase property via one of two different purchase structures, which are where their power comes from:

- **Forward purchase agreement:** This is an agreement to purchase where the developer agrees to sell an entire building to a single investor. The developer and investor enter a contract at an early stage of the development, sometimes even before planning has been secured. Under a forward purchase agreement, the investor will generally pay a deposit at the time of contract, and will then pay the balance of the purchase price upon completion of the building.

- **Forward funding agreement:** This is an agreement where the investor provides the finance to fund the costs of the development. The investor agrees to purchase the land and then makes monthly payments to the developer based on the amount of construction undertaken in the month. Once the building is complete the investor makes a final balancing payment, from which the developer derives their development profit.

An investor would expect to pay a lower price for a forward funding agreement than a forward purchase agreement, because they are accepting a greater amount of risk. However, with both a forward funding and forward purchase, the investor can secure the best terms which a developer is likely to give to a purchaser. Because the investor has removed *all* the sales risk from the development, the developer simply needs to finish the building and move on.

Large buyers and underwriters

Large buyers and underwriters are more opportunistic than institutional investors, and generally tend to trade their investments more regularly.

- **Large buyers:** Are typically looking for a combination of both yield and capital appreciation. They are generally seeking to benefit from generating a high discount simply by buying a lot of apartments from a developer in a single transaction and therefore reducing the developer's sales risk.

- **Underwriters:** Are a large group of buyers who have been around for a long time, but who are rarely discussed. They buy large volumes of apartments from a developer at a significant discount. They then re-sell the apartments to individual purchasers at a higher price, and the profit between the two is their 'margin'. They are no different from a retailer of widgets, which buys a lot of widgets from a manufacturer and then breaks up a large allocation of widgets and markets and sells them through their retail channel.

Retail investors

As a small investor, you fall into this category. Retail investors form an enormous part of the new-build development market. Retail investors fall below large investors in the pecking order. Retail investors are generally referred to as buy-to-let investors, or private landlords.

In 2018, the Ministry of Housing, Communities & Local Government (MHCLG) in England surveyed private landlords, something it does every four years, I have set out the findings below because they summarise the situation for most retail investors well.

Summary of MHCLG Survey 2018:

- 94% of landlords rent property as an individual, 4% as part of a company, and 2% as part of a company or organisation.
- 70% of landlords have let property for six years or more.
- The average amount of time a landlord had owned property was 11.5 years.
- 53% of landlords bought their first rental property intending to rent it out.

Ownership of Property:
Almost half (45%) of private landlords own one buy-to-let property, almost 40% own two to four properties, and more than 15% own five or more properties.

Figure 5.1: Ownership of Investment Property

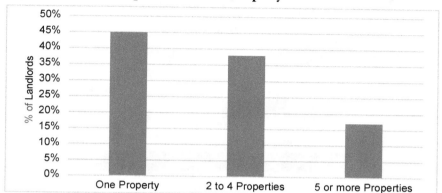

Reasons for becoming a landlord:

- 46% prefer property to other investments
- 44% to contribute to their pension
- Only 4% to let property as a full-time business

Landlords' motives to purchase:

- 47% as an investment for rental income
- 30% for capital growth
- 14% viewed their investment as a part-time business
- 59% long-term investment for pension

Figure 5.2: Landlords by Age

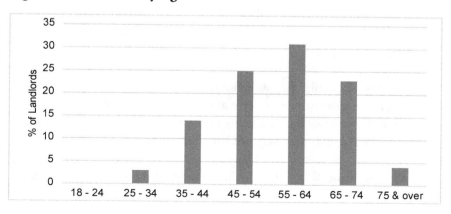

Figure 5.3: Rental income as a proportion of total income

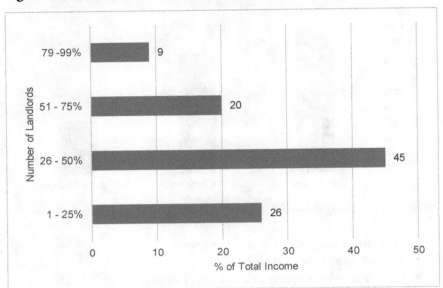

Owner-occupiers

Owner-occupiers have the weakest bargaining power with developers. Typically when purchasing a new-build development, first-time buyers or other buyers move from an existing property to the next rung up the property ladder. Several factors impact owner-occupiers' negotiating power and drive their decision-making in terms of their purchase:

- **Existing scenario:** Typically, they will be living in rented accommodation. They will have relatively limited options to purchase because they will need to look for a property that is either complete or close to completion at the time their lease ends.

- **Timing:** Typically, they do not have the confidence or capital to put down a deposit and reserve a property years off-plan. They are generally younger and less financially established, and they cannot take the risk that they may not get a mortgage.

- **Competition:** When they are in the market to buy, there is a much larger pool of buyers competing for a small amount of stock, because logically, there always will be in the market when developments are close to being completed. Typically, competition is high 6 to 9 months pre-completion of the development.

- **Reduced developer risk:** Developers will be far further through the sales cycle and therefore will be less willing to discount because they are likely to be relatively well forward sold, and they will have much lower sales risk.

- **Repayment elasticity:** Owner-occupiers are typically willing to pay more than an investor because they have greater repayment elasticity. Owner-occupiers can borrow a greater proportion of the value of a property at lower rates than investors. Their equation will favour the fact that they will no longer be putting dead money into rent. Therefore, they are likely to accept higher monthly payments at a lower interest rate, which means they can ultimately borrow more money.

- **Government schemes:** Governments around the world have introduced schemes to help younger people and first-time buyers get on to the property ladder. These are generally aimed at new-build property, because these stimulate the economy by creating jobs from new construction. This means owner-occupiers will have a financial incentive to buy, and developers will have an incentive to sell to them.

- **Emotional attachment:** Owner-occupiers have an emotional attachment, which is something unquantifiable. Investors do not, or at least they shouldn't be emotionally attached to real estate. For them, it is simply a transaction for which they risk capital with the expectation of a return. This is not the case for owner-occupiers, who have expectations about where they want to live and the type of property they want to make their homes in.

Market segmenting

Once a property agent and developer have established the sales profile and have built a broad concept of who the key buyers will be and when they are likely to buy in the purchasing cycle, they will determine how to segment the market and the best ways to deal with these segments.

Their profiles of different groups of buyers look like those in Table 5.2:

Table 5.2: Buyer characteristics

Purchaser Type	Characteristics	
Owner Occupiers	Pay the highest price Limited input into the scheme Purchase late in the sale process Low risk of failure to complete the sale	Large market Always in the local area Easy to find and access
Retail investors	Pay more than large investors, but less than owner-occupiers Purchase early in a sales campaign Low risk of failure to complete the sale	Smaller market All over the world Difficult and expensive to find and access
Large Buyers & Underwriters	Pay low prices, look to achieve a discount of 15% – 20% Purchase at the start or before sales and marketing campaign commencing Moderate risk of failure to complete the sale	Small market All over the world Easy to find
Institutional Investors	Will not purchase from a retail sales campaign Want input into building design Forward funding of forward purchase deals Low risk of failure for complete sale	Small market Generally focused on small geographic areas Easy to find

It is possible to map when these different buyer groups are likely to engage in the sales and marketing campaign – I call this the Buyer Spectrum.

Figure 5.4: The Buyer Spectrum

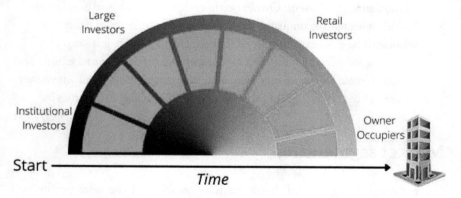

126

Sales campaign outline

When planning their sales campaign, the developer and agent need to think about who the potential purchasers are, and what they are looking for.

There are two variables with these buyer groups:

- The time when they are looking to buy; and
- The amount they are willing to pay.

Figure 5.5: Time when different buyers purchase

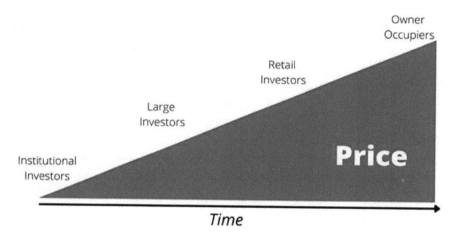

If you think of the blue triangle in Figure 5.5 as the purchase price, you know that institutional investors are likely to pay the lowest amount for the property, but want to buy early in the development process. Owner-occupiers will purchase late in the sales and marketing campaign and are likely to pay the highest price for the property. Somewhere in the triangle between the two are larger buyers, underwriters, and retail investors.

You also know that institutional investors want to have input into the design, and are unlikely to purchase once a sales and marketing campaign has commenced. Because they only typically purchase whole buildings, they cannot do this if one or two apartments have already been sold.

Therefore, there are only two options:

- Sell the entire development to an institutional investor *at a lower cost with less risk*; or
- Sell the development to the other purchasers – large buyers, underwriters, retail investors, and owner-occupiers – via a Retail Sales Campaign *at a higher cost with greater risk.*

Most developers initially go to the institutional market to find out if satisfactory commercial terms can be agreed upon. If this is not possible, they will execute a retail sales campaign.

Selling to an institutional purchaser

This is a relatively straightforward and low-cost process. Institutional investors are well-known and easy to find. They are sophisticated investors and do not need glossy sales brochures to make purchase decisions. They have access to high-quality market information, and can make decisions quickly.

The developer will likely appoint an agent to market the scheme to these buyers; they will prepare some basic marketing materials with enough information for the investors to do their due diligence.

Retail sales campaign

A retail sales campaign is vastly different from an institutional sales campaign, and there are three potential groups of purchasers to which the developer can sell its apartments:

- Large investors and underwriters
- Retail investors
- Owner-occupiers

We know that in planning their sales and marketing campaign, developers will have two primary sales milestones in mind:

- Achieve pre-sales to commence construction and get the development off the ground
- Be completely sold out by the completion

We also know that a developer will want to achieve the highest price possible for the apartments or properties they are building. Further, we know that owner-occupiers are only likely to purchase property in the final 6 – 9 months before completion.

So, in determining what their sales and marketing campaign should like, the developer will need to understand two key items:

- How many pre-sales are required to draw down funding?
- How many sales can they achieve in the final 6 – 9 months pre-completion, when owner-occupiers will be most active?

Consequently, the gap between these two sales targets is the final sales milestone (sales rate) which is the sales rate they need to achieve to have completely sold out before completion.

Example

Let's consider this in practice for Kingsley Tower and make the following assumptions:

- It contains 100 apartments and will take three years to complete from buying the land to finishing the building;
- Owner-occupiers will purchase at a rate of four apartments a month in the six months pre-completion;
- The retail sales campaign will commence two years before completion.

We are likely to see a divergence in how each of the two example developers plans their sales and marketing campaign.

Osborne Corporation uses internal funding and is likely to have a lower pre-sales target, as the perceived risk will be much lower. Their pre-sale target is 30%. The key milestones are therefore:

- Pre-sales Target = 30 Sales;
- Sales in final six months = 26 sales;
- Therefore, they will need to sell 44 apartments in the 18 months leading up to the final six months when domestic sales are active – i.e. 2.4 sales per month - to ensure that their apartments are all sold before completion.

Ashley's Homes has higher pre-sale targets, as their debt providers will see this as a riskier development. Their pre-sale target is 50%. The key milestones are:

- Pre-sales Target = 50 sales;
- Sales in final six months = 26 sales;
- Therefore, they will need to sell 24 apartments in the 18 months leading up to the final six months when domestic sales are active – i.e. 1.33 sales per month - to ensure that their apartments are all sold before completion.

In practice, the following will likely happen:
Osborne Corporation will:

- Have an onsite sales and marketing suite
- Have their own sales team
- Seek to push prices throughout the sales and marketing campaign

Ashley's Homes will:

- Use a property agent to deal with local sales
- Attempt to push sales prices, but sales will be their ultimate driver rather than price

Each developer will have the same basic sales profile, which is illustrated in the next section.

Typical sales profile

The retail sales and marketing campaign needs to be designed to appeal to those potential investors who are likely to be actively looking and willing to purchase at that point in the sales and marketing campaign.

This will depend on the size of the development and the price point. Generally, sales and marketing campaigns for most larger developments of 80 plus apartments will have six sales phases, during which different buyers are far more likely to be active:

1. **Pre-sales (institutions):** Developers will look for one large bulk deal or a series of larger deals with institutional and large investors.

2. **Pre-sales:** If the developer is not successful in agreeing a transaction with a large investor, they will need to achieve pre-sales with retail investors.

3. **Achieve Sales Rate (construction started):** The pre-sale target will have been achieved, and the developer will be looking to increase the price and/or decrease dealing margins. Large investors will not be willing to purchase at this point in the sales and marketing campaign. Retail investors and owner-occupiers are likely to be those making up the sales rate. The developer may or may not have a sales and marketing suite on-site or close to the development.

4. **Increase Sales Rate (construction started):** 6 to 9 months pre-completion, the developer will seek to increase their pricing. At this point they are likely to be unwilling to offer much discount if they are on track for their sales target. Owner-occupiers will start to view the development at sales and marketing suites.

5. **Completion:** This will be the final few months to completion, during which time the most active buyers are likely to be owner-occupiers, because it will be much easier for them to obtain a mortgage at this point.

6. **Post-Completion:** If the developer has not sold all of their apartments, they will now have 'stock apartments'. This is positive for owner-occupiers, as it means there are properties that they could immediately move into. From a developer's perspective, stock apartments cause a major issue, as the developer will need to keep the sales and marketing suite open which means they will continue to incur costs. In addition, they will not be able to recognise the revenue and profit that the sales would have generated. Many savvy investors will now re-enter the space looking for deals, as they can leverage the fact that they are in a strong position to complete a transaction quickly.

The shape of a developer's sales and marketing campaign will also depend on whether they intend to promote their development to international investors.

International investors

Most developers across the world promote their development to international investors in Asia and the Middle East. In determining whether to promote their development internationally, they will need to weigh up several different factors:

- **Depth of domestic market:** For most developers, there is not the depth of domestic market to achieve their required pre-sales target. Developers need to achieve pre-sales 18 – 24 months before completion, and there are very few owner-occupiers who will commit to purchase this far ahead of completion. In most markets, there are not enough domestic investors either.

- **Cost of marketing internationally:** International sales and marketing campaigns are hugely expensive. Developers need to weigh up the cost of marketing relative to the likelihood of success.

- **Speed of transaction:** Asia and the Middle East are well-known low-cost income tax locations, and are also locations with a significant amount of high-income earners. Many highly liquid investors do not want to invest in their home country because of a lack of opportunities. These offshore investors generally make far quicker investment decisions, making Asia and the Middle East an attractive location for developers to promote their developments.

- **Currency advantage:** Most Asian currencies are pegged to the US dollar, and many countries' investors can take advantage of currency fluctuations by investing offshore.

How do international investors purchase?

International investors purchase property off-plan in a completely different way to domestic investors and owner-occupiers. The majority purchase investment property via arranged sales events, typically:

- **Property investor shows:** There are many organised property investor events throughout Asia and the Middle East that developers and investors attend. They are held in large conference facilities.

- **Small dinner and cocktail events:** Individual developers hold smaller events for specific investors where they promote a specific development or a series of developments.
- **Investment seminars:** Property agents hold events on investing in international property.
- **Sales exhibitions:** Particularly in Hong Kong, Singapore, Malaysia, Shanghai, and Beijing, developers hold 2-day or 3-day exhibitions in 5-star hotels which are focused sales events for a specific new development.

The combination of the types of sales events that a developer holds in Asia and/or the Middle East depends on the price of the development and where the developer or agent expects to achieve the greatest number of sales.

Some countries, such as the United Kingdom, have specific rules and market conventions that require developers to launch the development first to their domestic market.

Sales and marketing materials

Developers need sales and promotional materials to help potential purchasers understand the proposed development. Unlike a property for sale in the second-hand market, there is nothing to see or physically visit for purchasers. Therefore, developers are likely to prepare more detailed information and point of sale materials.

The development of the marketing materials starts with the appointment of a marketing agency. These companies are experts at putting together highly compelling marketing and promotional materials designed specifically to capture your attention and convert you into a prospective purchaser.

These agencies spend hundreds of hours poring over the smallest details, from font type to brand name, to offer exactly the right message and materials. These will typically include:

- **Computer generated images:** These show what the development will look like when it is complete.

- **Floor Plans, building plans, and site plans:** Detailed plans showing the layout of the apartments and buildings so that buyers have a sense of what they are buying and how the apartment will work.

- **Development models:** Scale models are built of the development. These are shipped from event to event to bring the concept of the building to life.

- **Aerial photos and view shots:** Ariel photos enable buyers to understand the position of the development within the context of the surrounding area, and the view shots assist buyers in 'checking' the expected view from their apartment.

- **Marketing brochure:** Glossy coffee table brochures are produced to give buyers a sense of quality and prestige about the asset they are buying and the lifestyle they will lead if they choose to live in the property.

- **Short videos and fly-throughs:** Seductive short videos of the development and the surrounding area are produced to give a sense of the fantastic development which will be created, and are often used to sell an aspirational 'lifestyle'.

- **Digital assets and adverts:** A host of digital assets such as landing pages as well as adverts are created for press and digital advertising on social media.

Sales and marketing campaign costs

The cost of sales and marketing campaigns is much larger proportion of your cost base than you might imagine. Sales and marketing campaign costs fall within three core expense categories:

- Advertising and promotional expenses;
- Events; and
- Logistics.

Advertising and promotional expenses

All sales organisations work on what is generally referred to as a sales funnel. This refers to a process through which potential prospective purchasers are taken where they are found, qualified, and hopefully ultimately purchase the product or service which the organisation is selling.

Figure 5.5: Sales funnel

The basic premise of a sales funnel is that a developer will need to make a significantly higher number of potential purchasers aware of the product or service they are selling than the number of products they have to sell.

From a real estate perspective, typically agents and developers will work on the following metrics:

- Awareness – 1,000 potential purchasers
- Interest – 100 potential purchasers
- Decision – 10 potential purchasers
- Action – 1 sale

To put this in perspective, to sell 100 apartments, the developer will need to get their product in front of 100,000 potential purchasers. This is not the public – it refers to the people actively engaged in thinking about buying real estate.

Awareness phase

In the initial 'awareness' phase of the sales and marketing campaign, a significant amount of cost is involved. How much money is spent in this initial phase will depend on who is driving the campaign:

- **Developers:** They have no incentive to spend more money on advertising and promotion than they need to. They can generate some brand recognition from advertising internationally. However, most will be far more interested in keeping their costs as low as possible to drive profitability.

- **Property agents:** The motive is different for property agents, as they are not spending their own money. Their remuneration comes via a commission, and advertising expenses are separate expenses borne by the developer. Any advertising they do for the development includes both their logo and contact information. There is no incentive for them to restrict the money spent on advertising, because it allows them to do two things:
  - Promote their brand in the media using someone else's money! This is referred to as Vendor Paid Advertising (VPA) in the property industry; and
  - It helps them to build their customer database.

Advertising and promotions
These vary depending on how often they are shown, the time they are shown, and the length of the promotional period. Broadly, advertising for off-plan property comes in the following forms:

Outdoor media
Outdoor media include things like billboards, outdoor signs, signage in train stations, airports, and shopping centres. Outdoor advertising is generally purchased in blocks of weeks or months, and is very expensive. A prominent billboard or selections of advertising in a major train or underground station may start at $US 10,000 per week, and can even cost more than $US 100,000 per week.

Because of its cost, outdoor media is typically only used for large developments for short periods in a very targeted way. However, this form of media is still used. Many developers have promoted in Heathrow Airport or major tube stations to capture a significant amount of interest.

Digital media
Digital media is a broad area of advertising and promotion, and covers several different activities from banner advertising on prominent websites and targeted email campaigns to selected databases through to social media.

There is a general perception that digital advertising is cheap. It can be if it is not targeted, and simply broadcasts generally. However, highly targeted digital advertising is hugely expensive because it targets extremely specific groups of people.

For example, a targeted email campaign may cost up to USD 0.20 per email - which may not sound like a lot of money. However, if a company is sending tens of thousands of emails every week, these small costs can add up to a significant amount of money.

The costs are even higher to run a cost per click (CPC) advertising campaign in Asia. Consider the following data on promoting property search terms on digital media.

Table 5.3: CPC Google ad costs (May 2021)

Location	Key Words	Average Cost Per Click (USD)
Singapore	Buying property in Melbourne	7.71
Singapore	Buying property in London	4.52
Hong Kong	Buying property in London	34.02
Hong Kong	How to buy a house in Melbourne	40.57

If the marketing campaign for Kingsley Tower relied on meeting half of the required prospects (50,000) in paid Google advertising campaign, the cost would be $US 1,701,000 – just to encourage potential buyers to click on an ad!

Press

Press advertising has fallen out of favour over recent years as digital media has become more dominant. However, it is still used for property promotion, because a high proportion of the demographic who buy property tends to be older. The average age of a first-time home buyer in the United Kingdom is 33, and the average age of more than 59% of landlords is 55 years old - this latter demographic is more likely to read a newspaper.

The costs for print media can be huge. Pricing is generally based on the size of the ad, the page it is on, the section of the paper it is in, the day it is published, and whether it is in colour.

Large print advertisements in national papers start at circa. $US 25,000 per advertisement, and can quickly increase if the advert is in colour in a prominent position within the paper. When you consider that the average development may use several weeks of press advertising in multiple countries, the cost can easily become significant.

Interest and decision phases

The interest and decision phase(s) promoting property overseas are different to that of a traditional sales and marketing campaign. The objective of property agents is to have both phases occurring at the same time. They want potential investors to enquire about a property and decide to purchase in a very short time.

There are two reasons why property agents are trying to do this:

- **Marketing costs:** marketing costs to promote international property projects are far higher than those for a domestic sales and marketing campaign. This is because the property is located offshore, so there is a much smaller pool of potential investors than for a property located in the domestic market. Therefore, property agents need to spend a lot more money on the awareness phase to meet a small proportion of the population.
- **Lack of urgency:** there is no real urgency for investors to buy offshore, particularly in countries like China, Hong Kong, Singapore, and Malaysia, where overseas properties are constantly being marketed.

To overcome the high marketing costs and the lack of investor urgency, property agents focus on very short sales and marketing campaigns where all potential investors are pushed into focused sales events.

Sales Events

Event-based sales campaigns in Asia are a popular method of achieving sales in the new-build industry. This is because they are an easy way to get a significant amount of people together in the same place at the same time, and explain and sell the property. These small events are used to create a sense of urgency, and are typically held in many locations and formats, such as:

- **5 Star Hotels** in major city centres, such as the Mandarin Oriental in Hong Kong, the Regent Hotel in Singapore, and other hotels and restaurants in major locations;

- **Organised exhibitions for new developments**, where many developers attend, such as the Excel centre in London or the Exhibition Centre in Hong Kong. These investment shows are held regularly throughout the world; and
- **Small dinner and cocktail events** at prominent retail locations such as expensive retail shops, luxury car showrooms, and expensive restaurants.

Property exhibitions have been held in Asia for over 20 years, and have gained traction over the past ten years as developers have had a greater need to secure off-plan sales before they can draw down funds and begin constructing the building.

As the GFC hit property markets globally, developers from around the world have been required to look offshore for buyers, as their local markets were not deep enough to pick up the supply. Exhibiting property in Asia is now a mainstay for developers from all over the world.

Table 5.4: Hong Kong property exhibitions 2019 & 2020

Year	Number of Exhibitions	Number of Projects Promoted	Number of Cities Promoted	Number of Countries Promoted	Number of Agents Promoting
2019	984	365	57	21	85
2020	913	335	44	13	128

On average in Hong Kong in 2020, there were 17 exhibitions per weekend, with properties for sale from 13 different countries.

As more and more developers flock to Asia to sell their properties, the competition between developers has skyrocketed. What does this mean? It means that each developer must spend more and more on promotional activities to stand out from the crowd.

Branding is especially important for developers, and as such, there is little point in a developer promoting a scheme with apartments starting at US$ 500,000 in a 3* hotel outside a city centre. Therefore, developers are forced to pay for expensive 5* hotels that can cost $USD 100,000 for the weekend to entice well-heeled buyers in a suitable environment to sell their project.

Setup and logistics

As you might imagine, it is not enough to hire an empty hotel room and simply sit and talk to buyers. A significant amount of work and collateral are required to fill the room:

- Lightboxes
- Televisions (hire from the hotel)
- Model or models
- Boxes of brochures
- People

The costs of setting up these events, and then shipping all the above (including the people!) to multiple destinations where the event will be repeated, require an awful lot of planning, and a significant amount of money. But, for all the reasons I've explained in this book, for developments to be built and get off the ground, developers have had no choice but to follow this format of exhibitions.

What does a typical international marketing budget cost?

The sales and marketing costs for developments vary significantly, depending on the size of the development, where it is marketed, and whether the scheme is launched internationally.

To provide a guide as to what an international marketing campaign might look like, I have set out the costs of a typical sales and marketing campaign for a mid-sized development with exhibitions in different Asian locations.

Table 5.5: Typical exhibition costs

Centre	Detail	Cost (USD)
Singapore	3 day exhibition	250,000
Kuala Lumpur	2 day exhibition	150,000
Hong Kong	3 day exhibition	300,000
Guangzhou	2 day exhibition	150,000
Shanghai	2 day exhibition	150,000
Beijing	2 day exhibition	100,000
	Shipping	100,000
TOTAL COSTS		1,200,000

As you can see, the costs of hosting these international events are massive - and that's without any guarantee of success. However, developers have no option but to host these events, and they have no way of paying for the events other than adding the cost to the price of the apartments.

Don't forget, there will also be sales and marketing for the portion of the scheme launched in the domestic sales market as well. This is just the cost to sell the portion of the scheme which is required to be pre-sold before construction commencing.

There are other issues with exhibitions too:

- **Unforeseen circumstances:** The success of a 'launch' will hinge on the results of one weekend, which completely unforeseen circumstances can impact, such as a typhoon, or a protest. Despite the months of planning and the unrecoverable costs incurred, a developer may ultimately achieve no sales if they are impacted in such a way.

- **Competition:** Several developers may all be in competition on the same weekend, not just by exhibiting that weekend but also from those who are advertising future events. It may just be that they cannot compete effectively against other developers promoting their projects that weekend, and the exhibition fails.

Ultimately, the developer is spending a significant proportion of their marketing budget on an international sales launch because they must achieve sales. However, there is no guarantee of a return in the form of sales. This is a problem for you, the investor, as the cost of the exhibition needs to be paid for by someone.

Because developers only derive income from the sale of a property, they must cover the costs of selling that property in the cost of the property itself. Hence, the cost of the international marketing campaign is covered within the cost of the property, which is, of course, paid for by you, the investor.

Example: Kingsley Tower

Let's put these costs into perspective with Kingsley Tower. The sales targets were between 30 and 50 apartments, meaning the cost for sales and marketing will be approximately US$ 24,000 to US$ 36,000, assuming the developer hits their sales targets. But what if they don't? The cost per sale can start increasing significantly.

Let's narrow it down further, to an exhibition in Hong Kong that costs $US 300,000. Let's assume an average sales value for each property of $US 500,000, and an average commission of 3.0% of the gross sales price.

Table 5.6: Sales outcome of property exhibitions for developers, investors, and property agents

Number of Sales	Investors	Property Developer		Property Agent	
	Cost (US$) Incurred Per Sale	Event Costs (US$) Incurred	Agency Fees Incurred (US$)	Costs (US$) Associated with event	Fees (US$)
0	0	300,000	0	0	0
1	300,000	300,000	15,000	0	15,000
2	150,000	300,000	30,000	0	30,000
3	100,000	300,000	45,000	0	45,000
4	75,000	300,000	60,000	0	60,000
5	60,000	300,000	75,000	0	75,000
6	50,000	300,000	90,000	0	90,000
7	42,857	300,000	105,000	0	105,000
8	37,500	300,000	120,000	0	120,000
9	33,333	300,000	135,000	0	135,000
10	30,000	300,000	150,000	0	150,000

Try it for yourself
If you want to see the full impact of the cost of marketing campaigns on sale prices, download our calculator at **www.proptechpioneer.com/propser** which will show you how quickly these costs can escalate.

Action phase
Once investors have been through the awareness, interest, and decision phases, property agents try to quickly get investors into the action phase. The objective here is to get investors legally committed to a purchase as quickly as possible.

By creating a frenzy-like atmosphere in an exhibition room, property agents can create a sense of high-intensity excitement. They aim to create the sense that if an investor leaves the room, they will miss their opportunity to buy and someone else will step in from a long queue of investors, happy to take up the opportunity that they were silly enough to walk away from.

By bringing solicitors, financial advisers, and letting agents with them, they create a scenario where all the necessary ingredients exist to get an investor to commit to a deal and exchange contracts to purchase a property.

At the time, it almost sounds too good to be true! But the reality is that these events take place all the time, and it is because this is possible that developers will continue to find property agents to run these events for them.

CHAPTER 6

Other Purchase Costs

In addition to the purchase price of investment property which includes baked-in sales and marketing costs, there are a whole host of additional costs which you need to be aware of.

Some of these costs are relatively obvious, such as stamp duties and other taxes imposed by regulatory authorities. However, other costs are less obvious - such as unnecessary costs due to over specification, agency fees and how they are imposed, as well as the costs involved with purchasing currency, etc.

Purchase taxes and charges

The purchase taxes and charges associated with buying property are extremely high, and vary significantly between different countries. Although the names of each change between countries, as an investor you pay three basic charges with a real estate purchase:

- **Conveyancing fees:** The legal fees associated with instructing a conveyancer to act on your behalf;
- **Stamp Duty:** A tax charged by the government; and
- **Registration and transfer charges:** An administrative charge to transfer ownership.

The largest of these three costs is stamp duty, which changes depending on the type of buyer you are (e.g., first-time buyer, owner-occupier, investor), and in some situations, on where you live.

It is difficult to fully cover all of the different taxes which may be levied on investors, as they change from time to time - in the UK, they have changed virtually every year for the past five years!

In this section, I have focused on taxes and charges involved with purchases in Australia (NSW), New Zealand, and the United Kingdom, because this will give you a really good snapshot of how these costs work. In addition, for the United Kingdom, because the costs of taxes vary between countries I have focused on the taxes imposed on the purchase of property located in England and Wales.

However, in my library, I regularly update buyer guides and country guides. These can be found at: **www.proptechpioneer.com**

Australia

In Australia, each state and territory maintains a central register of all land which shows the owner of the land. This title is the official record.

Conveyancing fees

Conveyancers use relatively standard fee structures, and their fees are generally charged in three categories:

- **A fixed professional legal fee:** The cost of the conveyancer's time;
- **Search fees:** The cost of obtaining legal information for due diligence; and
- **Additional costs:** Professional and search charges.

Because the Australian Title system (Torrens System) is computerised and relatively straightforward, the costs associated with conveyancing there are relatively low.

Table 6.1: Average conveyancing fees NSW ($AUD)

Location	Fixed Professional Legal Charge	Standard Searches	Average Total Estimate
New South Wales	$750 – $1,000	$350 – $450	$1,100 – $1,450

Stamp duty, registration and transfer fees

Stamp duty is different in each of the Australian states and territories, and varies depending on whether the purchaser is an investor or a homeowner, and whether they are Australian or have an Australian VISA. In New South Wales, Stamp Duty is called 'Transfer Duty'. It is charged when a person or company purchases a property.

Purchasers must pay the transfer duty within three months of signing a contract for sale or transfer (including off-plan purchases). There is an exemption for off-plan purchases for permanent Australian residents (who have spent more than 200 days in the last 12 months in Australia), Australian citizens, and New Zealand citizens who intend to live in the property. They can defer payment for up 12 months after the agreement to purchase is signed or until the property has been completed, whichever occurs earlier.

Table 6.2: Stamp duty rates NSW ($AUD)

Purchase Price			Rate of Stamp Duty (Transfer Duty)
$0	to	$14,000	1.25% of the purchase price
$14,001	to	$30,000	$350 plus 2.4% of every dollar over $14,000
$30,001	to	$80,000	$415 plus 1.75% of every dollar over $30,000
$80,001	to	$300,000	$1,290 plus 3.5% of every dollar over $80,000
$300,001	to	$1,000,000	$8,990 plus 4.5% of every dollar over $300,000
$1,000,001	to	$3,000,000	$40,490 plus 5.5% of every dollar over $1,000,000
$3,000,001		and over	$150,490 plus 7% of every dollar over $3,000,000

Foreign buyer surcharge

For all purchases made after 1 July 2017, foreign buyers are subject to an additional surcharge of 8% of the purchase price.

Mortgage registration fee

There is a mortgage registration fee of $AUD143.50 in instances where a mortgage is registered on the Title.

Land transfer fee

There is a land transfer fee of $AUD143.50 for each transaction.

New Zealand

New Zealand introduced the Land Transfer (Compulsory Registration of Titles) Act in 1924 which brought most of the land in New Zealand under the Torrens system, and by 1951 the register was complete, although there are still some small parcels of land which fall outside the register.

Unlike Australia, where property titles are administered at state level, New Zealand is not divided into separate states. It simply has a national government and sixteen local regional councils. The Torrens system in New Zealand is administered at the national level.

Conveyancing fees

Conveyancing fees are quite low in New Zealand, and are typically between $NZ900 – $NZ1,500.

Stamp Duty

New Zealand does not have a Stamp Duty on the purchase of a property. Nor does it have any foreign buyer surcharge; however, the New Zealand government imposes restrictions and costs on a developer if it sells a property to foreign purchasers.

Where a developer in New Zealand wishes to sell off-plan property to foreign purchasers, they need to apply to the government for an Exemption Certificate. To be eligible for an Exemption Certificate, the residential development must meet the following specific requirements:

- The development must have 1 or more multi-storey buildings;
- Each building must consist of more than 20 apartments;
- The purchaser cannot live in the property;
- The purchaser must on-sell the property within a timeframe set by the Overseas Investment Office;
- Only 60% of the development can be sold to overseas purchasers;
- The developer must pay a fee of $NZ 2,040.

These rules do not apply to purchasers who hold Singaporean citizenship. as a trade agreement exists between the governments of New Zealand and Singapore.

Transfer charges

In New Zealand, there is a fee for the lodgement and registration of an instrument and for every time a change to property title occurs such as a change of ownership; these fees are set out below.

Table 6.3: Transfer charges New Zealand ($NZ)

Fee for...	Manual	Auto-registration
Lodgement and registration of an instrument	$176	$80
New titles (issue a record of the title), each title	$135	$135

United Kingdom (England and Wales only)

The United Kingdom does not use the Torrens system for property titles. Its property ownership and registration systems are much older and far more complex. Adding a further layer of complexity, Scotland and Northern Ireland have different systems and rules to those of England and Wales. Given that the majority of investors are focused on England and Wales, I have focused on England and Wales in this section. Land records in England and Wales are recorded by HM Land Registry.

Legal fees

Legal fees in England and Wales are charged in broadly the same way as those in Australia and New Zealand. They typically have three components:

- **Professional legal fee:** The cost of the solicitor's time. There is no specific convention; however, conveyancers will usually charge either a fixed fee related to the purchase price of the property (which is generally in price bands) or a percentage of the purchase price.
- **Search fees:** The cost of obtaining legal information for due diligence such as council and utility information.
- **Additional costs:** These costs are generally referred to as disbursements.

Typically, the cost of legal fees is approximately £2,000 to £3,000,

Stamp Duty

In England and Wales, Stamp Duty is generally referred to as Stamp Duty Land Tax (SDLT). The tax is payable by the purchaser immediately after the completion of the purchase of a property.

England and Wales have SDLT regimes for property in England and Wales, which are:

- First Time Buyer SDLT
- General SDLT

First Time Buyer SDLT

Specific SDLT rates apply to any person(s) purchasing their <u>first</u> home. The rates are set out below.

Table 6.4: First time buyer SDLT England and Wales

Purchase Price	First Time Buyer SDLT
Up to £300,000	Zero
Between £300,001 and £500,000	5% of the portion of the purchase price between £300,001 and £500,000

If the purchase price of the property is more than £500,000 then the property falls outside the First Time Buyer SDLT and the General SDLT rates will apply.

General SDLT

In England and Wales SDLT is charged via a progressive system that applies to all property, and additional surcharges apply depending on whether the purchaser is buying an investment property or second home, and if they are a foreign purchaser or not. The additional surcharges are added to the SDLT, and are:

- Second Homes and Investment Property Surcharge
- Non-resident Surcharge

These surcharges are outlined in Table 6.5.

Table 6.5: England and Wales

Purchase Price			SDLT	UK Residents (Second home or Investment Property)	Non-Resident Purchasers
£0	to	£125,000	0%	3%*	5%
£125,001	to	£250,000	2%	5%	7%
£250,001	to	£925,000	5%	8%	10%
£925,001	to	£1,500,000	10%	13%	15%
£1,500,001		and above	12%	15%	17%

* For purchase prices of £40,000 or more.

Multiple dwellings relief

There is the additional benefit of Multiple Dwellings Relief (MDR). Under the MDR rules, the relief identifies the average price paid for residential units, and the average price determines the rate of SDLT (with a minimum charge of 1%). This rate is then applied proportionally to the total consideration paid for all the residential properties.

MDR rules require that all the dwellings be purchased from the same vendor at the same time. MDR applies to leasehold and freehold property.

If any of the properties being purchased are sold within three years of MDR being claimed, then the SDLT payable on the remaining properties needs to be recomputed, and any additional SDLT is required to be paid.

Acquisition of six (or more) dwellings in a single transaction deeming rule

A deeming rule applies to the transfer of six or more dwellings in a single transaction which treats them collectively as non-residential for SDLT purposes. The total consideration for all units is added up, and then the non-residential rate of SDLT is applied to the total. The non-residential rates are set out below.

Table 6.6: Non-residential SDLT rates

Property or lease premium or transfer value	SDLT Rate
Up to £150,000	0%
Next £100,000 (i.e. the portion from £150,001 to £250,000)	2%
Remaining amount (i.e. the portion above £25,001)	5%

MDR and six (or more) dwellings in single transaction deeming rule

If a purchaser buys six or more dwellings in a single transaction, they can elect for either:

- Multiple Dwelling Relief (MDR); or
- Non-residential SDLT rates to apply

Take an example where a purchaser buys ten residential properties in a single transaction from a developer for £5,000,000 at an average of £500,000 per property.

The residential rate of SDLT on each property is as follows.

Table 6.7: Normal SDLT rates (second home or investment property)

Banding	SDLT Rate	SDLT Due
First £125,000	3%	£3,750
Next £125,000	5%	£6,250
Balance £250,000	8%	£20,000
Total SDLT Due		£27,000

The total SDLT for all ten properties is 10 x £27,000 = £270,000

If the non-residential SDLT rate is applied, then the SDLT is as follows.

Table 6.8: Calculation of SDLT

Banding	SDLT Rate	SDLT Due
First £150,000	0%	0
Next £100,000	2%	£20,000
Balance £3,750,000	5%	£187,500
Total SDLT Due		£207,500

The total SDTL applying the non-residential rate in this example is £207,500, so the purchaser would opt to pay on a non-residential basis rather than seeking MDR.

Transfer charges

In addition to legal fees and SDLT, the purchaser is also required to pay Land Registration fees. These are fees payable to the Land Registry for the registration of the purchaser's title. This is done as per the table below.

Table 6.9: England and Wales transfer charges

Purchase Price of Property	Fee
Between £100,000 – £200,000	£190
£200,001 – £500,000	£270
£500,001 – £1,000,000	£540
£1,000,000+	£910

International comparison of purchase costs and taxes

Purchase costs and taxes are incredibly important considerations for investors, particularly those purchasing offshore. Below I have set out a table with a comparison.

Table 6.10: Comparison of international purchase costs and taxes in Australia, New Zealand, and England and Wales

	Australia ($AUD)	New Zealand ($NZ)	United Kingdom
Legal Fees	Between $750 and $1,500 depending on property and state	Between $750 and $1,500 depending on property and state	£2,000 - £3,000
Stamp Duty	Progressive tax regime based on the purchase price	Nil	Progressive tax regime based on the purchase price
First Home Buyer Grants	Yes	No	Yes
Surcharge for Investor and Second Home Buyer	No	No	3%
Surcharge on Non-Resident Buyer	Yes (depending on the state, up to 8%)	No	2%
Transfer Charges	$143.50	$176	Between £190 and £910 depending on the purchase price.

To help to put this into context, I have compared the cost of purchasing in each country based on purchase prices in USD.

Table 6.11: Comparison of SDLT

	Australia (NSW)	New Zealand	United Kingdom (England)
	FX Rate USD = 0.65	FX Rate USD = 0.60	FX Rate USD = 1.25
USD 500,000	769,230	833,333	£400,000
Stamp Duty	59,533	0	37,500
USD 1,000,000	$1,538,462	$1,666,666	£800,000
Stamp Duty	122,071	0	85,000
USD 1,500,000	2,307,692	2,500,000	£1,200,000
Stamp Duty	192,947	0	154,688

To illustrate the difference between these countries, I have also shown the cost of purchasing at different price points.

Figure 6.1: Comparison of Stamp Duty (international investors)

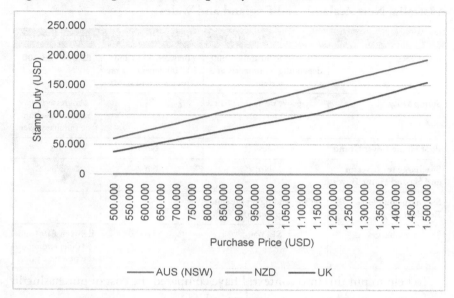

Specification

The specification is an important consideration for investors. The reality is that when procuring their construction systems, unless a developer can determine with certainty that they have a clear target market, they will not design their specification for any specific buyer.

The specification refers to the type of materials that builders and developers use in development. When people talk about the specification, from a new-build perspective there are generally two types:

- **Internal specification:** This refers to the interior of the property being purchased. It includes the internal fittings and fixtures, and the type and quality of materials used in fitting out the property. This will include things such as sanitary ware, white goods, and quality of light fittings, etc.

- **Building and development specification:** This refers to the specification of the building and development. These are features and characteristics which relate to the entire building.

Buyer groups

If you think about buyer groups who are not retail investors, their different specification requirements are interesting:

- **Institutional Investors:** Typically looking to own the property for a long period, so many have their own fit-out specifications and guidelines. These will relate not only to the specification of the units, but also the internal layouts of the space as well as the unit mix. These developers will typically look for good quality, durable fit-outs. However, because they also generate income from selling services to tenants, they will want large communal areas and generally well-specified kitchens, bathrooms, and high levels of tech gadgetry, as they typically have younger occupiers.

- **Large Buyers:** This is a diverse group of buyers. Some will be buying in bulk to achieve larger discounts, and they intend to retain the units over the long term. This group of investors will therefore want a good quality, durable fitout that lasts for a long period. Others in this group, such as underwriters, will seek to 'trade' the properties - and they will be less concerned with the specification.

- **Owner Occupiers:** Owner-occupiers are buying the property for their own use, and probably intend to hold the property for a long period. Any additional costs associated with the fit-out can be amortised in their mortgage, so they are likely to be quite willing to pay for upgrades and modifications to the space.

As a retail investor, the specification which best matches you is that of the institutional investors. But what does that mean? It means you want quality fixtures and fittings which are durable and will therefore last for a long time, and you want a specification that will appeal to a broad range of tenants. What you do not want is to pay for a series of expensive fittings and fixtures which are either over-specified or do not incrementally increase the rental income.

Specifications are typically agreed upon for institutional and large buyers. They can negotiate with the developer in the early stages of the design of the building, because generally these large investors engage in discussions to purchase in the early stages of development.

Most properties you will see for sale will be specified for owner-occupiers. This is because developers know that this group of purchasers will pay the most for their product. This group of purchasers will typically want to see a property or marketing suite before they commit to purchasing.

Competitive market

In many scenarios, there will be a significant amount of development taking place at the same time in the same location. This creates competition between local developers, who are all competing to attract the same pool of owner-occupiers.

Let's consider Metropolis and compare two or more of the comparable properties used to come up with the pricing, and think specifically about Kingsley Tower and Comparable F and their different characteristics:

- **Institutional:** Both properties are very similar, in that they have a similar set of rights and obligations. If they are leasehold (more common in the UK), the only real difference will be that perhaps the term of one lease is longer than the other. However, even if you compare a 999-year lease to a 125-year lease, there is no significant difference.
- **Economic:** They both have similar economic characteristics.
- **Physical:** From a location perspective they are both very similar, as they are in similar locations relative to the station, and have similar outlooks at ground level.

In such a competitive environment, developers need to create ways to differentiate their products from their competitors. They do this through their building specifications. Developers spend a lot of additional money on expensive fittings, finishes, and building amenities to set their products apart from competitors. These high-quality specifications are attractive to purchasers who intend to own and use the property for themselves over the long term.

This is not the case for investors, for whom expensive fit-outs often do not bring any additional rental income. However, they can add a significant cost to the purchase price of the development. Unless you are purchasing in an expensive part of a city where a is premium paid by tenants for a high-end specification it's best to steer clear of them.

You are not going to live in the property

You need to remember one thing when you are purchasing an investment property: **you are not going to live there** – it is an investment. Above all, your property needs to have a good quality specification which can be easily and cheaply maintained.

In my experience of renting properties out, tenants do not aspire to be tenants for their whole life. They typically hope to own their own home one day. This means that they are not going to want to spend all of their monthly income on rent. They will want to put a little aside each month to save towards a deposit to buy a home of their own.

Tenants will typically want a good quality property to live in which is well maintained, with a landlord who responds when the boiler needs to be fixed. The latest wine fridge or tech gadgetry might be nice for them to have; however, the circumstances in which tenants would be willing to pay additional rental for these features are extremely limited.

Also, remember that expensive equipment is generally more expensive to maintain. Expensive fridges and instant boiling taps need to be regularly serviced and their filters replaced. It's most likely that they won't be maintained by the tenant and will need repairs, and you will end up having to pay to have it done.

What is the right specification?

This is one of the few questions which only you can answer. Your answer will depend on the type of property you are purchasing and the local rental market. You need to do your research in this area by:

- **Looking on real estate portals:** To see the quality of fittings and fixtures and the level of the specification provided.
- **Speaking to rental agents:** They have their finger on the pulse and know what tenants want.

In doing your research, you should compare some new-build developments - but don't compare the newest ones. Compare a couple that are a few years old, try to search for some which you know were expensive and which had high-quality fit-outs. My guess is that you will find that the rents being asked by their landlords are not dissimilar to those for other well-maintained properties.

I have set out my thoughts on what I think is necessary for a good quality rental product, from experience - but I suggest you do your own research!

Table 6.12: Internal specification

Item	What you need	What you don't need
Kitchen		
Appliances	Good quality well-known brand appliances, with warranties and good energy ratings. Spec should include integrated appliances with a dishwasher	Branded stainless steel appliances, wine coolers, under-unit lighting, branded mixer taps
Worktops	Good quality, long-wearing worktops	Marble worktops
Upgrades	Not required	
Bathroom		
Ironmongery	Good quality well-known tap and shower units. The bathroom is where you are most likely to have to make repairs, so make sure they are a common brand	
Sanitary Ware	Good quality sanitary ware	Tenants usually do not care where the sink or bath was made.
Tech Gadgets	Not required	TVs built into mirrors, etc., are expensive to maintain and replace if something goes wrong
Heating and Cooling		
Heating	Underfloor heating is expensive to use but will save wall space, which is very important in smaller spaces If you can, the best thing to have is a central heat exchange which the building runs off.	Complicated unknown heating systems, which have not been used by the developer before, or are not common in the market. Let someone else be the guinea pig!
Air-Conditioning/ Cooling	A must in warmer climates and in taller buildings where the windows cannot be opened	
General Fitout		
Flooring	Engineered wood or tiles are the longest wearing	Avoid carpets completely if you can; they look dirty quickly and are expensive to keep maintained
Switches and socket	Consider adding additional power sockets and TV terminals	Integrated lighting systems and dimmers, etc.
Tech Gadgets	If integrated wi-fi is an option, do this	Wired speakers and other tech gadgets are all very expensive. They will date quickly and are expensive to keep maintained

Table 6.13: Building specification

Item	What you Need	What you don't need
Concierge	As more and people are ordering online, this is an important feature if available	
Gym	No	Gyms in buildings are rarely used; they are typically a compromise on equipment etc., and will not generally have free-weights due to insurance risks Tenants who want to use a gym will join one
Swimming Pool	No	These are very expensive to keep and maintain
Cinema Room	No	These are rarely used. Generally, a huge amount of money will be spent on expensive projectors and speakers
Outdoor Areas	Yes, small play areas for children and outside communal areas add a significant amount of utility for tenants	

Agency and transactional costs

I don't think the average investor buying off-plan fully appreciates the agency and transactional costs involved in some purchases. As a purchaser, you need to recognise that you will pay a fee to purchase property indirectly - there is no way around that. Even if you buy directly from a developer, you will still pay a fee to purchase as they have salespeople to pay.

The key is understanding these costs, how they work, and how much *you* as the investor are paying. Agency and transactional costs are incurred in three areas:

- Property Agency Fees
- Referral Fees
- Underwriter Costs

Property agency fees

In understanding the fees that property agencies charge, you firstly need to understand how they work.

Local property agencies

Local property agencies are smaller independent agents or franchised businesses. There are many of them, and you will likely recognise their logos. These companies usually focus on the local secondary market, which is where their principal income comes from. However, some will also get involved in the sale of new-build development.

These agencies are well established, have strong brands, and are well known within the local community for their participation in the secondary market. They generally have large sales office networks covering small geographic areas, and lots of salespeople who know the local market. These agencies have relatively small offices in suburban locations, and they have relatively low overheads.

They charge lower fees for the sale of an off-plan property than international property agents do. This is because they are rarely involved in international transactions or transactions which cover complex sales scenarios. Therefore, their fees are more closely related to the local secondary market than to fees for new-build sales. Property agency fees in the secondary market are generally lower, because typically there is less work involved in the sale as there is a physical product to sell, and there is also less work involved in the physical marketing of an individual property.

Large multinational property agencies

Large multinational property agencies have offices throughout the world. They have broad geographical reach but typically do not have a deep local sales capacity. These companies are usually involved in the off-plan sales market because of their involvement in the land market. These property agencies refer to this type of agency work as 'project marketing', because they only typically market and sell new property developments.

These companies have strong brands, and are well regarded throughout the market globally as experts in property and matters related to it. They are large and very cumbersome, which means that they cannot act in a nimble fashion to deal with changing conditions in the market. They have very high costs, because unlike smaller local property agencies they are in central city locations where office rents are high, and they have a huge amount of corporate infrastructure.

Referral fees

Referral fees are generally a significant cost that purchasers are not always aware they will have to pay. They are typically for two services:

- Sales referral fees
- Referral fee for property-related services

Sales referral fees

Sales referral fees are common, as regardless of how large an agency is or how many salespeople a developer has, they are always under pressure to achieve new sales. Because of the fierce competition generating new sales leads, property agents use referrers to introduce them to new potential investors. These third parties are called referral partners, runners, or channel partners – the names may vary from company to company, but the function is the same. These sales referral parties could be accountants, lawyers, financial service providers, education consultants, or sometimes they may simply be referred to as a runner - someone who coordinates referrals for property sales.

A developer will expect an agent to be absorb any referral fees within their own fee. However, the issue is now that as markets have softened around the world, it is far more difficult to sell property, and therefore the cost of referral fees has increased significantly as developers try to sell more and more apartments internationally.

In some instances, the referral party will seek a fee that is even greater than the agent's fee in the first place. This leaves you with two scenarios. First, the developer will pay a top-up fee, and the agent will pay part of their fee, together with the top-up fee to the referral parties. More commonly, the developer will simply pay a referral fee and an agency fee.

The net result as a purchaser is that you will ultimately be paying two parties to meet the same developer. This will mean that the cost of the fees will limit any discount from the purchase price that you might enjoy.

Third-party referrals

Another way that property agents can make additional fees is through referrals for alternative services. Purchasers typically don't buy a new-build development by itself; they also buy additional related goods and services which are required to get the property onto the market. These are typically things such as:

- Property Management and Letting
- Furniture
- Currency when the property is purchased offshore
- Accounting services
- Establishment of company structures and vehicles

It is common for agents to have relationships with third-party providers who provide these services. And, rather than simply pass this work on to their partner, many will take a referral fee for introducing the purchaser to this service provider. This is a practice known as 'Clipping the Ticket'.

Underwriter costs

Underwriters work with developers early in the sales and marketing campaign before a developer has taken the property to market. They work with the developer when the developer is concerned about its sales risk. The underwriter will step in to mitigate this risk – at a price.

An underwriter will agree to purchase part or all of the development at an agreed price referred to as the 'Strike Price'. The strike price will be at a significant discount to what they believe to be the price the property will sell for on the open market. The underwriter then markets the property through various channels with a margin on top of the market price, and therefore receives the difference between their selling price and the strike price.

What are the costs?

I have spent quite a lot of time explaining different versions of these agency structures, but what is the point, I hear you ask? Well, the point is that you need to know about the costs because they can vary dramatically!

I am not saying that any of these costs are good or bad. I just think it is important for you to recognise what the different structures are when you come across them, so you can have an idea of what they are. This will enable you to make your own informed decision as to what you would like to do.

The key thing is that many property agents, even the big ones, use various combinations of these fee structures. So, what do they look like?

Typical property agency fees

If the agent is instructed to sell the development internationally, it typically gets paid additional fees to cover the additional work involved in coordinating sales across multiple centres and paying additional teams of people. These additional fees could be anywhere between 1% to 5%, bringing the total fees up to between 2.5% to 10% of the net sales price of the property.

Higher fees tend to be paid by smaller developers, for lower-cost properties, and for properties in smaller cities. For example, most agents would expect to be paid a higher fee to sell an apartment in Manchester or Perth, Australia, than an apartment in London or Sydney.

Globally, fees tend to fall within the ranges set out below.

Table 6.14: Comparison of typical property agent fees (Australia, New Zealand, and UK)

	Domestic Fees	International Fees
Australia	2 – 3.5%	3 – 10%
New Zealand	2 – 3.5%	4 – 6%
United Kingdom	1.5% – 2.5%	2.0% – 7%

Hybrid agency fee structures

The hybrid agency fee is the most complex of all the various fee structures. These are used by developers who want to incentivise an agent to sell as many apartments as possible as quickly as they can. In this model, they will give an agent a selling fee that incorporates their anticipated price (base price), a dealing margin in the fee, and generally they will give the agent the ability to do whatever they like with these fees.

In the hybrid fee structure, the developer will allow the agent to set its own fee, which they will do by setting broad parameters for the agent to work with; these will typically be:

- **Base price:** The developer will set out for the agent the minimum price it will be willing to accept for a given unit;
- **Minimum fee:** It will set a minimum fee for the agent;
- **Dealing margin:** It will give the agent a dealing margin to negotiate with.

The combined fees costs are added together to form the 'Asking Price'. The agent will then be free to do whatever it likes with these costs provided they do not go below the minimum price.

Therefore, the agent can use the dealing margin and part of their fee to 'entice' buyers to buy the property. Likewise, they can choose not to pass any of the dealing margin on to the purchaser, and try to charge them the full asking price. In this scenario, the agent's fee will be the minimum fee together with all the dealing margins. They can use any combination they like.

These hybrid fee structures are common in international sales where developers may be new to the market or unwilling to take substantial risks on marketing expenses. The highest combination I have seen of this nature has been a 5% agency fee and an 8% dealing margin. In this scenario, the maximum fee that the agent could achieve for a sale is therefore 13% of the net asking price.

Because salespeople are driven and highly incentivised by the commission, there is minimal incentive to find scenarios that help to move volume. Most would prefer to sell each property at the highest price possible, and to keep as much of the dealing margin as possible as their fee.

Referral fees

Referral fees are a huge hidden cost for investors. They are typically in the following ranges:

- **Property sales:** Between 3 to 10% of the net value of the property
- **Additional services:** Between 12.5% and 30% of the additional service being offered

Underwriter costs

Underwriters will typically seek to achieve a discount on what is considered the market value, of 12% to 20% of the property value. Additionally, they will generally add a marketing premium in the region of 5 to 10%.

This means that the total difference between what a developer is willing to sell to an underwriter and what the ultimate end buyer will pay may be as high as 30% of the value of the property. This is a risk that this is being taken by the underwriter and they are being rewarded for bearing that risk. You need to be aware of who you are dealing with, and what they are getting for purchases.

Furniture

Whether or not to purchase furniture will be a significant consideration for some investors. In some markets such as the United Kingdom, it is common practice to rent out a property with furniture. In other markets such as Australia and New Zealand, it is uncommon.

Furniture is a rapidly depreciating asset. By that, I mean that most of its value has gone once it has been installed. This is because:

- People do not generally pay a great deal of money for second-hand furniture; and
- Pieces of furniture are very bulky items and are difficult to move and store

Additionally, furniture is essentially a binary decision for both investors and prospective tenants. This is because:

- **Landlords:** Need to furnish an apartment to let it to a tenant who wants to rent a furnished apartment. If it does not have furniture, they simply will not rent the property

- **Prospective tenants:** A prospective tenant either wants furniture or not. For all but a few very fussy tenants, they will not particularly care what type of furniture it is. They are not bothered by the brand, colour, or style. Provided it is clean, functional, and not completely outlandish, they will happily live with it.

So, what does this mean for an investor?

As an investor, if you do not need furniture, do not buy it! If you do, your furniture should be:

- Good quality
- Neutral in colour
- Have easily obtained spares and replacements

How much should you pay?

Furniture providers tend to be specific to the new-build industry. They tend to provide furniture in specific packs for specific units, and then install all the furniture on a single day.

These furniture providers are different from your average furniture retailers, because:

- They do not have large showrooms or warehouses which they need to maintain, which are expensive. Likewise, they do not have the same staff and overheads as a typical furniture retailer.

- They would usually not typically meet investors without property agents, and therefore agents typically seek a 'referral' fee from the furniture provider. This can be between 10% – 20% of the value of the furniture.

I have no problem with furniture providers making a profit, nor should you as an investor. However, you should be mindful of what you are paying, and how you meet this provider of furniture. If you have met them through an agent, ask how much the referral fee is.

Currency rates

Currency is an important consideration for international investors. If you are buying a property in another country, the developer will only accept payment in their local currency. To pay the developer, you will therefore require local currency to pay a deposit and any other payments. Purchasing currency can be far more expensive than you might imagine.

Those requiring currency will use their local high street bank to purchase it. This can be an expensive option. Most people perhaps do not realise that they are paying a significant premium to purchase it from their bank. Most banks will charge a commission of approximately 3% to buy their currency; 3% might not sound like a lot of money, but in the case of a purchaser buying Plot 1 Kingsley Tower who needs 35% as a deposit on the purchase price of £450,000, the commission will be £4,725. This is the cheapest example in the building, and the currency commission could be considerably more!

There are many online retailers of currency that are all perfectly safe to use. I recommend that you shop around when purchasing currency, as an extremely easy cost saving can be achieved.

Part 2 Recap

We have covered quite a lot of ground in this section, I have provided a quick recap below as well as two purchase examples.

Price

There is no universal price - there are simply different versions depending on your perspective. These are:

- **Open market value:** Established by a valuer
- **Book value:** Used by a developer
- **Asking price:** Used by property agents and developers
- **Purchase price:** The price paid by a purchaser
- **Total purchase price:** The total price a purchaser pays including purchase costs.

Cost

As an investor, you need to think about 'price' as a series of costs. Costs fall into four key categories:

- **Absolute costs:** The cost of all of the items that the development would not exist without
- **Variable costs:** Costs that change depending on how the developer's costs change
- **Dealing costs:** The difference between the developer's book value and the asking price
- **Facilitation and completion costs:** Costs which you pay to purchase the property.

Some costs can either be saved or avoided, but there is no way to pay nothing. So, where can costs be saved? As an investor, you can achieve cost savings and avoidance in the following areas:

- **Developers' variable costs:**
  - Sales and marketing campaigns
  - Specification

- **Facilitation and completion costs:**
  - FX Rates (Purchase Costs)
  - Furniture & Fittings
  - Agency Costs

- **Dealing costs:** The dealing cost involved in the transaction

Worked example

To demonstrate the importance of understanding how purchase costs work, it is helpful to consider two examples. To emphasise the point, I will use both extremes of the spectrum. However, there will be differences.

Let's consider Plot 1 Kingsley Tower, in scenarios where Buyer 1 gets no advantage from savings, and Buyer 2 can maximise all the savings available. The following are constant:

- Asking Price – £400,000
- Dealing Margin – £11,618
- Book Value – £388,382
- Avoidable Specification Costs – £5,000
- Furniture Pack – £5,000 (full retail)
- Marketing Costs – £24,280
- Estimated Monthly Rental – £1,500 per month
- LTV 70%

Let's assume that Buyer 1 purchases through a referrer (on top of the agent) who charges a fee of 5% and that the agent receives a fee of 2.5%. Additionally, we assume that 3.5% of the referral fee is paid by the developer, and that the agent reduces their fee to 1%. Finally, that Buyer 1 can negotiate a discount from the asking price of £5,000.

Their total purchase price could therefore be calculated as follows:

Table P2.1: Buyer 1 Equation

Item	Cost (£)
Purchase Price	395,000
Furniture Pack	5,000
Currency Costs	3,555
Stamp Duty	29,500
Lease Registration	270
Legal Fee	1,000
Currency Costs	3,555
Total Purchase Price	434,325
Initial Gross Yield	4.14%

Table P2.2: Developer Equation for Buyer 1

Item	Cost (£)
Purchase Price	395,000
Agent Fee 6%	23,700
Marketing Expenses	24,280
Avoidable Specification Costs	5,000
Net Return to Developer	341,500

Now let's assume that Buyer 2 purchases through the property agent who charges a fee of 2.0%, and that they purchase before the development is marketed. They reduce the avoidable specification and negotiate directly with the furniture company and save the 30% referral fee, and they buy their commission from an online broker at 1%. Additionally, because the developer has no additional risk or referral costs, they are willing to pass on all the dealing margin.

Their Total Purchase Price would be calculated as follows:

Table P2.3: Buyer 2 Equation

Item	Cost (£)
Asking Price	400,000
Less	
Dealing Margin	11,618
Marketing Costs	24,800
Avoidable Specification	5,000
Net Purchase Price	358,582
Stamp Duty	25,585
Lease Registration	270
Legal Fee	1,000
Furniture Pack	3,500
Currency Costs	1,075
Total Purchase Price	393,927
Initial Gross Yield	4.5%

Table P2.4: Developer Equation for Buyer 2

Item	Cost (£)
Purchase Price	358,582
Agent Fee 2%	7,171
Net Return to Developer	351,410

My example is a simple one, but I think it illustrates the potential for savings here:

- Buyer 1 paid £434,325, generating a gross initial yield of 4.14%, and the developer received £341,500

- Buyer 2 paid £40,398 less, which is equal to 26 months' gross rental income, yet the developer still received £10,000 more. In addition, they had less risk because they did not have to risk £24,800 in marketing expenses or incur finance costs on this or the specification cost.

Of course, these expenses and scenarios are always different. However, these costs are in fact drawn from a real example, and I think the comparison helps to highlight how much dead cost there is in some of this new-build expense.

You are going to say "it is all very well for you to give me this example, however, I am not going to be able to replicate this".

My response would be that you should consider two things:

- If you do not ask you do not get. This may be far easier to negotiate than you think – you just need to create the scenario.
- The great thing about being an investor is you do not have to buy. If you cannot create this scenario, then find a property where you can!

PART 3

Purchase and Operational Considerations

Having considered 'price' together with the costs associated with purchasing an investment, the logical next step is to consider the actual process involved in purchasing, as well as the operational issues you will need to consider as you operate your investment.

For most people, the purchase process and the day-to-day operation of a rental property will be unfamiliar. While many will have purchased your own home, this is not something you will have done regularly. There are several factors which investors need to consider when determining where to buy and what their strategy will be for investing. I categorise these into broad areas and present them here in the order they are likely to arise.

- **Property tenure:** What are the different forms of property tenure, what protections do you have as an owner, and additionally what obligations exist with ownership? What restrictions exist on foreign investors? I have also covered the main forms of ownership in Australia, New Zealand, and the United Kingdom.
- **Purchase process:** How does the purchase process work? What are some of the typical considerations you will come across, and how can you ensure that you put yourself in the best possible position?

Particularly, what contractual issues should you be thinking about when buying off-plan?

- **Operational issues:** All sorts of operational issues will come up as you develop and manage an investment property. The costs involved will be one; however, other issues will arise, such as whether to use a managing agent. And equally importantly, does it make sense to buy a new-build or a second-hand property, or to refurbish a property?

CHAPTER 7

Property Tenure

We covered property tenure and its origins in Chapter 1: The Real Estate Market. However, it is also useful to look at the practical applications of different forms of tenure and their impact, rather than in just discussing them in the abstract. Tenure simply refers to how property is owned, and the rights of the owner (as the registered proprietor of a property).

There are many forms of tenure, providing different rights and obligations which run with them.

Freehold

In most European countries, the highest form of property ownership is freehold ownership (ownership in 'fee simple').

With freehold tenure, the owner of the property owns it outright, including both the land and the improvements built on it. The owner of the freehold is named as the 'registered proprietor' on the title. The benefits of owning freehold property are:

- As the owner, you are not subject to any obligations which are imposed by a lease;
- You have no party superior who you need to deal with;
- You do not need to pay ground rent, service charges, or other landlord charges;
- You do not require any approval or permission to deal with the title or the buildings (other than normal regulatory requirements).

As the freeholder, you are responsible for maintaining the land as well as the built improvements on it, which can be more costly.

Subordinate forms of ownership

Below freehold, various subordinate interests can be granted by the freeholder. These forms of ownership are indeed subordinate to freehold ownership. However, this does not mean that subordinate forms of tenure are necessarily worse than freehold ownership.

In many scenarios, subordinate interests are created for practical reasons. For example, with a block of apartments it is simply not practical to create multiple freehold interests, as there is only one parcel of land upon which all of the apartments are built. The most common forms of subordinate tenure are share of freehold, leasehold, common hold, and strata title.

Share of a freehold

Share of freehold is as the name implies. Instead of a single freeholder, the freehold is jointly owned between several shared freehold owners, referred to as 'common holders'.

Share of freehold is established in two ways:

- The freehold is split jointly between common holders within a block of flats or apartments. Within this structure, the maximum number of owners can be four; or
- A company is established to own the freehold and each of the tenants holds a share of that company.

In both situations, the owners of a share of freehold have both a level of ownership and control over the freehold interest in the land. Therefore, the owner of a share of freehold interest will have a share of ownership of the common areas of the building, such as the roof, walls, stairs, and hallway.

It is the responsibility of common holders to maintain the building, including its common parts. Collectively, the common holders are also required to insure the building.

The benefits of owning a share of freehold are:

- Greater control over decision-making concerning the property in all areas including maintenance costs and obligations. Therefore, you cannot be victim to overcharging by an aggressive freeholder. With other common holders, you can negotiate service fees, find the best value building insurance, and negotiate better maintenance prices

- Generally, it is anticipated that the owner(s) of the shared freehold have a higher level of investment in the property, and therefore they are likely to maintain the property to a higher standard
- As a common holder, you have a level of control of the lease, including the costs associated with extending it
- Theoretically, it is easier for the owner of a share of the freehold to ensure that decisions are made by the common holders for renovations and repairs to their property.

Your obligations in owning a share of a freehold property are:

- Administration of the annual accounts and ensuring that the building is properly insured, which can be time-consuming
- Because maintenance tends to be done on an ad-hoc basis, the service charge can fluctuate dramatically if there are large repair items that need to be attended to.

Commonhold properties

Commonhold ownership is a type of freehold ownership in England and Wales. It helps flat owners to acquire full ownership of their property as an alternative to having a lease. With commonhold properties, the owners within a block of flats club together to form a Commonhold Association Company that then owns the building.

Commonhold is a similar type of ownership to strata title ownership in Australia. Commonhold ownership was introduced in the UK in 2002; however, it has never really become commonly used.

Leasehold

The difference between holding a property leasehold and freehold is that the leaseholder has a long-term interest over their area of a property. The property is held by way of a lease agreement that gives the lessee (the tenant) the right to occupy the property for the lease term. Most leasehold agreements are quite long – generally, they are greater than 99 years.

With leasehold, a contract (lease agreement) is created between the tenant and the landlord. The agreement provides the tenant with conditional ownership of a part of the building – generally an apartment and other specific areas, such as car parking and/or storage space. The area 'owned' by the tenant is referred to as the 'demised area'.

The lease agreement outlines the rights, responsibilities, and obligations of both the leaseholder and the landlord. The landlord is required to manage, maintain, and repair the building structure, common areas, exterior, and the grounds the building sits on. The tenant is required to keep their demised area in good order, behave in a 'neighbourly' way, and not undertake certain actions without the permission of the landlord. These might include anything from structural alterations to the demised area to having a pet.

With leasehold property, the landlord has the right to charge a ground rent for the property, which is typically charged annually. You need to be aware of this obligation, as well as the review mechanisms which exist to review the rent.

As a tenant, the main advantage of a leasehold property is that the freeholder is required to maintain the common areas of the building as well as the land itself.

The disadvantages of having a Leasehold Property are as follows:

- If you, the leaseholder, want to make any structural changes to the property, you will usually require the permission of the freeholder
- There may be restrictions on what you can do to the property, such as not being able to sublet, or not being allowed to own a pet
- As a lease is a wasting asset and is used over time, therefore the closer it gets to expiry the less it is worth
- You are required to pay annual maintenance fees, annual service charges, and your share of insurance costs
- You are required to pay an annual ground rent
- If you do not fulfil the terms of the lease, you can be in breach of the lease and legal action can be taken against you

Strata title

The strata title system was created in Australia and has subsequently been adopted by other countries around the world. Strata title allows individual ownership of part of a property called a 'lot', combined with shared ownership in the remainder of the property called the 'Common Property'. The common property typically comprises foyers, driveways, and gardens.

The ownership is created through a legal entity called the owner's corporation - or body corporate, strata company, or community association, depending on your state or territory of residence and the type of scheme. Each owner owns part of this legal entity.

Community title

Community title is specific to Australia. There are two forms of community title: a community title scheme, and a community strata scheme.

A community title scheme is similar to a strata scheme in that when you buy a lot, you own that lot and share ownership and responsibility for the common areas on the property. A community title requires a minimum of two separate lots as well as common areas. These common areas could simply be a driveway or communal land. In a residential setting, a community title is typically used for large housing estates or housing schemes that share common land.

A community title scheme is created by registering a community, neighbourhood, or precinct plan managed by a community association as collectively held by all of the lot owners. The common area in a community title scheme is called the association property. Unit entitlement is based on site values which determine unit owners' voting rights and contributions to maintenance and insurance levies.

The main difference between strata and community titles is how the boundaries are defined. Strata titles apply to structures such as apartment blocks, townhouses, duplexes, and units whereby each specific area is defined by a structural aspect of the building. In contrast, community titles typically involve multiple buildings (such as houses) and the boundaries are related to surveyed measurements of the land.

A community scheme can also include strata-titled buildings, which means that sometimes, the by-laws of both the strata scheme and community scheme apply. All by-laws in a community title scheme are detailed in a management statement, which differs from plan to plan. As every community scheme varies in nature, the by-laws are therefore far less standardised than strata scheme by-laws.

For the maintenance of the property, the rights and decision-making process are similar to strata title. Owners are required to pay levies for maintenance depending on the size of their unit or lot, and all owners have voting rights on any proposed changes and developments which they can exercise at general meetings.

One of the major differences between strata and community title ownership is how insurance is managed. With a strata title, insurance is compulsory for the building and public liability, including the common area managed by the body corporate. The entire building structure is therefore covered by strata insurance, and each unit owner is then only responsible for the content's insurance of their unit. However, in community titles there is no obligation on the owners to maintain and insure other lot owners' buildings. Instead, the owner of each lot is responsible for the insurance of any building on that lot. The community corporation is thus only responsible for insuring any common areas or buildings, such as driveways and service infrastructure.

Unit title (freehold strata title or stratum estate)

New Zealand uses a form of strata title called unit title, and this is the most common form of ownership in apartment buildings in New Zealand. Unit titles can be either Stratum in Freehold - where the owners own the underlying land - or Stratum in Leasehold, whereby the owners lease the land from a third party.

Cross lease

Holding a cross lease ascribes two interests in the property - a share of the freehold title (with the other cross leaseholders), and a leasehold interest in the area of the building (typically the apartment) that you occupy. Leases are typically for 999 years. This form of title is similar to Share of Freehold in the UK.

Common forms of ownership Australia, New Zealand, and the United Kingdom

In the table below are the most common forms of tenure in Australia, New Zealand, and the United Kingdom. Other countries have other forms of ownership tenure, and property owners need to be aware of what they are and the rights and obligations that run with them.

Table 7.1: Common forms of ownership (Australia, New Zealand, and the UK)

	Australia	New Zealand	United Kingdom
Apartments	Strata Title	Strata Title	Predominantly leasehold for new-builds in England and Wales (not Scotland)
Houses	Most houses are owned freehold or community title	Freehold	Freehold, although there are some leaseholds in England and Wales

UK (England and Wales) issues with leasehold

In England and Wales, there are two important elements of the lease that you should consider: the term remaining on the lease, and the ability to extend it.

If fewer than 70 years are remaining on the lease, it will be more difficult to obtain a mortgage. This is because most lenders will usually request that a buyer has a lease with a lease term for 30 years beyond the end of the mortgage term, which can be up to 40 years. However, lenders will start getting nervous with 80 years remaining on the lease. Likewise, if you are selling a property with a lease term of fewer than 70 years remaining, it will be harder to sell for the same reason.

It is possible to extend a lease. However, the freeholder has the right to charge a premium for the lease extension; also, the costs of the premium will vary depending on the property and its assessed value. Both a solicitor and surveyor will be required to extend the lease, so there will also be professional costs to pay.

If you would like more information on extending leases in the UK, look at: **www.proptechpioneer.com/lease-extension-calculator**

Restrictions on foreign ownership

Many countries have restrictions on property ownership for foreign nationals. Each country has its own rules. If you are thinking about investing offshore, you must fully understand how the property ownership rules work in the country you are considering investing in. This should not ring warning bells for you, though, as offshore investing is a great way to invest in property, where:

- You want to avoid unfair tax treatments in your home country; you can create company structures to purchase offshore and simply pay local income tax in the country the property is located
- You cannot purchase property in your home country due to investment restrictions or expensive tax surcharges
- You want to diversify your risk and returns
- You want to enhance your return through currency gains.

Below, I have set out how international property ownership works in Australia, New Zealand, and the United Kingdom.

Australia

In Australia, foreign purchasers cannot purchase existing or 'second hand' properties. However, they can buy new-build property, subject to Foreigner Investment Review Board (FIRB) approval.

Certain non-resident buyers may not require FIRB approval before purchasing residential real estate in Australia, such as:

- Australian citizens (regardless of whether they are resident in Australia or not)
- New Zealand citizens
- Holders of an Australian permanent visa; or
- Foreigners purchasing property as joint tenants with an Australian citizen spouse, New Zealand citizen spouse, or Australian permanent resident spouse.

The FIRB assesses applications from foreigners who wish to purchase property in Australia. For new developments, foreign buyers generally need to apply for approval before purchasing their property.

A new dwelling is defined as:

> *A dwelling that will be, is being or has been built on residential land, has not been previously sold as a dwelling and has either: not been previously occupied or if the dwelling is part of a development, was sold by the developer of that development and has not been occupied for more than 12 months in total.*

There are fees to apply for FIRB approval; the fee depends on the purchase price of the property.

Table 7.2: FIRB fees ($AUD)

Purchase Price	FIRB Fee
Less than $1 million	$5,700
$1,000,001 to $1,999,999	$11,500
$2,000,000 to $2,999,999	$23,100
$3,000,000 to $3,999,999	$34,600
$4,000,000 to $4,999,999	$46,200
$5,000,000 to $5,999,999	$57,700
$6,000,000 to $6,999,999	$69,300
$7,000,000 to $7,999,999	$80,900
$8,000,000 to $8,999,999	$92,600
$9,000,000 to $9,999,999	$104,100
$10,000,000 or higher	Amount dependant on specific purchase price

New Dwelling Exemption Certificate

A developer can obtain a New Dwelling Exemption Certificate. This allows them to sell dwellings in a specified development to foreigners, and means that foreign buyers do not require individual foreign investment approval to purchase.

Developers can apply for a New Dwelling Exemption Certificate if the development:

- Consists of 50 or more dwellings
- Has development approval from the relevant government authority
- Was planned in such a way that foreign investment approval was sought to purchase the land, and any conditions are being met.

Where a developer holds a New Dwelling Exemption certificate, it limits the number of apartments that can be sold to foreign buyers to 50% of the total apartments. If the 50% quota is reached, any additional foreign buyers will require approval from FIRB on an individual basis.

Sale contracts differ between those with pre-approved New Dwelling Exemption Certificates and those buyers in the process of obtaining FIRB approval. For those seeking their FIRB approval, sales contracts should be 'subject to FIRB approval'.

Penalties
Strong penalties exist for breaches of the FIRB rules and requirements. Such breaches can result in criminal prosecution.

New Zealand
Generally, only New Zealand citizens and residents are permitted to buy residential property to live in. Foreign buyers can purchase new-build apartments for investment, but not to live in themselves. There are a limited number of scenarios where overseas buyers can purchase for owner-occupation.

Overseas buyers can purchase apartments off-plan in large apartment developments in three ways.

Table 7.3: Overseas buyers' rights to off-plan property in New Zealand

	To buy	For Owner Occupation	Must on-sell
Transitional exemption certificate	✔	✔	✘
Exemption certificate	✔	✘	✘
Individual application	✔	✘	✔

Transitional Exemption Certificate
Foreign buyers may buy an apartment in a development that has a Transitional Exemption Certificate without needing any further consent. The purchase must be the first sale (i.e., not an assignment or re-sale property), and settle before 22 August 2023. There are no other restrictions - buyers can live in the apartment and do not have to on-sell it. The New Zealand government publishes a list of developments with Transitional Exemption Certificates on its website.

Exemption Certificate
Foreign buyers may purchase apartments in large developments (i.e., those of 20 units or more) which have been granted an Exemption Certificate without needing to obtain further consents. Certain criteria and rules apply: buyers must purchase the property before the construction of the apartment is complete, and are not permitted to live in the apartment.

A developer is only permitted to sell 60% of the scheme to foreign buyers under the terms of the Exemption Certificate. The developer must maintain records and provide a copy of the certificate to purchasers before they enter into a sale and purchase agreement.

Individual applications

If a development does not have a certificate and a foreign buyer wants to buy an apartment even though the development is already over the 60% limit for an exemption certificate, it is possible to apply for one-off consent. The development must have one or more multi-storey buildings as a single development, where each building will consist of a minimum of 20 apartments.

In this scenario, the buyer is not permitted to live in the apartment, and importantly, they must on-sell it within a timeframe set by the Overseas Investment Office. The fee for this consent is $NZ 2,040. In practice, the Overseas Investment Office has not asked investors to sell their property within a given timeframe; this does not, however, mean that they will not start to do so in the future.

Penalties

If these requirements are not adhered to, purchasers may face significant penalties and may be required to dispose of the property.

Exceptions for Singaporeans

Singaporean nationals are not subject to these restrictions due to the Free Trade Agreement between the two governments. Singapore Permanent Residents may apply for consent for a home to live in, but certain rules apply.

IRD (Inland Revenue Department) Number

Foreign buyers must obtain an IRD Number to buy, sell, or transfer property in New Zealand. Purchasers must have an IRD before settlement.

To apply for an IRD number, buyers must have a New Zealand Bank account, or a Customer Due Diligence form completed by a New Zealand reporting entity, to submit with their IRD application form.

For mortgage purposes, a New Zealand bank account and an IRD number are required.

United Kingdom

There are no restrictions on foreign investors buying property in the United Kingdom. However, most large developers in the UK have committed to domestic market developments before any global sales and marketing campaign can take place.

CHAPTER 8

The Purchase Process

Buying property off-plan can be an overwhelming process. It is not something that most people do on a regular basis, and therefore it is not common to have a lot of experience with the process. Additionally, there is much more to consider with real estate than other assets. There are three principal differences between the purchase process for real estate and other assets, which create complexity:

- **Solicitor or conveyancer:** In most countries around the world, it is not possible to buy a property without a conveyancer or solicitor. This is because you need someone to deal with the legal complexities involved with the land and the building, and with the different rights transferred with the institutional characteristics of the land and property.

- **The process is not universally the same:** One of the things which makes the purchase of real estate quite confusing is that the processes, laws, and terminologies relating to property vary across different countries.

- **Transaction costs:** Buying property is an expensive process, not only for the property itself. The costs and taxes associated with the transaction are huge. In some cases, they can be up to 25% of the purchase price.

The good news is that this process doesn't have to be overwhelming.

Purchase process for new-builds

When it comes to new-builds, we can break the process down into five manageable parts, and if you think of the process like this you will find that it does not matter where you look at buying property - as essentially, the off-plan purchase process will always follow these five steps.

Figure 8.1: New-build purchase process

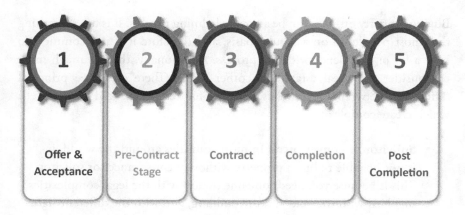

1	2	3	4	5
Offer & Acceptance	Pre-Contract Stage	Contract	Completion	Post Completion

Offer & acceptance

After you have negotiated with a developer or agent to buy a property, you will make an offer to purchase the property and the offer will be accepted. This is the starting point in the purchase process. At this point, the following will happen:

- **Reservation agreement:** A short agreement will be agreed upon between you and the developer setting out the broad terms of the agreement to purchase the property, together with any conditions to which the purchase is subject, such as obtaining finance, or the sale of another property, or a building inspection.
- **Reservation fee:** You will pay a reservation fee to reserve the property.
- **Legal representation:** Each party will appoint a solicitor or conveyancer to act on their behalf.

At this stage, even if a reservation deposit and reservation agreement have been signed, neither you nor the developer is likely to be legally bound to purchase the property. It would only be in highly unusual circumstances that you as the purchaser are legally bound to proceed with the transaction. If this is the case, the developer will likely be required to make this clear at the time. At any time before the exchange of contracts, either you or the developer can simply decide not to proceed with the transaction for whatever reason. However, if you have paid a reservation fee and you decide not to proceed, you should expect to forfeit some or all of that fee.

Pre-contract

At this point, the developer's conveyancer will submit a draft contract to you and your conveyancer, together with the documents relating to the title of the property. If the property being purchased is leasehold or strata-titled, there will also be lease documents or strata or body corporate documents. This is often referred to as a 'legal pack' or a 'sales pack'.

Your conveyancer will then carry out several pre-contact investigations relating to the property. These will be both technical and practical, and seek to ensure that the legal title is satisfactory. They will also explore items such as:

- Water and sewerage charges payable;
- Any service charge or strata payments;
- Searches with the relevant local government authorities concerning planning permission and other local matters.

If the property being purchased is leasehold or in a strata corporation, they will review the lease to ensure that no adverse conditions within the document prevent the property from being used for your intended purpose.

After your conveyancer has completed their checks, they will report back to you on the property. If there are any defects with the property title or issues with the property, they will advise you of these as well as possible ways to remedy these issues.

If you are satisfied with their advice, they will then request that you do the following:

- Sign a copy of a Sale and Purchase Agreement (sales contract)
- Provide any funds required to cover the deposit on the property; this will typically be 10% of the purchase price.

They will also ask you to confirm the following:

- Your proposed completion date – because the property is a new-build and therefore under construction, the completion date will not be known, and therefore this will be an estimated completion date and completion will take place within a period after the developer has given notice to complete to the purchaser;
- That you either have a mortgage in place or are confident of generating the funds to pay for the property;
- That you are happy to exchange contracts.

In most countries, the developer, property agent, and conveyancers will be required to undertake some type of Anti Money Laundering (AML) check on you. These searches are now common and will be required to demonstrate the following:

- Your identity, with some or several forms of photo ID;
- Your home address, with utility bills or something similar;
- Your source of funds to buy the property, to demonstrate they are from legitimate sources.

These checks are normal. and are undertaken simply so that the developer, property agent, and conveyancers can demonstrate that you have not taken part in any criminal or terrorist activity, and that your money has come from legitimate sources.

Contract

At this point, both parties will be in a position to 'contract'. The form of the contract will depend on the country you are buying in, and the tenure of the property (freehold, leasehold, or strata-titled).

This process is referred to as an 'exchange of contracts', because the contract consists of two identical parts - one part is signed by you, the buyer; the other by the developer. The two conveyancers then 'exchange' their signed contracts, and your conveyancer pays the deposit money to the developer's conveyancer.

At this point, both parties are *legally bound* by the contract, and therefore to proceed with the transaction. If either party fails to complete the purchase they will be in breach of the contract. The damaged party could sue the other for damages.

It is important to note that at this point in the process you now have a legal interest in the property. Therefore, you should insure the property. If the property is being purchased freehold, then the building will also need to be insured. If the property is leasehold or strata-titled, the building will be insured by the group managing and maintaining the building. In this case, you will simply need to insure the contents of the building, such as the internal fixtures and fittings including the kitchen and bathrooms, etc.

Completion

'Completion' is the point at which the contract is fulfilled (completed) You will take possession of the property, and the developer will receive their full payment.

The developer will issue notice to you that the property is ready for completion, known as a *Notice to Complete*. Notices to complete cannot typically be given unless building regulations have been met and approved, and warranty and insurance certificates have been issued. Your conveyancer will ensure that this is all in order.

On the day of completion, your conveyancer will pay the developer's conveyancer the balance of the purchase price due and then the title documents and keys to the property will be handed over. There is no need for either party to be physically present at completion; indeed, it is quite uncommon for this to be the case.

If you delay completion, you will be liable to pay interest at a penalty rate on the balance of the purchase price. The developer can also serve a Notice to Complete which requires you to complete within a fixed period.

If you fail to complete then you are in breach of the agreement and the developer can treat the contract as being at an end. The developer is then entitled to keep the deposit that has been received from you to cover any expenses they have incurred and for any subsequent loss incurred on any sale at a lesser value.

Post completion

After completion has taken place, the title deeds will be handed over to your conveyancer and they will apply for your registration as an owner of the land after the payment of stamp duty. This process can take several months depending on the country and the time of year. At the end of this process, the Land Registry register will show that you are now the owner of the property (the Registered Proprietor).

Potential issues when buying off-plan

There is one obvious difference between purchasing an off-plan new-build and buying a second-hand property, which is that when buying new-build property off-plan, the property does not yet exist. This fundamentally changes two things: the protection buyers have, and how the sale contract works.

Overview of buyer protection and contractual issues

Buyer protection

With second-hand property, you can physically inspect the property. It is expected that you will have undertaken due diligence and satisfied yourself as to the structural integrity and soundness of the property for the intended purpose.

After completion has taken place on the contract, if issues with the property subsequently arise, then these are typically your problem unless you can demonstrate the property agent or vendor has misled you in some way. In the second-hand property purchase process, you can mitigate your risk to some extent by:

- **Building Inspections:** You can instruct a building surveyor to undertake an inspection and survey of the property to determine if any defects or maintenance issues need to be addressed.
- **Insurance:** In some circumstances you may be able to get insurance against any structural issues and items of major repair which arise post-purchase.

However, in practice, your ability to mitigate risk is limited as the protection provided by both building inspections and any insurance products is relatively limited. This, in turn, is because uncovering potential issues within a building based on a visual inspection is difficult. Additionally, there is generally an assumption that second-hand properties will require more maintenance and work than new properties. So, you need to accept that there will be some requirement for maintenance.

This is not the case with new-build property when buying off-plan. It is not possible to physically inspect the workmanship of the developer and their contractors before entering the contract.

Contractual issues

The building is still being built and therefore nothing exists yet, so you are entering a contract to purchase something which will be built in the future. Because of this, there are several issues you need to consider which could occur during the construction period, along how the contract will deal with them, such as:

- What if construction is delayed?
- What if the developer runs out of money and gets into trouble, or goes into bankruptcy?
- What if you cannot afford to complete?
- What your circumstances change and you need to sell the property?
- What if you cannot arrange finance for the property?
- What if the apartment has defects or is not as advertised?

These are all important issues to be considered when entering into a contract to purchase property off-plan. When buying off-plan, everyone expects things to go exactly as planned. However, things do sometimes go wrong, so consideration needs to be given as to what will happen if they do.

Buyer protection

The specific level of protection given to investors varies across countries and developments. You need to be very sure that you know what your rights are and the obligations of the developer before you sign an agreement. Generally, you will find that less developed markets will have lower protection for investors.

As a buyer, you should be most concerned with two items, specifically:

- **Deposit protection:** Is any deposit you have paid against the purchase of property protected if a developer gets into financial trouble?
- **Insurance and building warranties:** What happens if something goes wrong with the building after you have completed the purchase?

Most countries have rules and regulations which deal with these issues. However, they vary significantly between countries. By looking at the different approaches taken in Australia, New Zealand, and the UK, you will get a sense of what these different approaches are, and why you need to do your due diligence.

Australia

The Australian conveyancing process has strong and effective consumer protection legislation. There are various protections in place for purchasers which are implemented on a state-by-state basis. These protections are provided by way of deposit protection, cooling-off periods, and building insurance.

Deposit protection

Deposit protection is largely consistent across Australia. Any deposit paid by a purchaser for a property is held in a Trust Account either by a conveyancer or by an estate agent in most states. In some states these funds can be released to the developer, but only with the agreement of the purchaser.

The only exception to this is in NSW. By NSW law, deposits and any other instalments must be held by a stakeholder (usually the real estate agent) in a trust or controlled money account during the contract period. The money *cannot* be released to the developer before settlement, meaning that deposit and instalment monies are protected in the event of the developer's insolvency.

Cooling off period

Most states in Australia (excluding WA and Tasmania) have a 'Cooling-Off' period for real estate contracts, which is a limited period when either the buyer or developer can terminate a contract.

How does it work?

Once you have exchanged contracts and paid a deposit on the property, the cooling-off period begins. At any point, during the cooling-off period, either party can get out of the contract by providing written notice. However, if you pull out of the contract, you will not get your whole deposit back in some states and territories.

The process for the cooling-off period is as follows. The property agent or developer must give you:

- An unsigned copy of the contract at least one business day before the agreement is signed;
- A copy of the consumer guide regarding agreements when selling a residential property at least one business day before the agreement is signed; and

- You must then sign a waiver form approved by the Office of Fair Trading before signing the agreement.

The length of the cooling-off period and the amount of sale price, which is forfeited if you withdraw from the purchase, depends on the state in which the property is purchased.

Table 8.1: Cooling-off periods in Australian states

	Cooling-off Period (Business Days)	% of Sale Price Forfeited
ACT	5	0.25%
NSW	5	0.25%
NT	4, if the purchaser is not represented by a conveyancer or solicitor	Nil
QLD	5	0.25%
SA	2	Small holding deposit is forfeited (up to $100)
TAS	There is no mandatory cooling-off period.	100%
VIC	3	0.2%
WA	There is no mandatory cooling-off period	100%

The cooling-off period starts on the day you receive a copy of the signed contract and ends at 5pm on the last day of the cooling-off period. If public holidays or a Sunday fall within the period, they are not counted as business days and are therefore excluded from the cooling-off period.

During this time, your conveyancer can make inquiries to detect further problems. These inquiries may include building and survey reports, or the certificate of compliance. If there are any problems, you have the option to terminate or 'rescind' the agreement.

If you want to rescind the agreement during the cooling-off period, you have to write to the agent or developer to advise them of this. No explanation of the reason(s) for cancelling the contract is required. This notice must be issued within the cooling-off period and will not be effective if it is issued after the cooling-off period has expired.

There are three ways you can issue a letter of termination:

- Give it personally to the agent;
- Mail or deliver it to the property agent's business address; or

- Deliver it to a place assigned in the agreement should cancellation take place.

Waiving the cooling-off period

Under the Property, Stock, and Business Agents Act 2002, purchasers can waive their cooling-off period. Under the Act, only the buyer has the right to waive the cooling-off period following strict guidelines.

If the purchaser wants to sign a waiver of the cooling-off period, they must give the seller a 66W certificate in compliance with the Conveyancing Act 1919. The purchaser's legal representative must sign this certificate.

Waiving the cooling-off period might make your offer more attractive to the developer; however, you should exercise caution before doing so. You need to make sure that you are absolutely confident about your ability to pay for the property. You can not only waive the cooling-off period, but you can also reduce or extend it with the developer's agreement.

Insurance and building warranties

Each of the Australian states has different insurance and building warranties for new-build developments. Investors buying property in Australia need to be aware that the protections in place to protect purchasers are not as strong as those in New Zealand or the United Kingdom. Therefore, you need to ensure that you have undertaken adequate due diligence to ensure that you have enough protection. A state-by-state breakdown of insurance and building warranties is contained within our Australia Buyers Guide, available at **www.proptechpioneer.com/buyer-guides**

New Zealand

In New Zealand, deposits and warranties are covered at a national level.

Deposits

Buyers typically pay a deposit of 10% on signing the sale and purchase agreement. Deposits are protected, as they are held in a trust account by a stakeholder until settlement, when they are released to the developer. You should always ensure that this is detailed within your contract before signing a Sale and Purchase Agreement.

Building warranties

New Zealand law provides various protections for purchasers of new residential property. All residential building work in New Zealand, no matter how big or small, is covered by the implied warranties set out in the Building Act.

These warranties:

- Last for 10 years
- Apply whether they are stated in the contract or not
- Also apply to work done by subcontractors employed by the main contractor.

The implied warranties are as follows:

- All building work will be done properly, competently, and according to the plans and specifications in the approved consent
- All the materials used will be suitable and, unless otherwise stated in the contract, new
- The building work will be consistent with the Building Act and the Building Code
- The building work will be carried out with reasonable care and skill, and completed within the time specified, or in a reasonable time if no time is stated
- The home will be suitable for occupation at the end of the work
- If the contract states any particular outcome and the homeowner relies on the skill and judgement of the contractor to achieve it, the building work and the materials will be fit for purpose and be of a nature and quality suitable to achieve that result.

12-month defect period

The New Zealand Building Act also gives purchasers an automatic 12-month repair period from the date of completion. In practice, this means that if you provide written confirmation of the defect within 12 months of completion, the developer must repair it within a reasonable timeframe. If there is a dispute, then it is the developer's responsibility to prove that the defective work or products are not their fault.

The warranties do not apply if a defect is caused by:

- Events beyond human control
- Accidental damage caused by others - but not subcontractors or anyone that the developer is legally responsible for
- You (the owner) not carrying out normal maintenance
- You (the owner) not carrying out repairs or arranging to have them done as soon as practicable after a defect becomes apparent
- You (the owner) not following the developer's advice.

If the developer goes out of business, you are not protected. However, you may still have legal rights against the subcontractors. This highlights why it is so important to buy from a reputable developer with a good track record. In terms of activating warranties when they are breached:

- Most breaches can be resolved through the negotiation process set out in the contract
- If your developer does not fix the breach within a reasonable timeframe then you should seek legal advice as you may be able to arrange for another tradesperson to make the repair and have the developer pay the costs
- If the warranties are breached and the building will not be safe for occupants, or it lacks the expected quality set out in the contract, your developer may have to pay you for the loss of value to your property, or they might have to re-reimburse you for their faulty building work
- You may also have the option to cancel your contract
- You can take the developer to the District Court or the High Court. To be successful in court, you will have to show that you have suffered loss or damage because of the actions of the developer. The court can award you compensation for the breach.

United Kingdom
There is a high level of protection for purchasers in the United Kingdom through a Consumer Code and a Construction Guarantee.

Consumer Code for Home Builders
The Consumer Code for Home Builders specifies that a reservation agreement is issued that details the purchase price, exactly what is included within that figure, and the nature and estimated cost of service charges or management fees.

Construction guarantee

Most reputable developers in the United Kingdom provide a construction warranty guarantee, which is a form of insurance against defects. **Buyers should be wary of purchasing a newly constructed property without this.**

This cover protects the first 10% of the purchase price paid as a deposit to the developer if the developer becomes insolvent and is unable to complete the property. You should ask your conveyancer to check that the developer has a construction guarantee in place. It is important to note that the warranty typically only covers the first 10% of the purchase price, and the policy will not cover any stage payments paid beyond this.

Various companies offer protection; the NHBC warranty is by far the most common. These policies vary depending on the provider. The cover usually includes a 2-year builder warranty period backed by the provider's resolution service and guarantee, followed by an 8-year insurance policy covering physical damage to the home caused by a failure to build to certain technical requirements.

If the completion date on the build is 'unreasonably' delayed, then purchasers may have the right (under the Consumer Code for Home Builders) to withdraw from the purchase and claim a full refund of all monies paid.

Contractual considerations

In addition to the deposit protection building insurance, as an investor purchasing off-plan property there are many contractual considerations that you will need to give some thought to. Unless you are regularly dealing with new-build property, it is unlikely that you will think about these - and there some traps you could unwittingly fall into.

Rather than trying to unpick a contract, it is probably easier to go through the questions that are likely to come up in the process. Unfortunately for many investors, these questions often arise after a contract has already been signed.

What if the building is delayed?

Construction is a complex process, and many things could go wrong which could cause delay. Many of these delays will be beyond the control of the developer. Remember, though, that there is no incentive for them to delay completion, as they do not get their money until the contract completes.

Construction delays, and therefore delays in completion, can occur due to adverse weather conditions, delays in the supply of materials, or for any number of other reasons. It is impossible to plan for every eventuality, no matter what you do. For example, not many people would have foreseen the delays created by the recent COVID-19 lockdowns.

For new developments, contracts generally include a clause called a short stop and a long stop date; these are important dates for you to understand:

- **Short stop date:** This is the date by which the developer expects to have the building or apartment finished, and is the earliest date by which the property can be completed.
- **Long stop date:** Sets a fixed date by which the development will need to be completed. Should the developer not serve the completion notice by this date, then the purchaser will have the option to cancel the contract, and any deposits and stage payments will be returned to them. In some countries, long stop dates are typically referred to as 'Sunset Clauses'.

Both dates will be important considerations for you as a buyer-investor. On the one hand, the developer can't absolutely guarantee the date by which the building will be complete, and it is reasonable for them to have some flexibility to complete due to delays which may be beyond their control. However, on the other hand, as a buyer, you will also want to ensure that you are not tied to a contract that has no specific deadline.

A reasonable long-stop date will be 12-18 months after the short stop date. A period longer than this will be problematic for you, for two reasons:

- As an investor, not only do you have the right to bring the contract to an end if construction goes beyond the long stop date, so too does the developer. You run the risk of waiting for 2 to 3 years for a development to complete just to have the development not go ahead.
- There is an opportunity cost. If you wait for a development to complete and it does not go ahead, you will receive your deposit back. However, if this should happen then the potential upside which you would have received if the market increased between the time you initially invested and the long stop date will have been lost. In this scenario, you are losing a significant amount of potential capital appreciation - and because of how markets move, this may be far more

than the rent you would have earned over that period. There may well be scenarios where the market has grown rapidly and therefore prices have increased considerably.

Occasionally, unscrupulous developers may try to push construction beyond the long stop date. In some states of Australia, the sunset clause requires the consent of the purchaser for it to be exercised. You may wish to consider this in reviewing the sale and purchase agreement.

What if the developer runs out of money and goes into bankruptcy?

It is not completely uncommon for developers to run out of money during the construction period of a development and go into administration or bankruptcy. I have been the property agent on some projects which failed to complete, and believe me, this was not a pleasant experience for anyone - especially the purchasers.

As an investor, you need to consider this possibility when purchasing an investment. Just because the market is going up in value, that does not mean that this cannot happen. Indeed, in many scenarios, developers will find themselves in trouble when the market is going up in value. They may well find that excessive competition means they have paid too much for the land, or that the construction cost is more than they anticipated.

Thankfully, in many countries there is protection in place for purchasers. However, how much protection you have will come down to the country you are buying in.

If you purchase an apartment or property in a new development, even if you are lucky enough to get all your money back, there will be a significant amount of time involved and therefore an opportunity cost. This is because if a development goes bad it will not happen quickly - a developer will try extremely hard to complete a building. So, it may take a long period for them either to go into bankruptcy or pass their long-stop date. You will then have to invest a significant amount of time in recovering your money. Not only will this be a painful process, but there will be an opportunity cost in relation to the capital appreciation you could have made on an alternative property.

What if your circumstances change and you need to sell the property?

First, do you have the right to sell? Unless you have legally completed on your property, you may not automatically have the right to sell it.

Generally, sale and purchase agreements will have one of three arrangements:

- **No right to sub-sell or assign:** If your agreement says this, then you have limited options. If the agreement does not include the right to sell before completion, this will have been done for a reason. Most likely, it will have been because the developer has a lot of apartments to sell and they do not want to compete in the open market with their development. If you are in this situation, I would have a conversation with the developer. All good developers will have a strategy to deal with these scenarios.

- **Right to assign your contract:** You have the right to 'assign' the benefit of your agreement to another party. In this scenario, the new purchaser will assume your position in the contract. There are two things you need to be aware of with assignments:
  - Generally you will need the developer's permission to assign the contract, so you need to understand the process, and which scenarios the developer could decline.
  - More importantly just because you assign your interest in the contract, this does not mean you no longer have any obligations in the contract. If the new purchaser fails to complete the transaction, you will be required to 'complete' and purchase the property.

- **Right to sub sale:** This is your 'cleanest' possible way to sell an off-plan property. In this situation, you simply sell the property to a third party. Generally, there will be limited recourse from the developer if the new purchaser fails to perform their obligations under the agreement.

Another thing you need to consider if you want to sell is whether or not you can use the developer's images. Remember that if you want to sell before completion there will be nothing to photograph, or at best a half-built property.

Marketing materials cost a lot of money, far more than you might imagine – the cost of getting the photography and computer generate images are all costs the developer has assumed to sell and promote their property. These materials are the *Intellectual Property* of the developer. You do not have the automatic right to use them to sell your property, and nor does anyone else. Developers have staff regularly calling agents and asking them to stop the unauthorised use of images.

What if you cannot afford to complete?

In some circumstances, investors will not be able to afford to complete a transaction for various reasons. The reality is that life happens, people lose their jobs, fall on hard times, and so on, so there are many reasons why a purchaser may simply not be able to complete the purchase of a property.

For new-build investors, it is difficult to obtain a mortgage offer from a bank before entering a contract. Banks generally do not offer mortgage terms until six months prior to the completion of a property at the earliest, because they are concerned that the property market may change during the period the property is being built. Therefore, you may commit to purchasing a property and later find out you are unable to obtain a mortgage.

Unfortunately, for an investor, if your circumstances change and you are not able to complete the purchase (because you cannot obtain a mortgage), you do not have the automatic right to pull out of the contract. Your only options are either to sell your interest in the property (assuming you have the right to do so), or simply not to complete.

If you fail to complete, you will likely forfeit any deposit you have paid. The developer can also sue you for any loss they have incurred as a result of you not completing the contract. However, in reality they are unlikely to do so, especially if you are investing offshore.

What if the property is not what you were told it would be?

Before completion, most reputable developers will ask the buyer to 'snag' a new property. This is an inspection that allows the buyer or their representative to check that the developer has met all their obligations under the terms of the contract. It may include a range of things from checking the dimensions of rooms, to checking the paint finishes. If any defects are recorded, then the developer should arrange for them to be remedied.

In many instances, a letting agent can carry out the snagging fixes on behalf of the purchaser. You need to ensure that this process is thoroughly undertaken, and that you spend as much time as required to deal with any snagging issues. This is the time when the developer is going to be most amenable to resolving issues. After all, they are waiting for your money.

Cost escalation clauses

You should be aware of the costs escalation clause in the sale and purchase agreement, the lease agreement in the event of leasehold, and any strata or service charge costs. I have set out the common issues below:

- **Construction cost escalations:** It is not uncommon for some developers to include cost escalation clauses, which increase the cost of the property to the purchaser if construction costs increase. You should not agree to a clause like this, as you would be taking on the risk of the construction, future value, and cost increases.

- **Ground rents:** Particularly in the UK, many developers have written leases for leasehold property that have highly onerous rental review provisions for ground rents. Within some of these agreements ground rents are stipulated to be doubled every 10 to 25 years, whereas typically these review provisions are linked to the Consumer Price Index.

- **Service charges and strata costs:** It is worthwhile reviewing the lease agreement to ensure that the provisions concerning the way the service charge is calculated are fair and reasonable.

Should you buy as an individual or as a company?

There are some practical issues that you need to consider when it comes to ownership. Not only can forms of tenure be different for real estate; you can also own real estate in different ways. You will have two questions to answer:

- Should you purchase as an individual or as a company?
- If you purchase as an individual, how should the property be held?

Buying as a company

You will have the opportunity to purchase a property via a company or a trust. Companies and trusts are legally recognised as separate entities from their owners, which means that you can create a separate legal entity in order for it to own the property on your behalf.

Trust and companies can be complex structures when used for investment property, and can be created for multiple reasons to achieve specific objectives.

Trusts versus companies

A company and a trust are two different kinds of legal entities, each of which have specific attributes. They are formed for different purposes, and have different characteristics in terms of their control, setup, and assets.

I give a brief explanation below of the differences between a trust and a company. However, if you are considering buying via a trust or company then you must get independent advice.

Trust

A trust is an organisation or firm created by a fiduciary relationship in which one party, known as a trustor, gives another party, a trustee, the right to hold title or assets for the benefit of another business or individual, the beneficiary.

Trusts are established to provide legal protection for the trustor's assets, to make sure those assets are distributed according to the trustor's wishes, and/ or to avoid or reduce inheritance or estate taxes. Funds not distributed from a trust are taxed.

Within a trust there are:

- **A trustee:** The person or people who own the assets in the trust. It is the trustees' job to run the trust and manage the trust property responsibly.
- **A beneficiary:** The person for whom the trust is set up. The assets held in trust are held for the beneficiary's benefit.

As an investor, if you put assets into a trust then they no longer belong to you provided that certain conditions are met. This means that when you die, their value normally will not be counted towards inheritance, and therefore will not be taxed. Instead, the cash, investments, or property belong to the trust. In other words, once the property is held in trust, it is outside anyone's estate for inheritance tax purposes.

Another potential advantage is that a trust is a way of keeping control of assets, and ensuring asset protection, for the beneficiary, A trust avoids handing over valuable property, cash, or investment whilst the beneficiaries are relatively young or vulnerable.

The trustees have a legal duty to look after and manage the trust assets for the person who will benefit from the trust in the end.

Company

A company represents a combination of assets and individuals with a common goal of earning profits to increase the wealth of its shareholders. A company is a separate legal entity.

The sole purpose of a company is to manage its business interests to generate a profit for its shareholders. In contrast, a trust may be formed with a variety of other aims.

Why use a company or trust structure?

There are many reasons why investors will use a company or trust structure. I explain the main ones below.

Mortgage Interest Relief

In United Kingdom, under the terms of Section 24 of the Finance (no. 2) Act 2015, buy-to-let investors are no longer able to claim mortgage interest, or any other property finance, as tax-deductible. Instead, rental profit is taxed with a maximum deduction for finance costs of 20% (the basic rate of tax).

Many countries have looked at the UK to see the impact of these changes on landlord behaviour. New Zealand has also recently introduced laws that have the same effect. Therefore, for many individuals looking to purchase an investment property, it is likely to be more tax-efficient to do so via a company structure.

Companies pay significantly lower tax rates

For high-income earners there may be significant tax advantages in owning via a company rather than individually, because as an individual income tax is payable on rental profits, whereas companies pay corporation tax. However, as an individual, you will still have to pay income tax on any income that the company pays to you as an individual (typically in the form of dividends or as a salary).

Below are the top income tax and corporation rates for Australia, New Zealand, and the United Kingdom.

Table 8.2: Top income tax rates and corporation taxes (Australia, New Zealand and United Kingdom)

	Top Income Tax Rate	Corporation Tax
Australia	45%	30%
New Zealand	33%	28%
United Kingdom	45%	19%*

*Recent changes announced in the UK budget mean that this will increase to 25% for profits over £50,000 after 1 April 2023.

Multiple shareholders

A company can have multiple owners (shareholders), which is a way of taking advantage of multiple individuals' income-tax-free allowances. Therefore, you can pay your spouse and/or children (depending on their age) via a salary or dividend. Each can use as much of their tax-free allowance as they like.

There is no requirement for a company to make equal payments of dividends, salaries, or profits to shareholders. Additionally, these payments can change every year, thereby allowing you to take the most tax-efficient approach.

You can retain company profits and reinvest them without paying tax

If you own an investment property in your name, you will pay income tax on any profit which is generated, regardless of what you do with it.

However, if the property is held in a limited company then all the profits (after corporation tax) can be kept within the company. The point is that you do not need to distribute this profit to other parties, who would then be subject to income tax.

Creditors do not have access to your assets

In the event of financial issues, creditors will only have access to the company's assets, so if the company's financial situation were to deteriorate, the owners of the company (its shareholders and directors) would be safe from creditors.

However, this protection may be quite limited because many lenders require owners to provide personal guarantees.

Lower stamp duty costs for sale of the company

There can be advantages of company ownership from a stamp duty perspective in the UK, as the owner can sell the company rather than the property. For example, this can be advantageous to the new buyer as the cost of stamp duty to sell a company can be as low as 0.5%, whereas stamp duty for a property can be as high as 18%.

Inheritance tax

In the United Kingdom, trusts can be used in certain circumstances to avoid the requirement to pay inheritance tax, assuming certain conditions can be met. This is not a consideration in countries such as Australia or New Zealand, which do not have inheritance or estate taxes.

Disadvantages of owning in a company or trust

There are many disadvantages to owning property via a company or trust, which is why getting independent advice is crucial.

- **Expensive:** It is expensive to set up a company, and particularly a trust. The costs of doing so may well outweigh the benefits, particularly if you do not plan to hold the property in perpetuity.

- **May not be significant tax advantages:** For many people, using a company to purchase property will only create significant tax advantages if their income within that country is already significant. For example, if you are a high-income earner and the income generated by the property will be taxed in the highest income bracket, or you do not want to use the income generated immediately, it makes sense to retain profits within a company. However, for others, particularly offshore investors, the advantages may not be as high.

- **More difficult to obtain a mortgage:** Most companies or trusts created specifically to buy property will not be able to borrow money easily. Therefore, the owner will most likely have to provide personal guarantees to obtain a mortgage.

- **Shorter mortgages:** Typically, mortgages offered to companies will be shorter than those available to individuals. The advantage of this will be that the total interest cost will be lower, and they will be paid off more quickly. However, the monthly mortgage payments will be considerably higher.

- **Potential tax issues:** If a company or trust is established specifically to purchase property, it may be viewed by the relevant tax authority as having been established specifically to avoid income tax. This means that it may well be taxed by the tax authority.

- **Costs not to let:** If you do not use the company or trust for the specific issue for which it has been created, then this can also create issues and tax liabilities. For example, a company that purchases a property to let it out in the UK needs to demonstrate that it is doing that.

Buying as an individual or with someone else

When buying a property individually, it can be easy to forget the legal protection you may need in the future. If you are buying with a spouse, friend or relative, or business partner, you will need to consider how you are holding the investment. When buying property together, those purchasers have the option either to register the property as joint tenants, or tenants in common.

Individual

When you purchase an investment property on your own, it is a straightforward process. You simply need to determine whether or not you should buy in your own name or via a company or trust.

Joint tenants

Under a joint tenancy, both parties own the whole of the property, not a quantified share.

This is the option most couples choose when they buy together. If one passes away, then the right of survivorship applies. This means that the surviving person from the relationship inherits the property on their partner's death. This means that the person who passes away are unable to leave their property, or a share of it, to anyone else other than their partner. However, when the surviving partner then dies, they are free to leave their property to whomever they choose.

Joint tenancy is generally the simpler of the two options, as it does not require working out exactly how much each partner contributes to the purchase price and simply splits the property equally between them.

If the relationship ends before one partner dies as they decide to split up, a couple who are joint tenants have options. They might choose to sell the property and split the proceeds 50/50, or one of them may choose to retain the property and buy the other out of their share.

Tenants in common

Tenancy in common is generally used by business partners for investment. The difference between tenancy in common and joint tenancy is that the owners can split ownership into specifically chosen amounts. Therefore, different investors can contribute different amounts to the purchase price and ownership costs, and the differences can be recognised via the split of ownership on the title.

This split can be fixed from the outset (for example, there might be a 25%/75% split of the purchase price). It can also be altered over time to reflect the contributions different parties make to the ownership of the property. For example, one of the partners may get a new job and start earning more, and as a result, they may increase their share of the ownership through increased contributions from, say, a 25%/75% split to 40%/60%, or any other combination. The appeal of tenancy in common is that changes in contribution over time can be reflected in the ownership of the title. Then, if the property is sold or the investors go separate ways, they know what percentage of the property belongs to them.

CHAPTER 9

Operational Issues

Operational issues are items that are likely to arise during your ownership of the property. In this chapter, I have covered the things you should think about as an investor.

Leasehold property

Investors will most likely be required to pay a ground rent on leasehold property if it is a new-build property. In relation to doing so, they should consider the following:

- Is the ground rent commercial?
- How much is it, and is the amount reasonable?
- How is it reviewed?

In 2017 in the UK, the Communities and Local Government Committee undertook a review of unfair practices in the leasehold market. The report which resulted from the review identified several concerns, which included:

- Onerous ground rents as well as the method and frequency of increases;
- High and/or unclear service charges and 'one-off' bills;
- Managing agents charging unexpected fees for permissions or consents;
- The costs of, and delays in, providing management information;
- Unbalanced dispute resolution mechanisms;
- Unreasonable costs to enfranchise or extend leases.

It is anticipated the UK government will make some changes to the leasehold system to deal with some of these issues. However, it may take many years for these changes to be implemented. They have been talking about building a third runway at Heathrow Airport since the 1950s! So, as an investor you need to ensure you have thought about the likely issues which may arise.

Ground rent

Concerns surrounding ground rents frequently appeared in the UK media in 2017 and 2018. The primary issue is that some leases allow for ground rents to double every ten years, thereby creating a highly burdensome rent review provision for leaseholders.

In the first instance, this may not sound like a significant amount of money; after all, most ground rents are relatively small amounts. However, if you think this through, for plot 1 Kingsley Tower if the ground rent is £300 p.a. and it has a review provision whereby every 10 years it doubles, then after 50 years the ground rent will be £9,600 p.a. When compared to a situation where the ground rental is an inflation-linked increase of 2% every year for 50 years (so at the end of the period, the annual ground rent will be £942 p.a.), the difference is material and will have a significant impact on your potential return and ability to sell the property.

Other issues

If you plan to own and let the property for the long term, you need to consider what might happen over that time. The reality is that you do not know what new technologies may emerge, and/or how the world will change.

Many leaseholders in the UK have been significantly financially impacted by having to resolve issues with having unsafe cladding attached to buildings removed following a tragic fire in Grenfell Tower in London in which many people lost their lives.

You need to review the lease agreement and consider:

- How difficult will it be to obtain freeholder consent to adapt to new legal and technological requirements?
- Who will pay the costs?

You also need to be confident that if things do change, you can adapt your property to those changes. To this end, you need to consider the following:

- How much are the permission fees involved in the application process?
- How long will it take the freeholder to deal with the issues?

Extending the lease

For leasehold property, the length of the lease should be a major consideration. This is predominantly an issue for UK (England and Wales) property, so I have focused a UK perspective, and specifically property in England in Wales. Things you need to consider are that:

- Short leases (under 85 years) are hard to sell
- Short leases (under 85 years) are worth less, and are harder to mortgage or re-mortgage
- Leases are a wasting asset - when they run out they are worthless.

A lease extension protects your asset against erosion by time and safeguards your investment. An extended lease is usually at nil (a "peppercorn") ground rent. Keep in mind that the longer you leave it, the more expensive a lease extension becomes, with increased costs rising year on year, and if a lease has less than 80 years remaining it will be more expensive.

The process you need to go through to extend a lease is called Leasehold Enfranchisement. Under the Leasehold Reform, Housing and Urban Development Act 1993, leaseholders have the right to extend their lease, subject to certain qualifying criteria being met. The process is complex, and I will not go into detail here; however, if you would like to understand the process I have detailed it at **www.proptechpioneer.com/lease-extension-calculator**

Service charges and strata management fees

Service charges and strata Management fees are not the same as ground rent. These are fees charged for the day-to-day management and upkeep of the common areas of the building.

These are all essentially the same, but are called different things in different countries:

- **Australia:** Strata Fees, charged by the Strata Corporation
- **New Zealand:** Body Corporate fee, charged by the body corporate
- **UK:** Service charge, charged by the landlord or their managing agent under the terms of the lease.

These fees will typically cover:

- Repairs, maintenance, and improvements to communal areas or the building structure
- Building insurance
- Management company costs
- The lighting, heating, cooling, and cleaning of communal areas
- Caretakers or concierges.

These fees are typically calculated proportionately to the size of the property relative to the others in the block or complex. All owners are required to pay for their share of the services, even if they do not use them all.

What services can you be charged for?

The services you can be charged for are set out in your lease, strata agreement, or body corporate agreement. These charges fall into several categories:

- **Administrative fund levies:** These are general daily and regular expenses. They cover most cleaning and gardening costs, any shared utility bills, body corporate insurance, and any general repairs or maintenance.

- **Sinking fund levies:** These fees cover larger expenses, and may include renovations such as the replacement of roofing or the repainting of walls.

- **Special levies:** If a task is required for the maintenance of the common property and it falls into neither administrative nor sinking levies, it becomes a special levy.

In addition, your agreement will also set out the following information:

- How service charges are calculated
- How charges are divided between owners
- Whether there is a sinking or reserve fund

Are there any limits to what you can be charged?

There are generally no limits to the level of service charges, but the freeholder/managing agent can only pass on reasonable costs to leaseholders/strata owners. Any works or services provided should also be of a reasonable standard.

Who pays the fee?

Strata fees and service charges must be paid by those who own an apartment or home. Tenants will not pay strata fees if they are renting. However, most landlords account for these costs by rolling them into the monthly or weekly rent charged for the property.

Can I simply not pay?

The short answer is no! An owner's obligation to pay strata levies (or service charges) is independent of any other matter between the owner and the body corporate or freeholder. Therefore, if an owner refuses to pay their levies, they will be in breach of their agreement. How this is dealt with depends on the country context:

- In **Australia**, the owner will become non-financial, and incur interest at 30% (or such rate set by the body corporate). As a "non-financial" member, the owner will also lose the right to vote at meetings and act on the committee.

- In **New Zealand**, the owner cannot object to a levy by not paying it. Interest can be applied to non-payments. The current penalty rate is 10%.

- In the **UK**, the freeholder can apply to the county court to recover service charges, and in extreme circumstances the owner could lose their property, although your freeholder must follow procedures and get a court order to repossess the property. It is likely that as an owner you could intervene before things deteriorate to that extent.

Is there a dispute process?

The dispute processes are as follows.

Australia

If an owner disputes a decision, action, or inaction of a body corporate, they must complain to the body corporate and seek clarification or remedy from the dispute. If the issue is not resolved at this level, then the owner may gather support from other owners to call an extraordinary general meeting. If this is not possible (in other words, the owner cannot generate sufficient interest from other owners), then the owner may apply for the matter to be decided by the Body Corporate Commissioner, or in limited circumstances, may lodge proceedings in the Magistrates or Supreme Court (depending on the type of complaint and parties involved – such as an insurance dispute over repairs, wherein the dispute relates to an insurer of a body corporate).

Even if the owner claims that the body corporate owes them money for something (such as repairs the owner claims to have been made relating to "common property" or damages associated with "common property"), the owner must continue to pay strata levies as and when they fall due, and take action against the body corporate separately.

New Zealand

If you are unhappy with the way the rules are being applied in New Zealand you can talk to a committee member, raise the issue at a general meeting, seek legal advice, or contact the government authority responsible for regulating strata issues for advice.

If you're not on the committee, you can voice your concern at the annual meeting, or do so in writing to the chairperson or the committee. However, your first step should be to talk to the body corporate manager themselves to explain your concerns, as they may have arisen out of a simple misunderstanding.

If you're a member of the committee, you can discuss the matter with your fellow members and establish a consensus of opinion regarding the performance of the body corporate manager. You can also examine the terms of their contract. It may be that the committee agrees that there has been under-performance – in which case it might set new performance benchmarks, or choose not to renew the contract.

UK

In the UK, owners have the right as leaseholders to challenge a service charge or services provided. They can do this even if they have already paid the charge in some cases. Common reasons for challenges to service charges include:

- High charges
- Work not done or done badly
- The owner cannot find out how their service charges are being spent
- The owner is being charged for services or works not covered in the lease

A tribunal can decide if a charge or proposed charge is reasonable. The freeholder must consult owners if they intend to:

- Carry out works that will cost individual leaseholders more than £250 per year; or
- Use a contractor to provide services for more than a year and that will cost individual leaseholders more than £100 per year.

Concerns relating to strata and service charge fees

Are strata and service charge fees a significant issue? The short answer is no. Most service charges and strata fees will be reasonable in the way they are managed and administered. As an investor, I think you should be far more concerned with the following things:

Tax deductible and marginal gain

In most countries your strata charges and service charge fees are tax-deductible, and while you do not want to pay excessive fees, these costs can be offset against your income from a taxation perspective. So, whilst there may be some margin gain to be had by driving down the cost of your service charge, it will not make a significant difference to your overall return.

Let me demonstrate using plot 1 Kingsley Tower, with an apartment which is 39 m² in a building of 6,500 m² in total. Say that the property has excessive cleaning costs for the common areas of £25,000 p.a., and therefore that the cost to the owner of Plot 1 is £150p.a.

Assume that by running a highly competitive tender process and pushing potential cleaning contractors, the building manager can find a company willing to do the work for £20,000 p.a. because the bidders see the value in getting a long-term contract.

Even with this 20% discount to this cost, the annual cost to the owner of Plot 1 Kingsley Tower will be £120 p.a. For the work required to achieve the 20% discount, they will improve their monthly financial performance by £30. Overall, the time spent to achieve this will not justify the financial outcome.

You want the building to be well maintained

Worse than an excessive service charge is a building where the service charge is too low to adequately maintain the building. Buildings can fall into a poor state of repair or cleanliness very quickly. This is particularly the case for larger buildings that have a lot of foot traffic with occupiers going in and out of the building.

A poorly managed building will typically create the following scenario:

- **Rental income:** Prospective tenants will not want to live in a poorly managed building, and the property will rent at a discount to other comparable properties.
- **Quality of tenant:** Better tenants want to live in better-maintained buildings.
- **Significant long-term cost:** By under-managing the building, the owners are not avoiding costs - just delaying them. Poorly managed buildings typically need more work over the longer-term and therefore there is greater cost.
- **Capital value:** The value of a poorly managed property will diminish over time. Whilst you may think it does not impact you if you do not want to sell the property, it will still impact you if you wish to arrange finance, etc.

Services to the building are more important

You should be more concerned about the physical services to the building rather than the specific costs to maintain items. Gyms, swimming pools, cinema rooms, and common facilities all cost a significant amount of money to clean, maintain, and insure. However, they generally will not increase rental income, as most tenants are not willing to pay a premium for these services. The costs involved in maintaining these unnecessary features will reduce the overall income which can be achieved due to the higher operational costs.

Should you use a managing agent?

Whether or not to use a managing agent to let your investment property is an important consideration for many investors. You will not make a return until you have a tenant in place. I think it makes far more sense to use a property manager rather than to manage the property yourself.

Above all, when you purchase an investment property you are establishing a business that is actively engaged in letting out rental accommodation; as such, your tenants are your customers. Whether or not you choose to let and manage the property yourself, you need to provide a high level of service to your customer. This includes maintaining the property and dealing with reasonable requests made by your tenant promptly. If you cannot (or are not in a position to) do this, I would get someone else to do it.

Types of property management

You have the choice of letting only or full management. When you consider appointing a property manager, these are the main considerations.

Letting only

With letting only, you are appointing a property agent to secure, vet, and contract a tenant to rent your property. If you appoint an agent to provide this service, they will typically provide the following services:

- Prepare particulars and market the property for lease
- Undertake viewings with prospective tenants
- Source a tenant
- Undertake reference checks on the potential tenant to confirm their suitability
- Draw up a tenancy agreement
- Conduct an inventory of the property, its contents, and its condition
- Move the tenant into the property

With letting only, once the agent has secured the tenant and moved them in ,you are then responsible for coordinating with the tenant from that point onwards.

Typically, letting agents will charge in one of two ways:

- A percentage of the annual rental (circa. 5 – 8%), or
- A fixed fee (circa. half to one month's rental).

Letting and management

With letting and management does as it implies. Not only will the agent provide those services set out above for letting the property, but they will also manage the property, which includes the following services:

- Collecting and passing on the rent, and chasing it up if it is not paid on time
- Inspecting the property regularly, and updating their client on its condition
- Taking care of the landlord's legal obligations, such as obtaining gas safety certificates
- Arranging and coordinating the repair and maintenance that is required
- Responding promptly to tenant requests and keeping them happy
- Handling rent increases, renewals, and check-outs.

Fees for full management are usually charged as a percentage of the rent, with something in the range of 7% to 15% being common. They might charge separately to find tenants in the first place, or this might be absorbed into the management fee.

What do you need to think about?

My advice is that you would be far better off having a property agent who can provide you with a full letting and management service, I will explain why.

- **Keeping a distance:** You should not underestimate the value of having a third party between you and your tenant. It is easy to get caught up in other people's day-to-day issues, and having a third party gives you some important distance. The role of a property manager is most importantly to collect the rent and ensure that the rental income you receive is in line with the market. As a landlord, you must provide the tenant with a clean, well-maintained property that is safe, and you respond to repairs promptly.

- **Legal obligations:** Governments are getting more involved in regulating the private rental market. The few landlords who behave badly and do not maintain properties give everyone else a bad name. This situation will not change, and more regulations will be introduced over time. As a private landlord, the consequences for getting it wrong can be both legally and financially severe. For example, not correctly registering a tenant's deposit can result in a potential fine of four times the deposit in the United Kingdom. Unless you can meet the existing regulations and keep up with changes to them, you are likely to be setting yourself up for failure.

- **Your costs are tax-deductible:** As a private landlord, your costs for employing a professional property manager are tax-deductible. So, why compromise your investment by doing this yourself when there is a marginal gain to doing so?

- **Service:** Like most things, it seems that people nowadays expect a far greater level of service than they used to. Social media has given everyone a voice, and many people like to use their new-found voice to complain! Tenants are no different – and bear in mind that while most requests will be completely reasonable, others will not. Either way, let someone else deal with it, as property managers are employed to give a good level of service in dealing with reasonable requests and to turn down ones that are not. Good tenants will understand what is and is not a reasonable request. The main thing a tenant will get annoyed with is a lack of responsiveness.

- **Access to internet portals and tenant pools:** The cost of accessing some of the large internet property portals to advertise your property can be high. For property agents, the expense makes sense because it is simply a cost of doing business. However, for you as an individual landlord, it will be far more expensive to use these services on a one-off basis. Additionally, numerous platforms and forums are used to attract tenants. It will be impossible for you to cover all these effectively.

- **Potential tenants will feel more comfortable dealing with a property agent:** One of the things which constantly comes up when tenants are interviewed is that they feel far more comfortable dealing with a professional agent managing a property. They will need to give deposits and a lot of personal information to rent a property, so they want to feel comfortable that the party is independent and trustworthy, and that someone will deal with issues with the property as and when they arise.

- **Higher rent:** Tenants are more likely to pay a premium for a professionally-managed property over one managed by a landlord directly. It is difficult to say how much, but some research suggests this may be as much as 10% more rent.

- **Difficult conversations:** Property managers are particularly good at having difficult conversations with tenants, something which can be challenging for many people, especially if you are not in the same country. They will have discussions about why rents need to be increased, or why a deposit needs to be retained to pay for property damage.

- **Knowledge:** Property agents are close to the ground - they are in conversations with tenants and people in the property industry every day. They will have come across most scenarios you can think of, and will help you with their deep knowledge. They know the best practices, know how to deal with disputes, understand the rules, and are a great sounding board for dealing with your investment.

- **Time:** Property managers will give you back your most valuable resource, time. Managing property is time-consuming: you need to keep records, respond to tenant inquiries, and coordinate repairs, builders, and handymen. Let the professionals take this off your hands.

Part 3 Recap

In this part, we covered forms of tenure, the purchasing process, and issues with operation and selling. Below, I have highlighted what I believe to be the key points you need to consider.

Tenure

There are many forms of tenure for real estate. In most western countries, the highest form of ownership is in fee simple, commonly referred to as freehold ownership.

Just because freehold ownership is the highest form of ownership, this does not necessarily mean that it is the best form in all circumstances. Other types of tenure have just as much merit, and in some countries or scenarios, it will simply not be possible for an asset to be held by way of a freehold interest, such as a block of apartments.

More important when considering what form of tenure works as an investor, is to establish the following:

- **Rights:** What rights and protections do you have to enjoy long-term ownership of the property?

- **Costs:** What are the costs associated with that form of tenure? It is important to remember that for some investors, freehold tenure will be cumbersome - because freeholders are responsible for maintaining the physical structure, which can be both costly and time-consuming. In contrast, with leasehold or strata ownership, both the costs as well the responsibility for management will be shared with other owners.

- **Dealing with the property:** What rights do you have to deal with the property? And whose permission will you require for renovations, etc.?

- **Ownership issues:** What issues are you likely to come across throughout your ownership? For example, if you are purchasing leasehold property, how long is the lease? What will it cost to extend it in the future if you have to?

- **Ownership structure:** How will the property be held? Individually, as joint tenants, tenants in common, or in a trust or company? These are decisions you will not be able to make without some external input, particularly if you are thinking about using a company or trust. For most people, tax considerations and long-term objectives will be the principal determinants of how to hold the property.

- **Foreign restrictions:** What foreign restrictions exist if you wish to purchase internationally? Could they potentially change in the future – and if so, how?

Purchase process

As an investor, you will need to give some thought to the purchase process, and you should be familiar with how it works. What can go wrong? If buying off-plan, you will need to consider what issues may arise during construction, what you would do as a result, and what the contract says.

Most people focus on everything going right and how well they will do. Do not worry about those things - worry about what could go wrong. Obviously, I am not advising you not to buy. But you should think about the whole process and have a plan to deal with possible problems.

Operational issues

Once you have purchased a property, you will need to secure a tenant, maintain and repair the property, collect rent, and make sure you comply with the relevant laws. You need to give some thought to how you will do all these things. You will need to consider the following:

- Are you going to use a property manager or go it alone? If you are going to use a property manager, what services will they provide? If not, how will you manage the property?
- How much will the services in the building impact the costs of managing and operating it? Are they worth it? Do tenants pay extra for these facilities, and if so, how much?

PART 4A

Financial Performance

So far, we have covered the operational realities of how the new-build market works. However, we are missing one vital element - financial performance. Measuring and tracking financial performance is how you move from a knowledgeable investor to a superstar investor!

It is impossible to make effective investment decisions without:

- Understanding how to measure financial performance, and
- Being able to use this analysis to compare different investments.

If you read the promotional materials and research reports prepared by property agents, you will notice that they refer to all sorts of data about historic market performance, future growth, and potential investment returns. This generic information is designed to bamboozle you with facts and figures, and provides limited value in your comparison of different investment opportunities.

Many people find measuring financial performance a complicated and overwhelming process; however, it does not need to be. Understanding how to map financial performance puts you in a *powerful position*, because it gives you the confidence to make decisions based on fact and logic. Learning these skills can be difficult; however, doing so will improve your effectiveness in making decisions by tenfold.

Let's go through the process step-by-step.

Financial objectives

Other than a loss, investment property is only capable of generating two financial outcomes:

- **Capital appreciation:** The difference in the value of your property at a given point in time less your costs to purchase the property; and
- **Income:** Rent paid by tenants.

How much of each of the above you are looking to generate will change over time as your investment objectives change. We will cover this in Part 5: Your property investment strategy.

You need to be able to calculate how much of the financial returns you get to keep, versus how much is absorbed by taxes and other costs. There are six key financial metrics you need to generate to determine which property best meets your investment objectives:

- **Cash required:** How much cash is required to purchase the investment?
- **Net cash flow:** How much cash will an investment generate after covering costs?
- **Net income after tax:** How much income is left after paying tax?
- **Capital appreciation:** How much capital appreciation will the investment generate?
- **Available equity:** How much available equity is your property generating which you can reinvest in other properties to grow your portfolio?
- **Net return on cash if sold:** How much net income does the investment return, relative to the cash required?

These key financial metrics come from a set of financial statements for potential property investment.

Financial statements

I know what some of you might be thinking: I am never going to be able to work these out, it would be too complicated and time-consuming! Do not get overwhelmed by the idea of financial statements. They are a powerful way of tracking the financial performance of a potential investment, and a great way to review potential investments.

If you buy an investment property, you are effectively creating a business. You are buying an asset that you rent to your customer (the tenant) to generate income and benefit from its increasing value over time. To track the performance of businesses, you record their financial data in the form of three financial statements:

- **Cash flow statement:** Sets out the net cash flow generated by your property over a specific period. It simply records the total amount of cash generated less the cash costs you incur to manage and maintain your investment.
- **Income statement:** Measures the financial performance of your property. It sets out how your property converts revenue into net profit.
- **Balance sheet:** Sets out your assets (the property you own) and your liabilities (your mortgage); the difference between the two is your owner's equity.

To demonstrate the power of these financial statements in making investment decisions, I am going to prepare them for the different scenarios of buyer(s) 1 and 2. I will also do so for plot 1 Kingsley Tower as though it was in either Australia, New Zealand, or England.

As powerful as the financial statements are, a word of warning. The financial statements do not represent what will happen; they simply represent a financial outcome based on a series of assumptions. How close the financial statements are to reality will depend on how good the assumptions you make were.

CHAPTER 10

Cash Flow Statement

Cash flow is the most important element of your investment. Your cash flow is the amount of money that flows in and out of your investment.

Many people get confused when they talk about cash flow, because they mix up profit and cash flow - which are not the same thing. It is important to recognise that the *cash flow statement* records when cash is collected. This is not 'profit', which is recorded in the *income statement* (as is explained in Chapter 11).

The cash flow statement has three elements:

- Income: Cash which the property generates;
- Expenses: Cash payments required to maintain the property and investment; and
- Net Cash Flow: The difference between the two.

A property has a *positive cash flow* if the income it generates is greater than the expenses incurred to maintain it. It has a *negative cash flow* if the expenses incurred to run it are greater than the income it generates. In this scenario, you would have to pay additional cash into the investment to meet its monthly expenses.

Income

Investment properties generate income in three ways.

- **Rent:** Your property will generate rent from tenants; this will mainly be for the property itself. But, you may also generate rent from other areas such as car parks or storage.

- **Income from sale:** If you sell the property, you will receive money from its sale.
- **Cash generated from released equity:** If the value of your property has increased, it may be possible for you to re-mortgage the property to extract some of the equity created.

Inputting income into a cash flow statement

To keep things simple, let's ignore cash generated from other sources, and just focus on rent.

I am going to use Plot 1 Kingsley Tower, and build a cash flow statement for the property. The property will rent for £500 per week, which equates to £26,000 a year.

Table 10.1: Cash flow statement, Plot 1 Kingsley Tower

	Year 1	Year 2	Year 3	Year 4	Year 5
Income					
Rent	26,000	26,000	26,000	26,000	26,000

Easy, right? Now, what are the factors which will impact rental income? There are two:

- **Rental growth:** Investors seek to increase rent over time. As the market improves, you will try and increase the rent. Let's assume that the rent increases by 3.0% annually.

- **Vacancy:** There will be times when the property is vacant and there will be no rent. You will try and keep the tenant for as long as you can. However, life moves on, and tenants come and go. In the United Kingdom the average period of a tenancy is 18 months, so let's assume this for Kingsley Tower. If a tenant vacates the property every 18 months and it takes two weeks to secure a new tenant, then over 5 years, there will be three periods of vacancy, each for two weeks.

You will note we have made three assumptions so far:

1. The rent will increase by 3%;
2. Tenants will stay for 18 months;
3. It will take two weeks to secure a new tenant.

This is exactly what you will need to do to build a financial picture of a potential investment. However, when you are making these assumptions in your financial statements, bear some things in mind:

- These are not what *will* happen; they are simply your *best* guess as to what is likely
- Do not overestimate figures – use *common sense* and be <u>conservative</u>
- Because these are estimates, it makes sense to blend them into your calculations rather than assume something will happen at a given point in time.

On vacancy, it makes more sense to blend this assumption into the cash flow. There are 60 months in a 5-year cash flow. For six weeks (1.5 months) the property will not generate rent.

Months of occupancy 58.5 / 5 = 11.7 months of the year the property is occupied.

Therefore, 11.7 months / 12 months = an occupancy rate of 97.5%, or alternatively, a vacancy rate of 2.5%.

Let's add this new information into the cash flow.

Table 10.2: Cash flow statement, Plot 1 Kingsley Tower

	Year 1	Year 2	Year 3	Year 4	Year 5
Income					
Rent	26,000	26,780	27,583	28,411	29,263
Rental Growth Rate		3.0%	3.0%	3.0%	3.0%
Vacancy Rate		2.5%	2.5%	2.5%	2.5%
Gross Income	26,000	26,111	26,894	27,701	28,532

Driving income performance

Hopefully, two things are obvious at this point. First, to drive your income performance, you will need to grow the rent. Second, periods of vacancy will have a highly detrimental impact on your income. Consider:

- **Rents:** These do not move in the way the cash flow suggests. Rents grow in slabs; it might be £2,167 per month for 2 years and then increase to £2,500 per month in year 3. If you have a terrible relationship with your tenant and do not maintain your property or you or they are just difficult to deal with, will the tenant be willing to pay more rent? Remember, there are lots of properties for rent!

- **Vacancy:** If you do not maintain your property, you will find that tenants will not want to stay as long in your property. And, you will need to do more work to your property in between tenancies, which means the property is vacant for longer. One month is 8.33% of a year, so the vacancy rate can hit you hard very quickly.

Assume for Plot 1 that we change our assumptions so that:

- There is no rental growth;
- Tenancies only last for an average of 12 months; and
- The gap between tenancies is one month – this will change our vacancy rate to 6.67%.

Our cash flow now looks like this.

Table 10.3: Cash flow statement, Plot 1 Kingsley Tower

	Year 1	Year 2	Year 3	Year 4	Year 5
Income					
Rent	26,000	26,000	26,000	26,000	26,000
Rental Growth Rate		0%	0%	0%	0%
Vacancy Rate		6.67%	6.67%	6.67%	6.67%
Gross Income	26,000	24,266	24,266	24,266	24,266

If this were the case, then a whopping £12,173 of potential income would be lost over 5 years. To put that in perspective, that is 47% of the first year's rental income.

Table 10.4: Cash flow statement, Plot 1 Kingsley Tower

Net Income	Year 1	Year 2	Year 3	Year 4	Year 5
Scenario 1	26,000	26,111	26,894	27,701	28,532
Scenario 2	26,000	24,266	24,266	24,266	24,266
Lost Potential Income	0	1,845	2,628	3,435	4,266

Expenses

Expenses are the other input into the cash flow, and are often the area where investors make the most mistakes. Most investors make two common mistakes when they track expenses:

- They underestimate the cost of expenses, and/or
- They do not include all the potential expenses in their calculations.

These errors give an inaccurate reflection of the expected return and create a false sense of security. You must undertake detailed due diligence when reviewing expenses to ensure that all expenses are effectively captured.

Cash expenses fall into four categories. I recommend that you track expenses in these groups, as doing so will make it far easier to assess investments:

- Purchase Costs
- Operating and Management Expenses
- Finance Costs
- Capital Improvements.

Purchase costs

We have covered purchase costs in Part 2: Purchase price and purchase costs.

Operating and management expenses

Operating and management expenses are the costs that are incurred in the day-to-day management of your property; they include the following.

Letting and management expenses
You will likely have a property manager to manage the property. Let's assume their fees are:

- Letting Fees - 2 weeks rental
- Management Fees – 6% of the gross income

In Australia, New Zealand, and the United Kingdom, there is also either GST or VAT to pay. Most property management fees are quoted net of these, which are:

- Australia – GST 10%
- New Zealand – GST 15%
- United Kingdom – VAT 20%

Therefore, for Plot 1 - Kingsley Tower the Letting and Management Fees are as follows:

- Letting Fees - 2/52 + VAT = 4.6%
- Management Fees - 6% + VAT = 7.2%

Council/property taxes
Council and property taxes are paid for local services such as street cleaning, refuse collection, street lighting, and other essential services. These charges vary between countries, and it is important that you understand what they are - and more importantly, who pays them.

Australia
In Australia, residential property is subject to two taxes:

- **Land tax:** A state tax which is assessed every year based on a property's value. In most states of Australia, residents do not pay land tax as there is an exemption for the primary residence. However, depending on the state, surcharge taxes do apply to foreign owners.

- **Council rates:** Municipal taxes levied by the local government, assessed each year on a property's value. Council rates are around $1,300 p.a. for an average Australian household.

In Australia, the landlord pays both land tax and council rates.

New Zealand
The local council and local regional council charge annual rates on every property for the services they provide. Rates are set annually, and are collected throughout the year in instalments. The landlord always pays property rates.

United Kingdom
In the UK, the ownership of residential property or land is not taxed. This is uncommon; but instead, a council tax is paid by the resident of the property, and only in the case of the property being unoccupied does the owner of the property become liable. Full details of UK council tax are available in the Buyer Guide for England and Wales at **www.proptechpioneer.com/buyer-guides**.

For Plot 1, Kingsley Tower, the council tax is £1,200 p.a. (payable by the tenant).

Body corporate/strata/management charges
We have covered these costs in Part 3: Purchase and operational considerations. For Kingsley Tower, I have assumed a service charge of £2.00 per ft^2 p.a., or £840 p.a.

Land lease/ground rent
We covered these fees in Part 3: Purchase and operational considerations. For Plot 1 Kingsley Tower, the Ground Rent is £300 p.a.

Insurance
As a landlord, there are several insurances you will likely pay.

- **Building insurance:** You will need to insure your property. This will be a requirement of your mortgage. Even if you do not have a mortgage, you should have insurance in case of a fire or other major event.
- **Contents insurance:** You will need contents insurance. This is because building insurance will only cover the physical fabric of the building, not the contents you own such as the carpets, blinds, kitchen, etc.
- **Landlord insurance:** You can get insurance against damage caused by tenants, or by tenants who fail to pay the rent.

With insurance, it is important to understand what your specific risks are, and ensure that you have adequate insurance against those risks. Equally, you do not want to over-insure yourself and pay unnecessary insurance premiums.

For Plot 1 - Kingsley Tower I am using an annual insurance estimate of £1,000 p.a.

Repairs and maintenance

Very few investors allow for repair and maintenance costs. These can be extremely high, particularly for older properties. Even if you have a new property, you should still budget for repair and maintenance.

If the property is brand new, I would suggest that you allow 1.5% of the annual rental. For older properties, the repairs and maintenance could be far more expensive. If you must regularly call out tradespeople to undertake repairs, the bills will soon stack up. For older properties, you need to budget more for repairs and maintenance. I would allow a minimum of 5%. However, the actual total could end up being significantly more.

Cleaning

Whether or not you need to include costs for cleaning will depend on the type of property you have. If you have a house or a larger block of apartments you will need to assume a cost for general cleaning. If you have an apartment, the general cleaning is likely to be covered by the tenant for the interior and by your service charge (strata or body corporate fees) for the common areas of the building. However, even if you do not have to pay for regular cleaning, you should still allow for some cost in between tenants.

For the sake of good forecasting, I have assumed that at Plot 1 - Kingsley Tower there will be a £300 cleaning cost in between tenancies.

Gardening

Gardening costs will only apply if you have one. If you own a single apartment within a block of apartments this will not be a concern, as these costs will be part of the service charge (strata or body corporate fees).

If you have a garden or an outside area, you will need to allocate a cost to maintain it. Even if your lease states that it is the tenant's responsibility to maintain the garden, you may well find you are better off maintaining the garden yourself.

Service contract and certifications

If you have air-conditioning or a new boiler, it will likely have a service contract which requires an annual check to maintain the warranty. Many countries require landlords to undertake annual gas and electrical safety checks. Whether this is required or not, I recommend that you have these done.

For Plot 1 Kingsley Tower I have assumed an annual cost of £200 p.a. to undertake an annual gas and electrical safety test.

Finance costs

If you have a mortgage, your mortgage expense will likely be your most expensive cash cost. In most scenarios, you will likely have two options for a mortgage, which are:

- **Interest-only:** You only pay interest on the capital you borrow, and at the end of the mortgage period you will still owe the entire amount of principal you borrowed when you purchased the property; or
- **Principal and interest:** Your mortgage payment will include both an element of interest as well as an element to pay down the capital you borrowed. At the end of the mortgage term, the capital which you borrowed will be reduced to zero.

The amount of interest you pay over the life of a mortgage can be enormous. You can build your own mortgage repayment schedule in Microsoft Excel, or download mine from: **www.proptechpioneer.com/prosper**

For Plot 1 Kingsley Tower, let's assume the following:

- Purchase Price £400,000
- Mortgage £300,000
- Interest rate of 4.5%
- Principal and Interest Mortgage

The monthly mortgage payment will be £1,530, and the total interest paid over the life of the mortgage will be £247,220. So, for a £300,000 mortgage, you have paid back a total of £547,220 (i.e., both the original principal and the interest). If you change the interest rate to 3.5%, 5.5%, and 6.5% you will see the following:

Table 10.5: Different interest rate impacts on mortgage payment

Interest Rate	3.5%	4.5%	5.5%	6.5%
Monthly Payment	£1,347	£1,530	£1,703	£1,896
Total Interest Paid	£184,968	£247,220	£313,212	£382,633
Additional Interest Paid	-£62,252	0	£128,244	£197,665

As this comparison shows, a 1% change in interest rates will have a significant impact on your monthly payments and the overall amount of interest you will pay. The difference between a 6.5% interest rate and a 4.5% interest rate is £197,665 over the term of the mortgage.

Capital items and improvements

Finally, you will need to give some thought to capital improvements. Capital items are assets and consumables which you purchase and which have a useful life of longer than one year. These are likely to be items such as:

- Furniture – For a furnished property, you will need to replace items from time to time
- Fixtures and fittings – White goods and appliances; new bathroom items such as washbasins and taps, etc.
- Renovations and new buildings – You may need to replace and update a kitchen or make other alterations and renovations.

Capital improvements are a significant cost for investors. For Plot 1 Kingsley Tower, I have assumed there are no capital items or improvements in the first 10 years, as it is a new property.

Completing the cash flow statement

With the information we have, we are now able to complete the cash flow statement. Where costs are not linked to a percentage of the rent, I have included an inflation factor of 2% to account for growth in costs over time.

Table 10.6: Cash flow statement, Plot 1 Kingsley Tower

	Year 1	Year 2	Year 3	Year 4	Year 5
Income					
Rent	26,000	26,780	27,583	28,411	29,263
Rental Growth Rate		3.0%	3.0%	3.0%	3.0%
Vacancy Rate		2.5%	2.5%	2.5%	2.5%
Gross Income	26,000	26,111	26,894	27,701	28,532
Expenses					
Operating and Management Expenses					
Letting Fees	1,196	1,201	1,237	1,274	1,312
Management Fees	1,872	1,880	1,936	1,994	2,054
Council Tax*	0	0	0	0	0
Body Corporate/Strata/Service Charge	840	857	874	891	909
Land lease/Ground Rent	300	300	300	300	300
Insurance	1,000	1,020	1,040	1,061	1,082
Repairs and Maintenance	390	392	403	416	428
Cleaning	300	306	312	318	325
Gardening	0	0	0	0	0
Service Contracts	200	204	208	212	216
Other	0	0	0	0	0
Finance Costs					
Mortgage	18,241	18,241	18,241	18,241	18,241
Capital Items and Improvements					
Furniture	0	0	0	0	0
Fixtures and Fittings	0	0	0	0	0
Renovations	0	0	0	0	0
Gross Expenses	25,539	25,600	25,752	25,908	26,068
Net Cash flow (before tax)	1,661	1,704	2,330	2,974	3,639

*Paid by the tenant

CHAPTER 11

Income Statement

Tax costs and benefits can be confusing; however, these are particularly important for you as a property investor, because a significant part of the value you can generate investing in property is created by the tax advantages it has. However, not all tax benefits are equal!

Which tax benefits you can access depends on certain key factors which you need to understand and factor into your investment strategy - which we will cover in Part 5: Your property investments strategy.

First, you need to understand how taxes are calculated. Tax costs and benefits are dealt with in the income statement, which measures your property's financial performance. It shows the revenues, expenses, profits, or losses over a specific period.

Your income statement has many components; income, cash expenses, non-cash expenses, profit (loss), tax, and net profit after tax.

Table 11.1: Typical property income statement

Gross Income	
Less	
Cash Expenses	
Operating and Management Expenses	
Interest Costs	
Non-Cash Expenses	
Depreciation – FF&E	
Depreciation – Capital Improvements	
Profit (Loss) Before Tax	
Income Tax	
Net Profit after Tax	

Gross income

Gross income is broadly defined in the same way in all countries. It is income that is generated in each period from renting the property out to a tenant. Gross rental also includes the rent-associated payments that are received, or you become entitled to, when renting out the property.

Expenses

This is where people get confused, because property agents use so many different terminologies. It does not matter where your property is located; it will have the same three groups of expenses from an income statement perspective. Where differences exist between countries, is in how these expenses are treated from an accounting perspective. Those are:

- Operating and management expenses
- Interest costs on finance
- Non-Cash expenses

Operating and management expenses

Operating and management expenses are the cash expenses that are incurred in renting and maintaining the property. In most situations, the operating and management expenses are fully deductible from a tax perspective, and are therefore included in the income statement.

Interest costs on finance

One of the reasons that real estate is such a popular investment is that you can recover the cost of interest incurred on your mortgage in many countries. It is important to note that only the interest portion of the mortgage payment is a taxable expense; the other part of the payment is reducing the amount of the capital you have paid (in a principal and interest mortgage).

Non-cash expenses

A non-cash expense is an accounting expense that does not involve the payment of cash. From a real estate investment perspective, non-cash expenses are allowances which investors can offset against their income to allow for the depreciation of their assets.

Except for the land your property sits on, your property consists of what is called wasting assets. Over time as they are used, their value diminishes; a sofa is a good example. Investment properties typically comprise of two different types of wasting assets:

- **Fixtures, Fittings, and Equipment (FF&E):** These are items in the property which do not form part of the fabric of the building itself. These include obvious items such as furniture; however, they also include less obvious items such as kitchen and bathroom fittings.

- **Capital improvements:** Property is an appreciating asset. However, it is only the land portion of the property that theoretically appreciates. From a tax perspective, you can depreciate the value of the capital improvements (the building) over time. To do this, you need to separate the value of the physical building from the value of the land on which it sits.

In practice, capital improvements have several components: the fabric of the building itself, and its fixtures and fittings. Each of these has different useful lives, and therefore the physical property will depreciate at different rates. The only way to determine this is by having a quantity surveyor prepare a depreciation schedule.

However, these differences will be relatively small, and if you assume that the asset which has the longest life itself is the fabric of the building, which is generally assumed to be 40 years, and then depreciate all the costs at this level, then you know that the situation will only improve with a *full depreciation schedule.*

From a tax perspective, there are two ways property investors can depreciate these assets:

- **Diminishing value method:** This depreciation reduces the value of an asset at a higher rate in the earlier years in which it is owned. This method is generally used where the value of an asset depreciates at a faster rate at the start of its useful life than at the end of its useful life. It is calculated by using the following formula:

Base Value x days held/365 x [0% of depreciation]/asset's effective life

- **Prime cost method:** The prime cost method, sometimes called straight-line depreciation, reduces the value of an asset evenly throughout its effective life. It is calculated using the following formula:

Base value x days held/365 x 100%/asset's effective life

Preparing an income statement

We can now prepare an income statement for Plot 1 Kingsley Tower. Let's go through each of its components.

Gross income
We have already prepared this in our cash flow (Chapter 10).

Operating and management expenses
We calculated this when we prepared the cash flow statement (Chapter 10); it sets out the total expenses less the cost of any mortgage payments.

Interest costs on finance
You can use my payment calculator (**www.proptechpioneer.com/investor-calculators**) to work these out. For our mortgage at Plot 1 Kingsley Tower, the interest component of the mortgage expenses are set out below.

Table 11.2: Plot 1 Kingsley Tower annual interest payments

	Year 1	Year 2	Year 3	Year 4	Year 5
Interest Payment	13,401	13,179	12,946	12,703	12,448

Non-cash expenses
We now need to calculate the non-cash expenses.

Fixtures, fittings, and equipment
The original cost to furnish the property was £10,000. Let's assume that the useful life of the furniture is 10 years - therefore, the calculation is.

Annual Depreciation - Furniture
= 10,000 x 365/365 x 100%/10
= 10,000 x 10%
= 1,000

Therefore, in the income statement, we would claim an annual expense of £2,000 p.a. for 10 years, to account for the useful life of the furniture.

Capital improvements

I am going to assume that the value of the improvements (excluding furniture) at Plot 1, Kingsley Tower is £130,000, and that the useful life is 40 years. Therefore, the calculation is as follows:

Annual Depreciation – Capital Improvements
= 130,000 x 365/365 x 100%/40
= 130,000 x 2.5%
= 3,250

Therefore, in the income statement, we would claim an annual expense of £3,250 p.a. for 40 years to account for the useful life of the capital improvements.

Income statement

We can now put all this information into our income statement for plot 1 Kingsley Tower.

Table 11.3: Income statement, Plot 1 Kingsley Tower

	Year 1	Year 2	Year 3	Year 4	Year 5
Income					
Gross Income	26,000	26,111	26,894	27,701	28,532
Expenses					
Operating and Management Expenses	6,098	6,165	6,324	6,486	6,652
Interest Costs on Finance	13,401	13,179	12,946	12,703	12,448
Non-Cash Expenses					
Depreciation – FF&E	1,000	1,000	1,000	1,000	1,000
Depreciation – Capital Improvements	3,250	3,250	3,250	3,250	3,250

	Year 1	Year 2	Year 3	Year 4	Year 5
Profit (Loss)	2,251	2,516	3,374	4,262	5,181

You will notice we can only get as far as determining the profit before tax, but not the tax itself. This is because how much tax is payable depends on several factors, including:

- The country in which the property is located
- Where the purchaser lives
- How much the purchaser earns

Accounting differences between countries

Countries around the world have completely different approaches to how they treat property investment. Understanding these differences is a key part of how you gain power as a property investor.

To demonstrate, I am going to use our three country examples: Australia, New Zealand, and the United Kingdom. I have chosen these countries because they represent three different approaches, as will become obvious.

In preparing the financial statements, I have adopted the costs set out below.

Table 11.4: Assumptions for financial statements

	Australia (AUD)	New Zealand (NZD)	United Kingdom (GBP)
Purchase Price	800,000	800,000	400,000
Capital Improvements Value	260,000	260,000	130,000
Furniture	20,000	20,000	10,000
Depreciation Type	Diminishing value	Diminishing value	N/A
FF&E Useful Life	10 years	10 years	10 years
Capital Improvements Useful Life	40 years	40 years	40 years
Operating and Management Expenses	14,596	14,596	7,298
Interest Costs on Finance	4.5%	4.5%	4.5%
Mortgage Type	P&I	P&I	P&I
Monthly Mortgage Payment	3,040	3,040	1,520
Interest Proportion of Mortgage	26,802	26,802	13,401

To make the examples more relevant, I adjusted for currency differences between the three countries and used an estimated exchange rate of £ 1 = $AUD 2 or $NZ 2 (obviously, the real-life rate varies). Therefore, I looked at the following:

Table 11.5: Assumed income for Buyer 1

	Australia (Domestic Income)	New Zealand (Domestic Income)	United Kingdom (Domestic Income)
Buyer 1	$AUD 100,000 p.a.	$NZ 100,000 p.a.	£ 50,000 p.a.
Buyer 2	Nil	Nil	Nil

Australia

Australia's tax rules treat companies and individuals in essentially the same way when calculating income tax.

Rental income

Rental income is simply the gross rental income generated in a given year.

Expenses

Expenses in Australia have different names; however, I have allocated these to the different cost settings I have set out earlier. Anything that is not included cannot be claimed by investors.

Operating and management expenses

Operating and Management expenses are referred to as 'Immediate Deduction Expenses' by the Australian Taxation Office (ATO). Immediate deduction expenses can be claimed for immediate deduction (in the year they occur). A detailed schedule is available in the Australia Buyers Guide at **www.proptechpioneer.com/buyer-guides**.

Interest costs on finance

In Australia, landlords can claim the *full* amount of interest charged on their mortgage. However, to do so the property must be rented out, or genuinely available for rental, in the income year for which the deduction is claimed.

While the property is rented, a landlord can also claim interest on loans taken out:

- To purchase depreciating assets
- For repairs
- For renovations

Non-cash expenses

Non-cash expenses in Australia are defined as "deductions for the declining value of depreciating assets". In Australia, if you purchase a new property, you are generally treated for tax purposes as having bought land, a building, plus various items of 'plant'. Plant are depreciating assets such as air-conditioners, stoves, and other similar items.

Therefore, the purchase price of the property needs to be allocated between the building (capital improvements) and other depreciable items. Investors can then deduct an amount equal to the declining value of each asset from the income generated in the year which the asset was held, for each year of the useful life of that particular asset.

These are classified as:

- Capital improvements (the building)
- Plant; and
- Various other depreciating assets.

Some items found in a rental property are regarded as part of the 'setting' (i.e. part of the building) for the rent-producing activity, and not as separate assets in their own right. If a depreciating asset is not considered plant and is fixed to, or part of, a building or a structural improvement, then it will generally be considered construction expenditure for capital works, and only a capital works deduction will be available for that item.

Capital improvements

Investors can depreciate the cost of a newly-built residential property purchased from a developer, or a residential property that has been substantially renovated if:

- No one was previously entitled to a deduction for the property; and
- The asset was installed for use or used at the property and you acquired it within six months of the property being built or substantially renovated.

Substantial renovations of a building in which all, or substantially all, of a building is removed or replaced are generally considered capital improvements. The renovations may, but do not necessarily have to involve. removing or replacing foundations, external walls into supporting walls, floors, the roof, or staircase.

Plant

In Australia, residential rental properties are a setting for income-producing activities, and so they do not fall within the ordinary meaning of plant. Items that form part of the premises are also part of the setting, and are therefore not eligible for deductions for the decline in value.

In determining whether an item is part of the premises or setting, the following needs to be considered:

- Whether the item appears visually to retain a separate identity;
- The degree of permanence with which it is attached to the property;
- The incompleteness of the structure without it;
- The extent to which it was intended to be permanent, or whether it was likely to be replaced within a relatively short period.

None of these factors alone is determinative, and they must all be considered together.

Examples

Wall and floor tiles are generally fixed to the premises, are not freestanding, and are intended to remain in place for a substantial period. They will generally form part of the premises. Expenditure on these items falls under capital works.

On the other hand, a freestanding item such as a bookcase may be attached to the structure only for temporary stability. It therefore does not form part of the premises, and may qualify for a deduction for declining value.

Articles

Plant includes items that are articles within the ordinary meaning of the word. A curtain, a desk, and a bookcase are considered articles.

Depreciation methodology

In Australia, investors can deduct the decline in value of a depreciating asset using either the prime cost or diminishing value method. Both methods are based on the effective life of the asset.

Calculating the effective life

Generally, the effective life of a depreciating asset is how long it can be used to produce income:

- Having regard to the wear and tear you reasonably expect from your expected circumstances of its use;
- Assuming that it will be maintained in reasonably good order and condition; and
- Having regard to the period within which it is likely to be scrapped, sold for no more than scrap value, or abandoned.

For most depreciating assets, you can either choose to work out the effective life yourself or to use an effective life determined by the Commissioner of Taxation.

Depreciation for the building

The depreciation claim for the plant, equipment, and building is often overlooked. You are normally allowed to claim a small percentage of the cost of the building and fixed structures on the property over time.

Usually, the rate is 2.5% from the time the property is built, the total claim is limited to the cost of construction, and you need to get a quantity surveyor to do the figures for you.

For example, for plot 1 Kingsley Tower, assuming that the value of the building is $260,000, the annual depreciation would be $6,500.

Depreciation for furniture

If the property is furnished, the Australian tax office allows a landlord to claim the cost of the furnishings as a tax deduction throughout its useful life.

These may be for furnishings installed at the time of purchase, or items bought during the rental period. Typically, an item of furniture can be claimed in the 5 to 10 years stipulated by the tax office.

Non-recoverable expenses

Investors cannot claim deductions on any of the following expenses.

- Acquisition and disposal costs of the property;
- Expenses not incurred by them (such as an item which is paid by the tenant which would otherwise be deductible);
- Travel expenses to inspect the property.

Australian income tax rates

In Australia, tax rates are different for resident and non-resident investors, and are set out below.

Table 11.6: Income tax rates (residents)

Taxable Income	Tax on this Income
$0 - $18,200	0%
$18,201 - $45,000	19% of each $1 over $18,201
$45,001 - $120,000	$5,092 plus 32.5% of each $1 over $45,000
$120,001 - $180,000	$29,467 plus 37.0% of each $1 over $120,000
$180,001 and over	$51,667 plus 45.0% of each $1 over $180,000

Table 11.7: Income tax rates (foreign residents)

Taxable Income	Tax on this Income
$0 - $120,000	32.5% of each $1
$120,001 - $180,000	$39,000 plus 37% of each $1 over $120,000
$180,001 +	$61,200 plus 45% of each $1 over $180,000

I have shown how the tax will be treated for each of the different scenarios set out above.

Preparing the income statement

Below, I have prepared both the tax calculations and the income statement for both buyers (residents and foreign residents) for Plot 1 Kingsley Tower located in Australia.

Table 11.8: Buyer 1, Australian resident

	Year 1	Year 2	Year 3	Year 4	Year 5
Gross Rental Income	52,000	52,221	53,788	55,401	57,063
Less					
Operating and Management Expenses	12,196	12,331	12,647	12,972	13,305
Interest on Finance	26,802	26,537	25,892	25,406	24,897
Less Non-Cash Deductions					
Building Depreciation	6,500	6,500	6,500	6,500	6,500
FF&E	2,000	2,000	2,000	2,000	2,000
Income/Loss before Tax	4,502	5,033	6,748	8,524	10,362
Personal Income	100,000	100,000	100,000	100,000	100,000
Total Income (including property income)	104,502	105,033	106,748	108,524	110,362
Income Tax					
$5,092 + 32.5% of every $1 over $45,000	24,430	24,603	25,160	25,737	26,335
Nominal Income Tax without Property					
$5,092 + 32.5% of every $1 over $45,000	22,967	22,967	22,967	22,967	22,967
Tax Incurred Due to Property	1,463	1,636	2,193	2,270	3,368

Therefore, for Buyer 1, the Income Statement would be as follows:

Table 11.9: Buyer 1, income statement

	Year 1	Year 2	Year 3	Year 4	Year 5
Gross Income	52,000	52,221	53,788	55,401	57,063
Less					
Operating and Management Expenses	12,196	12,331	12,647	12,972	13,305
Interest on Finance	26,802	26,537	25,892	25,406	24,897
Less Non-Cash Deductions					
Building Depreciation	6,500	6,500	6,500	6,500	6,500

	Year 1	Year 2	Year 3	Year 4	Year 5
FF&E	2,000	2,000	2,000	2,000	2,000
Income/Loss before Tax	4,502	5,033	6,748	8,524	10,362
Income Tax	1,463	1,636	2,193	2,270	3,368
Net Income after Tax	3,039	3,397	4,555	5,754	6,994

For Buyer 2, the tax calculation is different because there is no domestic income to consider. Instead, the tax liability is simply calculated based on the net income generated.

Table 11.10: Income Statement (Australia), Plot 1, Kingsley Tower

	Year 1	Year 2	Year 3	Year 4	Year 5
Gross Income	52,000	52,221	53,788	55,401	57,063
Less					
Operating and Management Expenses	12,196	12,331	12,647	12,972	13,305
Interest on Finance	26,802	26,537	25,892	25,406	24,897
Less Non-Cash Deductions					
Building Depreciation	6,500	6,500	6,500	6,500	6,500
FF&E	2,000	2,000	2,000	2,000	2,000
Income/Loss before Tax	4,502	5,033	6,748	8,524	10,362
Income Tax Payable					
32.5% of every $1 up to $120,000	1,463	1,636	2,193	2,770	3,368
Net Income after Tax	3,039	3,397	4,555	5,754	6,994

New Zealand

From a taxation perspective, New Zealand is slightly different from Australia in terms of the ability to recover costs and expenses. In 2021, New Zealand introduced changes to its tax treatment for rental property, the impact of which is that interest tax is now only deductible on new-build property. I have set out the rules for new-build property in New Zealand below.

Rental income
Rental income is simply the gross rental income generated in a given year.

Operating and management expenses
The following are allowable rental expenses:

- The cost of insuring your rental property
- The rates for the property
- Payments to agents who collect rent, maintain your rental, or find tenants for you
- Fees paid to an accountant for managing accounts, preparing tax returns, and advice
- Repair and maintenance costs
- Fees for arranging a mortgage to finance the rental property
- Fees for drawing up a tenancy agreement
- The cost of getting a valuation for mortgage purposes
- The costs of taking legal action to recover unpaid rent
- The costs incurred in evicting a tenant
- Mortgage repayment insurance
- Travel expenses for traveling to inspect your property or to do repairs
- Legal fees involved in buying a rental property, as long as the expense is $10,000 or less.

Finance charges
In New Zealand, investors can claim the full interest cost incurred in borrowing the funds for new-build property. Investors, however, cannot claim a tax deduction for the interest expenses incurred from the ownership of new-build property.

Non-cash expenses
In New Zealand, residential investment properties are divided into three parts: the land it sits on, the building, and chattels. FF&E is referred to as a chattel. A chattel is any item that does not form part of the building that can be depreciated. To determine what is a depreciable chattel, you need to consider the following:

- If the item is not attached to the building, then it can be depreciated separately;

- If the item is an integral part of, or firmly attached to, the building, then it is considered to be part of the building and cannot be depreciated.

The New Zealand Inland Revenue Department publishes a list of items that qualify as chattels, and which are therefore depreciable. A detailed schedule of these costs is available in the New Zealand Buyers Guide at **www.proptechpioneer.com/buyer-guides**

Investors cannot claim a depreciation expense for the depreciation of buildings, only for chattels.

To determine the depreciation deduction, you need to accurately identify the cost of each chattel. If you have purchased a new chattel, then the cost will be easy to identify: the cost is the price you paid. If you purchase a property with existing chattels, then you need to have a professional chattel valuation prepared.

Income tax rates

In New Zealand, income tax rates are the same for residents and non-residents, as below.

Table 11.11: Income tax rates

Income Threshold	Tax Rate
Up to $NZ 14,000	10.5%
Over $NZ 14,000 to $NZD 48,000	17.5%
Over $NZ 48,000 to $NZD 70,000	30.0%
Over $NZ 70,000 and up to $180,000	33.0%
Over $NZ 180,000	37%

Preparing the income statement

Table 11.12: Tax calculation, Buyer 1, Plot 1, Kingsley Tower

	Year 1	Year 2	Year 3	Year 4	Year 5
Gross Income	52,000	52,221	53,788	55,401	57,063
Less					
Operating and Management Expenses	12,196	12,331	12,647	12,972	13,305
Interest on Finance	26,802	26,537	25,892	25,406	24,897
Less Non-Cash Deductions					
Furniture	2,000	2,000	2,000	2,000	2,000
Income/Loss before Tax	11,002	11,533	13,248	15,024	16,862
Personal Income					
Total Income (including property income)	111,002	111,533	113,248	115,024	116,862
Income Tax					
Tax @ 10.5% (0 – 14,000)	1,470	1,470	1,470	1,470	1,470
Tax @ 17.5% (14,001 – 48,000)	5,950	5,950	5,950	5,950	5,950
Tax @ 30% (48,001 – 70,000)	6,600	6,600	6,600	6,600	6,600
Tax @ 33% (Over 70,000)	13,531	13,706	14,272	14,858	15,464
Gross Tax Liability	27,551	27,726	28,292	28,878	29,484
Nominal Income Tax without Property	23,920	23,920	23,920	23,920	23,920
Tax Expenses Due to Property	3,631	3,806	4,372	4,958	5,564

Table 11.13: Buyer 1 – income statement

	Year 1	Year 2	Year 3	Year 4	Year 5
Gross Income	**52,000**	**52,221**	**53,788**	**55,401**	**57,063**
Less					
Operating and Management Expenses	12,196	12,331	12,647	12,972	13,305
Interest on Finance	**26,802**	**26,537**	**25,892**	**25,406**	**24,897**
Less Non-Cash Deductions					
Furniture	2,000	2,000	2,000	2,000	2,000
Income/Loss before Tax	11,002	11,533	13,248	15,024	16,862
Tax	3,631	3,806	4,372	4,958	5,564
Net Income after Tax	**7,371**	**7,727**	**8,876**	**10,066**	**11,297**

Table 11.14: Income statement (New Zealand), Buyer 2, Plot 1, Kingsley Tower

	Year 1	Year 2	Year 3	Year 4	Year 5
Gross Income	52,000	52,221	53,788	55,401	57,063
Less					
Operating and Management Expenses	12,196	12,331	12,647	12,972	13,305
Interest on Finance	26,802	26,537	25,892	25,406	24,897
Less Non-Cash Deductions					
Furniture	2,000	2,000	2,000	2,000	2,000
Income/Loss before Tax	11,002	11,533	13,248	15,024	16,862
Income Tax					
Tax @ 14.5% (0 – 14,000)	1,155	1,211	1,391	1,578	1,770
Net Income after Tax	9,847	10,322	11,857	13,446	15,091

United Kingdom

In the United Kingdom, the tax benefits are less favourable than those available in Australia and New Zealand, because income tax on a rental property is not calculated in the same way.

Both rental income and operating and management expenses are broadly treated in the same way, but these are the only similarities.

Rental income

Rental income is simply the gross rental income generated in a given year.

Operating and management expenses

Operating and management expenses are referred to as "deductible expenses". In the United Kingdom, the following expenses are deductible in calculating income tax:

- Costs of repairs and maintenance (expenses incurred before 1st letting to put the property into good order may be allowable);
- Property agents' fees for managing the property;
- Ground rent, service charges, and other expenditure on common parts;

- Insurance premiums;
- Legal costs of renewing a short lease or tenancy agreements;
- Accountancy fees for preparing accounts and tax computations;
- Any unrecovered VAT on the items above.

Finance charges

In the UK, landlords cannot claim interest costs in the way most other countries allow.

As a landlord, you receive a tax credit of 20% of your mortgage interest cost which you can claim against your income tax liability. This has significant implications for investors when considering investing in the UK:

- A much smaller proportion of your interest costs can be offset against your income, thereby increasing your overall tax bill
- If you live in the UK, rental income can increase push you into a higher income tax band.

Therefore, for plot 1 Kingsley Tower, buyers 1 & 2 would receive a tax credit of £2,680 (£13,401 x 20%) in year 1.

This tax credit is treated as a form of tax relief rather than an as expense; therefore, it is treated differently to an expense. The amount calculated is netted off from the net tax liability.

Non-cash deductions

In the UK, landlords are not able to claim any non-cash deductions for the depreciation of capital improvements.

For FF&E, non-cash deductions are claimed on a 'renewal' basis. This means that you cannot claim a deduction for the initial installation of furniture, fittings, or equipment, but the costs of replacements can be claimed. This includes fixtures such as baths, washbasins, and kitchen units, etc.

Calculating tax

In the United Kingdom income tax is charged on UK rental income arising for individuals, non-UK resident companies, and trustees, irrespective of their residence and domicile status.

Income Tax is charged on rental income after the deduction of relevant tax-deductible expenses.

Personal allowances

For an individual British citizen, whether resident or not, there is an entitlement to personal allowances. The personal allowance is £12,500 p.a. from April 2019. The personal allowance is also available to EEA nationals, and individuals who are resident in, or nationals of, Thailand or Malaysia.

However, personal allowances are reduced by £1 for every £2 of income earned more than £100,000, so anyone earning a salary and rental profits above £125,000 cannot benefit from a personal allowance.

Rates of tax

The rates of UK tax on net rental profits for 2020/2021 are:

Table 11.15: Tax on net rental profits, 2020/2021

Individual	Basic Rate	£0 - £37,500	20%
	Higher Rate	£37,501 - £150,000	40%
	Additional Rate	Over £150,001	45%

Tax calculations

Therefore, how much income tax you pay will depend on your circumstances. Let's consider the following buyer profiles:

- Buyer 1 - UK resident earning £50,000 p.a.
- Buyer 2 - International investor (who does not reside in the EEA, Malaysia, or Thailand)

Table 11.16: Buyer 1, UK resident, tax calculation

	Year 1	Year 2	Year 3	Year 4	Year 5
Gross Income	26,000	26,111	26,894	27,701	28,532
Less					
Operating and Management Expenses	6,098	6,165	6,324	6,486	6,652
Rental Profit	19,902	19,945	20,570	21,215	21,879
Personal Income	50,000	50,000	50,000	50,000	50,000
Gross Income	69,902	69,945	70,570	71,215	71,879

	Year 1	Year 2	Year 3	Year 4	Year 5
Tax					
Tax free Allowance (£12,500)	0	0	0	0	0
Tax @ 20% (£0 - £37,500)	5,000	5,000	5,000	5,000	5,000
Tax @ 40% (£37,501 - £150,000)	12,961	12,978	13,228	13,486	13,752
Tax Relief					
Interest Costs	13,401	13,179	12,946	12,703	12,448
Interest Relief @ 20%	2,680	2,636	2,589	2,541	2,490
Tax Payable on Gross Income	15,281	15,342	15,639	15,945	16,262
Normal Income Tax without Property	10,000	10,000	10,000	10,000	10,000
Tax Expenses Due to Property	5,281	5,342	5,639	5,945	6,262

Table 11.17: Buyer 1 income statement

	Year 1	Year 2	Year 3	Year 4	Year 5
Gross Income	26,000	26,111	26,894	27,701	28,532
Less					
Operating and Management Expenses	6,098	6,165	6,324	6,486	6,652
Rental Profit	19,902	19,945	20,570	21,215	21,879
Income Tax	5,281	5,342	5,639	5,945	6,262
Net Income after Tax	14,621	14,063	14,931	15,269	15,617

Table 11.18: Buyer 2, overseas investor, tax calculation

	Year 1	Year 2	Year 3	Year 4	Year 5
Gross Income	26,000	26,111	26,894	27,701	28,532
Less					

	Year 1	Year 2	Year 3	Year 4	Year 5
Operating and Management Expenses	6,098	6,165	6,324	6,486	6,652
Rental Profit	19,902	19,945	20,570	21,215	21,879
Tax-free Allowance (£0)					
Tax @ 20% (£0 - £37,500)	3,980	3,989	4,114	4,243	4,376
Tax Relief					
Interest Costs	13,401	13,179	12,946	12,703	12,448
Interest Relief @ 20%	2,680	2,636	2,589	2,541	2,490
Tax Payable	1,300	1,353	1,525	1,702	1,886

Table 11.19: Buyer 2 income statement

	Year 1	Year 2	Year 3	Year 4	Year 5
Gross Income	26,000	26,111	26,894	27,701	28,532
Less					
Operating and Management Expenses	6,098	6,165	6,324	6,486	6,652
Rental Profit	19,902	19,945	20,570	21,215	21,879
Income Tax	1,300	1,353	1,525	1,702	1,886
Net Income after Tax	18,602	18,592	19,045	19,512	19,993

Therefore, Buyer 2 will be far better off from a taxation perspective in the United Kingdom than a resident investor. This is because the additional rental generated from Plot 1, Kingsley Tower has gone into a higher tax band, which is 40%.

CHAPTER 12

Balance Sheet

The balance sheet sets out your assets, liabilities, and your equity at a specific point in time. So, what does this look like for a real estate investor?
You have the following assets:

- **Appreciating assets:** These can go up in value, and are typically purchased as an investment strategy in the understanding that values should increase over time.

- **Depreciating assets:** These have a useful life, after which they have little or no value. They can be depreciated over their useful life from a taxation perspective.

So, if we take Plot 1 Kingsley Tower, we have two assets:

- Property (land and capital improvements); and
- Furniture.

Liabilities are typically the mortgage.
Therefore, for Plot 1, Kingsley Tower, the balance sheet would be as follows.

Table 12.1: Balance sheet, Plot 1 Kingsley Tower

Assets	Year 1 (£)
Furniture, Fittings & Equipment	10,000
Plot 1 Kingsley Tower	400,000
Total Assets	410,000
Liabilities	
Mortgage	300,000
Total Liabilities	300,000
Investor Equity	110,000
Total Liabilities & Investor Equity	410,000

We know that the balance sheet is a statement at a point in time, and that over time, several things will change on the balance sheet. They are most likely to be the following:

- **Property:** The value will grow through capital appreciation.
- **Furniture:** The value will depreciate (it is a wasting asset) .
- **Mortgage:** If the property is purchased using a mortgage, you will have to decide what type of mortgage to take out - either:
  - **Principal and interest:** Each of the monthly payments will include a payment towards the capital borrowed; or
  - **Interest only:** The investor will not be paying off any capital, they will only be paying for the use of the capital borrowed.

So, let's apply this to our example at Plot 1, Kingsley Tower, and make the following assumptions:

- **Property:** Value grows by 5% p.a.
- **Furniture:** We will ignore the value of the furniture, because even if you can depreciate it from an accounting perspective, the furniture has no value if you were to try to sell it second-hand. I recommend that you do this too when you compile a balance sheet, because in reality, it has no value outside of the property once you have purchased it; nor will ignoring it on your balance sheet impact your ability to depreciate it from an income statement perspective.

- **Capital improvements:** We will depreciate the building on the balance sheet, because then it will be picked up in our financial metrics with the capital gains tax calculations (see Chapter 13).
- **Mortgage:** P&I mortgage, so the amount borrowed is being paid down.

The two potential balance sheets are the same, except for the currency changes.

Table 12.2: Balance sheet, UK investor

Assets	Year 1	Year 2	Year 3	Year 4	Year 5
Property	400,000				
Capital Appreciation Rate		5.0%	5.0%	5.0%	5.0%
Capital Appreciation		20,000	21,000	22,050	23,153
Appreciated value	400,000	420,000	441,000	463,050	486,203
Total Value of Assets	420,000	420,000	441,000	463,050	486,203
Liabilities					
Mortgage	300,000	295,160	290,098	284,804	279,266
Total Liabilities	300,000	295,160	290,098	284,804	279,266

Therefore, the difference in total assets and liabilities is the investor equity.

Table 12.3: Investor equity

	Year 1	Year 2	Year 3	Year 4	Year 5
Investor Equity	120,000	124,840	150,902	178,246	206,937

CHAPTER 13

Other Taxes

As a property investor, there are also some additional taxes which you need to be aware of: Capital Gains Tax, and Inheritance Tax. Neither are operational taxes, as they are only incurred when the property is dealt with from a legal perspective. However, you should be aware of both.

Capital Gains Tax

When investors dispose of their property, any capital gain they have made is typically subject to a Capital Gains Tax (CGT). How the gain is calculated varies between countries. Additionally, the tax charged varies between countries, and depends on whether or not the investor is domiciled in the country of the property.

Australia

In Australia, a capital gain (or capital loss) is the difference between the property's purchase price and the amount it is sold for. These are measured *from the point at which the contract was entered.*

Rental properties are considered a Capital Gains Tax (CGT) asset in Australia, and therefore are subject to Capital Gains Tax. Although CGT is referred to as a separate tax, the gain is taxed as part of your income, and therefore it is added to your income tax costs in the year the sale is recorded. This date is referred to as a "CGT event".

Residents and non-residents

There is a difference between how residents and non-residents are treated in Australia concerning Capital Gains Tax:

- **Australian residents:** If the property is owned for more than 12 months before the CGT event occurs then the calculated capital gain is reduced by 50%.
- **Non-Australian residents:** Pay CGT on 100% of the calculated capital gain, regardless of how long they have owned the property.

Working out the capital gain

Every time a CGT event occurs, the capital gain or loss needs to be determined. To establish what the actual capital gain is, investors need to determine what the cost base for the asset is. The cost base of a CGT asset is the cost of the asset when it was purchased plus certain other costs associated with acquiring, holding, and disposing of it.

The Cost Base for most property therefore includes the following:

- Original Purchase Price
- Stamp Duty
- Legal Fees
- Cost of depreciation (if it was claimed)

However, investors cannot include any of the following:

- Council rates
- Insurance
- Land tax
- Maintenance cost
- Interest on money borrowed to buy or improve the property

Plot 1 Kingsley Tower

We can use Plot 1 Kingsley Tower once again to show how the CGT would apply for buyers 1 and 2.

In both scenarios, I have assumed the following:

- The property is held for 5 years and sold on the first day of the 6th year, and no other income is generated in the 6th year.
- The property value has grown to $AUD 1,021,025, assuming the value grew by 5% p.a. over the period it was held.
- An agent sold the property and was paid a fee of 2%.
- Legal fees of $ 2,000 were paid.

Calculating the cost base

First, we need to calculate the cost base.

Table 13.1: Cost base calculation ($AUD)

Item	Buyer 1	Buyer 2
Purchase Price	800,000	800,000
Stamp Duty	40,720	95,720
Legal Fees	2,000	2,000
Less		
Building Depreciation	32,500	32,500
Adjusted Cost Base	810,220	865,220

The total capital gain is then the net proceeds for the sale less the adjusted cost base. This is simply calculated as follows:

Sale Price = $AUD 972,405
Agent Commission = $AUD 19,448
Legal Fee = $AUD 2,000
Net Sale Proceeds = $AUD 950,957

We can then work out the calculated capital gain for both buyers:

Buyer 1
Net Sale Proceeds = $AUD 950,957
Adjusted Cost Base = $AUD 810,220
Capital Gain = $AUD 140,737

Buyer 2
Net Sale Proceeds = $AUD 950,957
Adjusted Cost Base = $AUD 865,220
Capital Gain = $AUD 85,737

Calculating the Tax Cost

The tax costs are different for buyer 1 and buyer 2 because buyer 1 is an Australian resident, whereas buyer 2 is not.

Buyer 1

Buyer 1 made a taxable gain of $AUD 140,747; however, because they are an Australian resident and have owned the property for more than 12 months, they receive a 50% reduction in capital gain. Therefore, their actual taxable gain is $AUD 70,374.

Buyer 1 earns an Australian Income of $AUD 100,000 p.a., and therefore, all of the taxable gains sit within two tax brackets: up to $AUD 120,000 is taxed at 32.5% ($AUD 20,000), and $AUD 50,374 is taxed at 37.0%. So, the tax on the capital gain will be $AUD 25,138, and Buyer 1 will receive $AUD 115,609 back after tax.

Buyer 2

Buyer 2 made a taxable gain of $AUD 85,737. Because they are not a resident of Australia, they do not receive the 50% discount on their capital gain.

Buyer 2's taxable gain is $AUD 85,737, subject to the foreign tax rates, and is taxed at 32.5%, equating to $AUD 27,865.

So, Buyer 2 will receive $AUD 57,872 back after tax.

New Zealand

In most scenarios, New Zealand rental property is not subject to a Capital Gains Tax. However, a Capital Gains Tax is payable in certain circumstances.

Intention rule and bright-line rule

If a property sale meets either the 'Intention Rule' or the 'Bright-Line Rule', then any gains are subject to tax. These rules are as follows:

- **Intention rule:** This rule says that it is the intention of the buyer when they buy a property to determine the tax situation at the point of sale. If the property was purchased with a firm intention to re-sell the property, then tax on any profits must be paid, whereas if the property was either owned by an owner-occupier or held by an investor as a long-term rental investment, there will be no tax payable in most cases. However, if individuals have a pattern of buying and selling property, then the government may consider them to be property dealers, and they may have to pay tax when they sell the property. There is no set number of properties that would need to be bought or sold before the intention rule would be triggered.

- **Bright-line rule:** This does not apply to properties purchased before 1 October 2015. It applies to properties purchased:
  - Between 1 October 2015 and 28 March 2018, and sold in the 2-year bright-line period; and
  - After 29 March 2018, and sold within the 5-year bright-line period

The bright-line period starts on the date the property's title is registered with Land Information New Zealand (LINZ), and ends when you enter into a sale and purchase agreement. For off-plan sales, the bright-line period is where the title has not yet been issued, and it begins when you sign the agreement to purchase the land. The bright-line rule applies regardless of the purchaser's intentions when the property was purchased.

Under these rules, any gains are treated as income, and are taxed on the calculated gain (or loss) by deducting the original purchase price, acquisition costs, disposal costs, and costs of capital improvements from the sale proceeds.

Residential Land Withholding Tax
Additionally, a Residential Land Withholding Tax (RLWT) may also be deducted for a property sale if the owner is offshore and has held the period for less than the bright-line period.

RLWT is calculated based on the lower of the following three methods:

- RLWT x (sale price – the vendor's acquisition costs)
- 10% of the sale price
- Sale price – security discharge amount – outstanding rates x RLWT.

Plot 1 Kingsley Tower
Clearly, a buyer in New Zealand would be likely to wait for the expiry of the 5-year Bright-Line period to avoid paying capital gains tax. Therefore, both Buyers 1 and 2 would simply receive the sale price minus the agent fees and legal fees, i.e. $150,957.

United Kingdom

In the United Kingdom, Capital Gains Tax (CGT) is charged upon worldwide gains realised by individuals and trustee residents in the UK. Unlike in Australia and New Zealand, Capital Gains Tax is not treated as income, and is separately taxed as a one-time capital event.

There is an annual exemption per individual (from tax on all gains) of £12,300 for the 2020/21 tax year. This CGT exemption only comes into play in the tax year that the gain is made.

Investors can deduct the following allowances from any taxable gain:

- The base value of the property;
- The Stamp Duty Land Tax paid when the property was purchased;
- Legal fees for buying and selling;
- Agent's fees;
- The cost of capital improvements made (where no deduction has been claimed against the rental income).

International purchases before April 2015

Before April 2015, CGT was not payable by non-UK resident individuals, trusts, and companies; however, this 'loophole' has since been closed. Effective from April 2015, any UK property sold by a non-UK resident (including trusts and companies) has been subject to CGT.

However, this creates an issue for properties purchased before April 2015 by offshore owners; in such cases, there are two possible calculation methods:

- Rebase the property to market value at that date. CGT is then charged on the difference between the net sale proceeds and the market value from 6 April 2015.

- Calculate the profit arising on the disposal of the property without rebasing the base cost, and then split this gain across the period of ownership. Only the period post-April 2015 is subject to charge. For example, if a property was purchased in April 2007 and was then sold in April 2017, then only two of the ten years are subject to tax and therefore tax is payable on only 20% of the gain, with the remaining 80% of the gain exempt.

Calculating the CGT liability

Calculating the CGT liability is relatively straightforward in the UK for properties purchased after April 2015. For those purchased before that date, it is likely that the investor will require a formal valuation undertaken by an RICS qualified surveyor, effective for April 2015 (this would need to be provided to the HMRC at the time of sale).

Individuals (regardless of whether they are domestic residents or international investors) can simply calculate their gain and net off any of the allowable deductions. They will then pay CGT at a rate of 18% to the extent the profit falls within the basic band of tax, and the 28% rate on any profit thereafter, in both situations allowing for the annual exemption.

Calculating the tax cost

The tax costs are the same for buyer 1 and buyer 2. However, in the future, the calculation could be different when there are different SDLT charges for international and domestic purchasers. Assuming this is the case, the taxable gain calculations would be as follows:

Table 13.2: Capital gain calculation

Item	Buyer 1	Buyer 2
Sale Price	486,603	486,603
Less		
Purchase Price	400,000	400,000
Stamp Duty	22,000	30,000
Legal Fees	1,000	1,000
Agency Fees	9,724	9,724
Taxable Capital Gain	53,879	45,879
less		
Taxable Allowance	12,300	12,300
Net Taxable Gain	41,579	33,579

In determining the tax payable, the following would be the calculation:

Buyer 1
Net Taxable Gain = £41,579
Basic Rate Tax £37,500 @ 18% = £6,750
And then £4,079 @28% = £1,142
Total Tax Payable = £7,891

Buyer 2
Net Taxable Gain = £33,579
Basic Rate Tax £33,579 @ 18% = £6,077
Total Tax Payable = £6,077

Estate and inheritance tax: UK

Estate taxes and inheritance taxes are triggered by death. The difference between the two is essentially who pays the tax:

- **Estate tax** is paid by the estate of the deceased before any money is distributed; while
- **Inheritance tax** is levied on the person who receives the money.

Several countries have various estate and inheritance taxes, such as Japan, South Korea, France, the United States, Spain, Ireland, Belgium, Germany, the Netherlands, Greece, Chile, Denmark, Finland, Iceland, Poland, Switzerland, Turkey, and the United Kingdom. Neither Australia nor New Zealand has any estate or inheritance taxes (and neither do Canada, Austria, Israel, Italy, or Mexico).

Inheritance Tax is charged in the UK upon death or, in some cases, on the transfer of capital from one individual to another. The estate of an individual domiciled in the UK is subject to inheritance tax on all of their worldwide assets. Even if you do not live in the UK, if you own property there then there is a good chance it is subject to inheritance tax.

Inheritance tax is extremely high. It is currently charged at 40% on the total value of an estate subject to the tax. The proportion of the estate subject to tax is the amount above what is referred to as the Nil Band Rate (NRB). The NRB is currently £325,000.

If you are considering buying property in the UK, you should research ways to mitigate your inheritance tax liability. You can read more on this at **www.proptechpioneer.com/buyer-guides**

Part 4A Recap

Going through Part 4, you will undoubtedly have realised that there are significant differences between how various costs and expenses work in different countries, and even between buyers. Having a clear understanding of these is crucial to developing your real estate investment strategy.

Below, I have summarised the differences between Australia, New Zealand, and the United Kingdom.

Table 4AR1: Real estate tax differences – Australia, New Zealand, and the United Kingdom

	Australia	New Zealand	United Kingdom
Management and Operating Expenses	Yes	Yes	Yes
Finance Expenses	Yes	Yes	Only 20% of the interest cost
Depreciate of Furniture	Yes	Yes	No, but can claim a one-time event for new purchases.
Depreciation of Plant	Yes, only for new	Yes	No
Depreciation of Building	Yes for new-build, no for second-hand property	Not building, but FF&E can be depreciated	No
Capital Gains Tax	Yes	Yes	Yes
Estate or Inheritance Tax	No	No	Yes

Now that we have prepared the different financial statements, we can pull the information out to track our financial metrics, and compare and contrast the different situations.

Information sources

First, let's go through where the information comes from:

- **Cash required:** This is simply the total cash that is required for you to purchase the investment property. We went through this information in PART 2. It is simply the total purchase price.
- **Tax payable:** This information was calculated in the income statement, and set out how much tax is payable annually for the income generated by the property. Importantly, if you are an international investor then you may have to pay additional tax in the country you live in.
- **Net cash flow after tax:** This is the net cash flow from the cash flow statement we have prepared. Importantly, a negative cash flow indicates a requirement for you to put more cash into the investment, whereas a positive cash flow means there will be surplus cash flow for you to use.
- **Capital appreciation:** This is how much the value of the property has increased in a given year. This information comes from the balance sheet.
- **Available equity:** This is the money that is generated by the investment, and which is available for redeployment. It is simply the owners' equity, less the deposit requirement of the mortgage - 75% in this case.
- **Net return on cash:** This is a figure which is calculated, and is simply the net cash flow after tax together with the capital appreciation in a given year, expressed as a percentage of the total cash required to purchase the investment. A higher percentage indicates a better-performing investment.
- **Net cash if sold:** In addition, we have talked about Capital Gains Tax, so to make a complete comparison, I will include the net income after CGT (if any), assuming the property is sold at the end of the cash flow period.

To make a like-for-like comparison between the different countries in order only to show tax implications, I have made the following adjustments:

- Converted AUD and NZD back to GPD at an exchange rate of 2 to 1;
- Ignored furniture in the balance sheet;

- Made the costs the same (in Australia and New Zealand, there would be no ground rent; in addition, the landlord would pay council rates, but this would have been compensated for by a higher rent).

Comparing the buyers

Table 4AR2: Australia Buyer 1

	Year 1	Year 2	Year 3	Year 4	Year 5
Cash Required	121,140				
Net Cash Flow (before tax)	1,661	1,704	2,330	2,974	3,639
Tax	732	818	1,097	1,385	1,684
Net Cash Flow (after tax)	930	887	1,233	1,589	1,955
Capital Appreciation	0	20,000	21,000	22,050	23,153
Total Return (after tax)	930	20,887	22,233	23,639	25,107
Return on Cash	0.77%	17.24%	18.35%	19.51%	20.73%
Available Equity	0	20,000	41,000	63,050	86,803
Net Return if Sold	57,805				

Table 4AR3: Australia Buyer 2

	Year 1	Year 2	Year 3	Year 4	Year 5
Cash Required	148,860				
Net Cash Flow (before tax)	1,661	1,704	2,330	2,974	3,639
Tax	732	818	1,097	1,385	1,684
Net Cash Flow (after tax)	930	887	1,233	1,589	1,955
Capital Appreciation	0	20,000	21,000	22,050	23,153
Total Return (after tax)	930	20,887	22,233	23,639	25,107
Return on Cash	0.62%	17.24%	18.35%	19.51%	20.73%
Available Equity	0	20,000	41,000	63,050	86,803
Net Return if Sold	28,936				

Table 4AR4: New Zealand Buyer 1

	Year 1	Year 2	Year 3	Year 4	Year 5
Cash Required	101,040				
Net Cash Flow (before tax)	1,661	1,704	2,330	2,974	3,639
Tax	1,815	1,903	2,186	2,479	2,782
Net Cash Flow (after tax)	-154	-199	144	495	856
Capital Appreciation	0	20,000	21,000	22,050	23,153
Return on Cash	-0.15%	19.60%	20.93%	22.31%	23.76%
Available Equity	0	20,000	41,000	63,050	86,803
Net Return if Sold	75,478				

Table 4AR5: New Zealand Buyer 2

	Year 1	Year 2	Year 3	Year 4	Year 5
Cash Required	101,040				
Net Cash Flow (before tax)	1,661	1,704	2,330	2,974	3,639
Tax	578	605	696	789	885
Net Cash Flow (after tax)	1,084	1,099	1,634	2,185	2,753
Capital Appreciation	0	20,000	21,000	22,050	23,153
Return on Cash	1.07%	20.88%	22.40%	23.99%	25.64%
Available Equity	0	20,000	41,000	63,050	86,803
Net Return if Sold	75,478				

Table 4AR6: United Kingdom Buyer 1

	Year 1	Year 2	Year 3	Year 4	Year 5
Cash Required	123,270				
Net Cash Flow (before tax)	1,661	1,704	2,330	2,974	3,639
Tax	5,281	5,342	5,639	5,945	6,262
Net Cash Flow (after tax)	-3,619	-3,638	-3,309	-2,971	-2,623
Capital Appreciation	0	20,000	21,000	22,050	23,153
Return on Cash	-2.94%	13.27%	14.35%	15.48%	16.65%
Available Equity	0	20,000	41,000	63,050	86,803
Net Return if Sold	45,988				

Table 4AR7: United Kingdom Buyer 2

	Year 1	Year 2	Year 3	Year 4	Year 5
Cash Required	131,270				
Net Cash Flow (before tax)	1,661	1,704	2,330	2,974	3,639
Tax	1,300	1,353	1,525	1,702	1,886
Net Cash Flow (after tax)	361	351	805	1,272	1,752
Capital Appreciation	0	20,000	21,000	22,050	23,153
Return on Cash	0.28%	15.50%	16.61%	17.77%	18.97%
Available Equity	0	20,000	41,000	63,050	86,803
Net Return if Sold	39,802				

Net cash flow

Below is a graphical representation of each of the different buyers and their net cash flow from the same investment with the same assumptions. The only differences are in where they are resident, and where they have chosen to invest.

Figure 4AR1: Comparison of net cash flow (after tax)

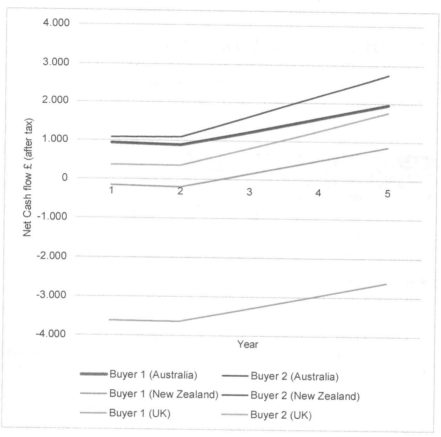

The cash flow comparison demonstrates the need to understand the market you are investing in. For the different scenarios, the situations are as follows:

- **Australia & New Zealand:** The ability to depreciate both FF&E and the capital improvements (Australia only) as well as the offset 100% of interest expenses make these two countries logical places to invest for long term income.

- **UK:** The inability to depreciate assets as well as the offset 100% of interest expenses make the UK a far less desirable location to generate long-term income. Although the international investor fares better if they build up a large portfolio, their income will decline as they move up tax brackets.,

Comparison of net return if sold

Below, I have included a comparison of the outcomes for each of the different investors if the property is sold.

Table 4AR8: Net cash receipt if property is sold

	Cash Returned £ (after tax)
Buyer 1 – Australia	57,805
Buyer 2 – Australia	28,936
Buyer 1 – New Zealand	75,478
Buyer 2 – New Zealand	75,478
Buyer 1 - United Kingdom	45,988
Buyer 2 – United Kingdom	39,802

As you can see, there is a significant difference in what is returned to the investor if the property is sold. For the investor, the key considerations are likely to be:

- **Australia:** A better option for domestic investors due to CGT relief, whereas for international investors it makes more sense to invest in Australia for the long term.
- **New Zealand:** Tax rates are favourable for both domestic and international investors, so the questions would focus on whether growth is achievable.

- **UK:** As a domestic investor trading makes sense, but not long-term ownership. For international investors, the CGT rates are attractive for short-term capital growth.

What happens if growth is zero?

I have painted a positive picture of what will happen if property prices grow by an average of 5% p.a. What if that does not happen? What if values do not go up at all?

Table 4AR9: Comparison of outcomes if growth is zero

	Year 1	Year 2	Year 3	Year 4	Year 5
Buyer 1 – Australia	0.77%	0.73%	1.02%	1.31%	1.61%
Buyer 2 – Australia	0.62%	0.60%	0.83%	1.07%	1.31%
Buyer 1 – New Zealand	-0.15%	-0.20%	0.14%	0.49%	0.85%
Buyer 2 – New Zealand	1.07%	1.09%	1.62%	2.16%	2.73%
Buyer 1 - United Kingdom	-2.94%	-2.95%	-2.68%	-2.41%	-2.13%
Buyer 2 – United Kingdom	0.28%	0.27%	0.61%	0.97%	1.34%

Discussion of financial metrics

The financial metrics presented here highlight some key areas you need to consider when you invest in residential property:

- **Purchase taxes:** How much are the purchase taxes you will have to pay when you purchase an investment? It is possible to offset these costs against taxes that are due when you sell your property. However, this will only be of benefit if you sell.

- **Interest expenses deductibility:** The extent to which you can offset interest expense will significantly impact your net income after tax. In the examples, we have considered the fact that both buyers 1 and 2 in the UK would have to put additional capital into the property to cover the additional taxes, because only a small proportion of the interest expense is deductible. In the UK, then, your strategy would need to be more focused on capital appreciation rather than generating ongoing income.

- **Non-cash expenses:** How much (if at all) you can depreciate both your FF&E and capital improvements will have an impact on your ability to generate a higher income after tax.

- **Tax brackets:** Tax brackets are an important consideration, particularly if you are investing in your own country, or if you already have several investments in a country. Moving from one tax bracket to another will have a material difference to your net return.

- **Capital Gains Tax:** You will only incur capital gains tax when you sell your property. However, if you are planning to sell or are forced to sell, it will become an important consideration. In some countries including New Zealand CGT is zero, whereas in the UK it is low, and in Australia it is very high.

PART 4B

Driving Financial Performance

Now that you understand how to track financial performance, your next challenge is determining what you can do to improve the financial performance of your investment. Unlike other forms of residential property, where redevelopment, alteration, and refurbishment are all options, these are not realistic options with new-build property. So, you have a relatively narrow range of options to improve performance. They are simply as follows:

- **Cash flow:** Free cash flow generated from your property will generate cash reserves for re-investment, and reducing and rebalancing debt obligations. It is only possible to grow the investment's cash flow by increasing income or *reducing costs.*

- **Tax costs and benefits:** Tax costs and benefits are one of the main reasons for investing in property rather than other investments. However, how income is treated can be very confusing, as a variety of different terminologies are used. Likewise, the tax treatments for investment property vary significantly across different countries.

- **Capital appreciation:** Over 30% of landlords invested for capital growth, according to a survey undertaken by the UK's Ministry of Housing, Communities & Local Government (2018). Further, capital appreciation creates additional equity for re-investment. You need to understand what drives capital appreciation, and how to look for signs of potential capital appreciation.

- **Debt reduction and management:** Debt is a useful tool for investors to use to purchase an investment property and build a property portfolio. For most investors, the cost of interest debt will be their largest expense. Clever management of debt is key to cost management and driving net returns. The ability to recover a debt is now changing in different countries; therefore, the liberal use of debt is not the "no-brainer" it once was.

- **Currency gains:** Significant gains can be generated through exploiting movements in currency rates. For many investors, taking advantage of opportunities presented by low points in currency has been the key to creating highly enhanced returns.

- **Ownership structure:** How property is held can have serious tax consequences from the perspectives of both income and any capital gain generated from a sale. Additionally, the ownership structure has impacts from an inheritance tax perspective in countries with an inheritance tax. Changing the ownership structure will generally create a stamp duty event, so getting the structure right from the outset is critical for long-term investors.

CHAPTER 14

Cash Flow Performance

To improve your cash flow, you can increase income, reduce vacancy periods, reduce costs, or do all three. So, how do you go about doing that?

Paid occupancy rates

There is limited research available about rental property performance, particularly for small investors. Some of the best research I have seen was produced by Molior, a leading UK research company. In this section, I have set out the findings of one of their recent reports.

Unit mix

The Molior Report compared 41 Build to Rent developments that were launched for rent in 2018. Collectively, those developments provided 4,150 apartments ranging from studios to five bedrooms. The majority of the apartments were one-bedroom (44%) and two-bedroom (38%) apartments.

Figure 14.1: Molior Report - unit mix

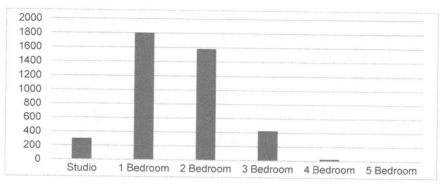

Communal facilities

Of the 41 schemes, 17 (41%) had no communal facilities. For those which had communal facilities, a concierge was the most common, followed by shared external space. Only five of the 41 schemes had a gym, a concierge, a residents' lounge, and outside space.

Figure 14.2: Molior Report – buildings' communal facilities

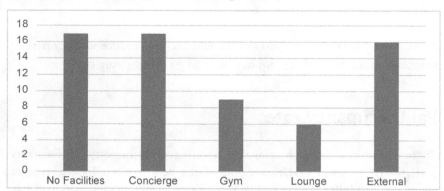

Let-up rates

The rate at which the properties were let is set out below on a unit per month rate, relative to those available for rent by private landlords.

Figure 14.3: Molior Report - let-up rates (units per month)

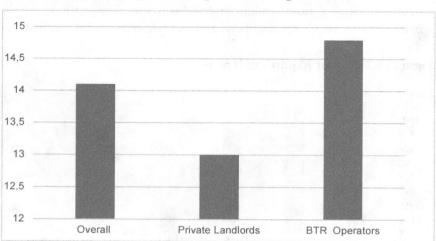

The average let-up rate of the blocks was 14.3 units per month. This dropped slightly to 14.2 in schemes without a concierge, and rose slightly to 14.5 in schemes with a concierge.

Figure 14.4: Molior Report - impact of concierge

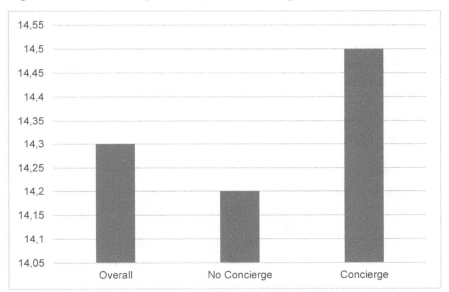

Rental performance

The Molior Report also considered which features impact the levels of rent achieved. In addition, Colliers International produces an Annual Rental Premium Report in which it presents the results of a survey of rented buildings across the UK. Both reports have found that having a concierge and a professional management company managing the property are the two factors that have impacted rents in the UK. On average, the reports have concluded that apartments with a concierge achieved a rental premium of circa 10% higher than apartments without a concierge.

In my experience as a private landlord, these are the only two factors that improve rental performance:

- **Professional management:** For several reasons, being able to deal with a professional property manager gives potential tenants far greater confidence than dealing with a property owner:
    - Tenants must pay a significant deposit order to let a property, and feel more comfortable paying this money to a private company rather than an individual
    - They feel that repair and maintenance issues are likely to be more quickly and professionally dealt with
    - Property managers are regulated, so there is a greater degree of scrutiny of how they behave.

  For these reasons, a tenant is more likely to rent in the first place and pay a higher rent if you have a property manager.

- **Concierge:** People (particularly younger people) are buying a far greater proportion of their household goods and clothing online. However, it is getting harder to pin couriers down to a specific delivery time with this greater demand. Having someone responsible for coordinating deliveries and other issues means that tenants do not have to lose valuable hours in their day waiting for parcels. This is a service that most tenants are willing to pay a higher rent for.

In contrast, the two reports found that gyms, communal facilities, media rooms, and club lounges did not significantly impact the rental paid by tenants. There is very little research available to suggest that occupiers use, or are willing to pay an additional rental for, these facilities in buildings. Unless they have little impact on both the cost of the property and more importantly the service charge, I would simply steer clear of these when purchasing a property.

Costs

Many costs will impact your cash flow. However, there are costs and there are COSTS. You are only going to be able to influence about 20% of the costs that materially impact your income and therefore profit, so just focus on those.

Council rates

Council rates are part of being a landlord, and you will want to own investment properties in areas that are well maintained by the local authority. In some countries, these costs are borne by the tenant, in others by the landlord. It does not matter who pays the costs. Either way, the cost will be factored into the rental equation:

- In countries where the tenant pays the council tax or rates, rents are generally lower to allow for the cost.
- In countries where this cost is borne by the landlord, rents are generally higher to factor in these costs.

You should be concerned about the level of council tax for your particular property relative to others in other council areas. In some situations, the differential can be significant. If the council tax is significantly higher than other options, then this will impact the amount of rent you can achieve, so make sure that these costs are in line with the market, as they are important.

Insurance

Insurance can be expensive, and one of the main reasons for this is that many landlords are over-insured. In other words, they have more insurance than they actually need.

To establish the right level of insurance, the best thing to do is determine what your insurance requirement is and to have multiple insurers quote to provide that level of insurance. Therefore, you should consider the following:

- **Building:** You will only need building insurance if you are the freeholder. If you are not, it will be covered in your service charge or strata fees.

- **Public liability insurance:** This form of insurance is not particularly expensive, and it is worthwhile having, but you will need a realistic estimate of how many people will visit the property. Public liability insurance becomes more expensive if you have high-risk tenant facilities, such as swimming pools and gyms, etc.

- **Contents:** Prepare a detailed inventory of the contents of your property, as even if you let the property unfurnished you will have contents such as carpets, blinds, and other soft furnishings. If you have an inventory, you can ensure that you only get cover for what you need, and that you have cover for all your fit-out.

- **Landlord insurance:** Rental protection insurance and landlord insurance against tenant damage are forms of insurance you may want to consider. In rare situations, you may find that tenants either damage your investment and/or do not pay rent, and you will have costs with both repairs and loss of rental. Particularly for first-time landlords, this can be an important expense to insure against.

If you have a clear idea of what the cost of these items is, and you have a good understanding of what your exposure is, then you will be in a better position to get a competitive set of insurance quotes.

Property agency fees

I believe you should use a property manager for both letting and management. However, I also think you need to get value for money and know what you are getting.

You need to shop around for agents, as the cheapest will not always be the best. Likewise, the most expensive may not necessarily be the best either. You need to ensure both that you are getting what you need from your property manager, and that you are not paying extra for services that should be part of the deal. These are the areas where you should pay particular attention:

- **Inspections:** Your property manager should be undertaking routine inspections, documenting these visits, and sending you the inspection reports. There should be no additional charge for this.

- **Advertising:** You should understand how much you are being charged to advertise your property to let. Some charges are fair, such as for listings on external portals. However, you should not be paying to list your property on the agent's website, to use their email databases, or for them to prepare a simple brochure.

- **Repairs and management:** You should not be paying any cost for coordinating basic repairs and maintenance, or paying a percentage of their value for coordination.

- **Renewals:** You should not be paying a new letting fee if the tenant renews their lease. There may be a minor administration charge, but this should be minimal.

- **Referral fees and mark-ups:** The property manager should not be charging any markups on any services or receiving referral fees from external parties related to activities with your property.

Body corporate and service charges

Body corporate and service charges can be extremely high, so you should consider that when you purchase a strata title or leasehold property. This can be particularly difficult for new-build property because the service charges will be estimates. Things which you need to consider are:

- **Facilities:** Managing facilities can be expensive. Swimming pools, excessive lifts, and cinema rooms are all unlikely to generate more rent, but they can cost you a significant amount of money. Steer clear of properties that have these facilities and leave those properties for owner-occupiers, unless you are very confident that tenants will pay for these services.
- **Ask questions:** You should ask your building/strata manager questions. They are getting paid, so make sure they are doing a good job.

Repairs and maintenance

The cost of minor repairs can become a considerable expense, particularly if you have a tenant who is not able or willing to repair minor niggles, and who wants the property manager to deal with them. The issue with these repair items is that the callout fees will soon add up, and will likely cost more than the work itself.

Work with your property manager to get a preventative maintenance program in place. Have a handyman go to the site annually to deal with maintenance issues, or to visit in between tenants. This will help with long-term tenant retention. Tenants will not leave for an alternative rental if they have a high level of service.

CHAPTER 15

Tax Costs and Benefits

Property investor taxes are one of the largest factors impacting the performance of your property investment. A sound understanding of how taxes work relating to owning and renting residential property is one of the material differences between good and great property investors.

Tax costs and benefits are an important area, and your approach to them will depend on what your strategy is. Broadly speaking, taxes fall into the following categories:

- Stamp Duty and Purchase Taxes
- Capital Gains Tax
- Income Tax
- Estate and Inheritance Taxes

Several things will ultimately drive your view on these taxes:

- Your purpose for purchasing – i.e., capital appreciation or generating an income
- Your view on potential market growth
- The point in the market cycle
- Interest rates

I have been through each of the different taxes in earlier chapters. Here, I simply want to point out some of the key considerations to you.

Stamp duty

Stamp duty can be extremely expensive! Sure, you can offset the cost of your stamp duty against capital gain for CGT, but this is only helpful if you are intending to sell your property.

Below, I have mapped out the effective cost of stamp duty for buying as a foreign investor comparing Australia (NSW), New Zealand, and the UK. I have used USD as the currency to make an effective comparison.

Figure 15.1: International stamp duty comparison ($US)

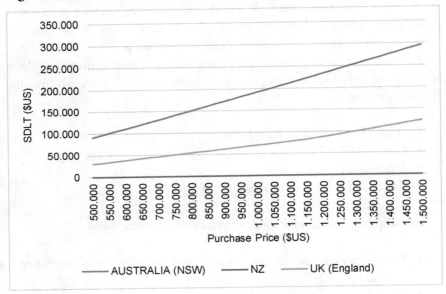

As the graph shows, the cost differential can start to become quite significant, particularly at the higher end of the scale. As an investor, you will need to consider stamp duty in the context of your overall investment objectives. Over the longer term the costs will be eroded, so if you have a long-term investment strategy this will not be an issue. However, if you are purchasing to benefit from short-term growth, you may have a completely different view.

Capital Gains Tax

CGT will only be an issue if you plan to sell. If you never sell, you will never have a capital gains event. So, you need to have a clear plan regarding what you intend to do and where you intend to invest.

If you have a relatively short-term growth plan, CGT will be a major consideration - and places like the UK where your CGT liability is lower are likely to be of more interest. On the other hand, if you have a long-term plan then the ability to depreciate the building in Australia is likely to be a more attractive option.

You should also consider the timing of the sale in countries where CGT is factored into income tax such as Australia and New Zealand. This is because if you generate other income in the year you sell, it will be added to your income and may push the gain from a sale into a higher tax bracket, creating a higher tax burden for you.

For many investors, simply re-financing to withdraw equity may be a more attractive option, particularly if significant gains have been made.

Income tax

Of the different taxes, income tax is the one you need to consider most carefully, as it is likely to be the tax which will have the greatest impact on your investment. You will need to consider:

- **Interest expenses:** Your ability to recover your interest expenses will significantly impact your income tax expense. For long-term investors, countries like Australia and New Zealand will be far more attractive, because of the ability to offset the full cost of interest expenses against your income, thus reducing your tax liability. If you have a short-term outlook and are just looking to buy and trade, this will be less of an issue.

- **Depreciation:** If you have a short-term trading strategy, depreciating your assets will not be an issue. However, if you are buying intending never to sell, you will clearly want to depreciate your assets to the fullest possible extent.

- **Tax brackets:** Having a view of how your income fits into different tax brackets will also significantly impact your net return. If the income your property generates changes your tax banding, it will become a significant tax consideration.

- **Company/trust structure:** If you have no intention of generating an ongoing income from your asset in the medium term, then using a company or a trust to hold the property may make sense. However, this can be complicated, so you need to consider its impact from a long-term perspective.

- **Tax domicile:** You need to consider how your tax domicile impacts your income tax. For some investors, generating income outside of your own country will be taxed as part of your worldwide income.

Estate and inheritance taxes

You will also need to decide from the outset your intention in purchasing your property. If you intend to sell the property during your life, estate planning will not be an issue except if you die prematurely. An issue will then be created with your estate. Regardless of whether you have a will, in some countries where you own property this will create either an estate or inheritance tax liability.

This will not be an issue if you were to purchase a property in either Australia or New Zealand, as there is no inheritance or estate tax in those two countries, and therefore there is no tax liability created. However, in the UK inheritance tax applies.

CHAPTER 16

Capital Appreciation

Capital appreciation should be a material consideration for you as an investor as it will give you greater options, such as releasing excess equity to purchase other investment properties.

Capital appreciation is simply the difference between how much you paid for the property versus its value at a given point in time. Capital appreciation is created in the following ways:

- **Real estate capital appreciation:** How much the property grows in value; and
- **Total purchase price:** Other things being equal, the less you pay in the first place, the greater the amount of that capital you get to keep versus paying to the developer!

We have already covered the total purchase price in Part 2.

As an investor buying property, you should be looking to achieve capital growth. The rate at which your property grows in value will not only increase the equity you have available; it will also have an impact on your ability to use the equity to purchase other property, or simply to use the equity gained as cash for other items by re-mortgaging.

Real estate appreciates for many reasons, the major ones being:

- Economic growth and public confidence
- Interest rates
- Demographics
- Infrastructure investment
- New planning approvals
- Government policies and subsidies; and
- The regeneration of a specific area

Economy and public sentiment

The domestic economy and economic sentiment will have a significant impact on property price growth. The more confident people are, the more comfortable they will feel in their employment prospects and the more willing they will be to purchase a property. The greater the demand, the greater the pressure on prices.

Interest rates

Interest rates have perhaps the largest impact on real estate values. Mortgage costs are typically the highest cost in purchasing a property.

Consider the example of the mortgage payments for Plot 1 Kingsley Tower. If you recall, the monthly mortgage payment was £1,520 per month. However, the vast majority of that was interest, £1,125, whereas only £395 was a repayment of the mortgage.

Over time, a larger percentage of the monthly payment is principal rather than interest, as is demonstrated graphically below. In the figure, the blue represents the interest portion and the red the principal payment.

Figure 16.1: Analysis of monthly mortgage payments

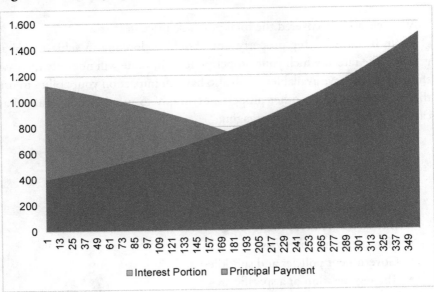

The lower the interest rate, assuming the same length of the mortgage, the lower the monthly payment and the lower the amount of interest paid. Therefore, when interest rates are low, demand for property generally increases as the cost to own property falls.

There is an inverse relationship between interest rates and rental prices, because as interest rates go up, fewer people can afford to buy. Rental prices increase as more people choose to rent than own property, and increased demand increases prices.

Demographics

One of the most notable changes in demographics in relation to real estate pricing is the change in the locations where younger workers and families are moving into. This puts upward pressure on pricing. Conversely, population aging over time can also apply downward pressure on pricing.

The issue with demographics is that major changes can significantly impact property prices for a period of years and even decades, and these changes will take many years or decades to reverse.

As an investor, you need to consider the following factors relating to changes to pricing and values:

- How will demographic changes increase demand for property in a location?
- Who will demand this property?
- What would be the impact on property prices if many people were to move out of a specific location?

Infrastructure investment

New infrastructure being built in a location increases demand for property in that location, because of the additional amenity it creates. There are numerous examples around the world where new infrastructure has increased house prices. For example, the new Crossrail line in London and the HS2 cross-country rail link in the United Kingdom have both had significant impacts on the price of the property that benefits from it.

It is not just large infrastructure projects which will impact value. Smaller, more local improvements, such as light rail extensions, new schools, and upgraded or new roads all impact the desirability of a location. If you consider the three characteristics of land value (physical, institutional, and economic), new infrastructure will change the economic characteristics of a location.

However, the impact of infrastructure investment will not happen at a single point. Generally, much of the value uplift will have taken place at the point of announcement, rather than when new infrastructure is finally delivered.

New planning approvals

Partially linked to both demographic changes and infrastructure investment, as locations become more desirable as residential locations, more and more residential development will take place. This is because as property values increase, potential development land will also become more valuable.

This will ultimately mean that more and more developers will seek to undertake planning applications for re-development. And, as more applications for new planning are made, there will be a corresponding increase in planning approvals. In many scenarios, this will generate a snowball effect, as more and more development takes place.

Government policies/subsidies

Often underestimated is the impact of government policy and subsidies. These are typically used to stimulate a part of the market, or to deter certain groups from participating in the real estate market. The issue for investors is that it is difficult to fully anticipate the impact of various government policies on a real estate market.

Initiatives can include changing tax regimes for certain groups, or giving subsidies to others. The most obvious examples of these are:

- **First home buyer subsidies:** Various subsidies have been introduced to try to help make first homes cheaper for first-time buyers. Many countries have introduced these policies. However, the policies have often had unintended consequences. Many of these changes have driven up values at the lower end of the market at a much faster rate, and as prices have grown at these levels, first home buyers have purchased at inflated prices.

- **Taxes on foreign and second home buyers:** Many countries have introduced measures to make purchasing new property for international and second home buyers more expensive. The theory behind this is that these investors were in a far better position to invest, and that this would therefore level the playing field. These policies have also had unintended consequences, as in practice they have slowed down new development. Ironically, this has put upward pressure on housing, and likewise changed the dynamic of the market. So, investors have simply focused more on the lower end of the market where the tax impacts are lower.

Not only do direct measures impact housing and property markets, but broader measures imposed by governments can equally impact property markets. For example, the decision of the UK population to leave the European Union (Brexit) has had a significant impact on the value of property. Likewise, new trade deals or other stimulants to the economy will do the same.

Legislation is also another factor that can have a sizable impact on property demand and prices. Tax credits, deductions, and subsidies are some of the ways governments can temporarily boost demand for real estate for as long as they are in place. Being aware of current and pending government incentives can help you to determine changes in supply and demand, and to identify potentially false trends.

Regeneration projects

Internal project regeneration is another form of potential capital appreciation. Particularly with larger projects, property developers will typically seek to increase pricing throughout the development process. This will generally account for what is referred to as the 'place making' which has taken place in the development.

The theory behind this is that at the start of a large regeneration project there will be less utilisation for early buyers, as there will be a significant amount of development still to take place. So, owners will have to put up with the disruption of the property development taking place around them. Additionally, many of the services to the development will also not come on stream until later in the development process. So, it is expected that prices will increase as greater utilisation takes place.

CHAPTER 17

Debt Reduction and Management

The use of mortgage debt is an important tool for investors. How to use debt and what it costs are important considerations.

What is a mortgage?

A mortgage is a debt instrument used to purchase real estate. The collateral of the real estate secures the mortgage, and the mortgage is registered against the title of the property.

In a mortgage, the mortgagor (the borrower) agrees to grant a mortgage (a charge on the land) to the mortgagee (the lender). Therefore, the mortgage is an encumbrance (limitation) on the right to the property. This is because the owner would need to pay off the mortgage in order to sell the property.

There are different types of mortgages, and different variables. I have set out the basics below.

Term

The term is the length of the time the capital is borrowed for, and therefore the time in which the capital needs to be re-paid. Typically, mortgage terms range between 25 and 40 years for individuals, but are much shorter for companies at between 10 and 15 years.

For a typical buy-to-let investment for a single apartment or house, mortgage terms are around 30 years. However, for more complex properties such as a block of apartments or less conventional properties, lenders take the view that the properties are riskier and more difficult to sell, and will want to lend investors money for a shorter term.

Loan to Value (LTV)

The loan-to-value ratio (LTV), sometimes referred to as LVR, is the amount of the mortgage expressed as a percentage of the assessed open market value of the property.

Lender requirements vary between different countries depending on where the investor lives and the type of property.

The LVR is an important indicator of a riskier loan. Higher LVR loans are considered riskier due to there being lower amounts of owner equity to absorb any potential declines in the value of the property. Typically, where a borrower has a mortgage with an LVR of higher than 80% they may be required to buy the lenders' mortgage insurance.

Conversely, a mortgage with an LVR of less than 80% is generally considered less risky and would expect to receive a lower interest rate, to account for the lower risk to the mortgagee. However, this is not always the case.

Interest rate

The interest rate is the rate at which the lender is willing to lend money to the borrower, and it will account for the relative risk they are accepting; this will generally reflect the following:

- Borrower's income
- Borrower's credit score
- Value of the property
- LVR
- Term of the mortgage

Interest rates are simply a reflection of the availability and cost of credit to the lender plus a premium for inflation and specific risk. The specific rate on offer reflects the return, in the same way as any other investor would seek a return for their cash.

Most banks will calculate their interest rates relative to a base rate. The base rate is typically the country's base rate or the cost of borrowing money at extremely low risk. Banks then add a risk premium to this base rate to allow for their estimated risk associated with the mortgage. This is often referred to as the 'variable rate', or floating rate.

The variable rate moves up and down in line with the market or a given index. Typically, this will be linked to a benchmark. The variable rate will include a spread to allow for the bank's risk, and is typically expressed as base rate plus that spread, for example the base rate plus 2% (or 200 base points).

In addition to the variable or floating rate, other interest options are available for some mortgages. The two most common are:

- Fixed Rates – whereby the interest rate of the mortgage is fixed for an introductory period such as 2, 5, or 10 years. When the fixed rate ends, the mortgage will revert to the bank's standard variable rate. Fixed rates are set at a premium to the variable rate at the time to reflect the risk the bank is taking. Rates may increase above the variable rate during that period, meaning that the bank could earn less.
- In some scenarios, it is possible to agree caps and collars on an interest rate, whereby a floor and ceiling is set to limit how much the interest rate could fluctuate over the term of the mortgage.

Types of mortgages

There are typically three types of mortgages available.

Repayment mortgage

With repayment mortgages, monthly payments include both an element of interest and payment towards reducing the capital owed. At the end of the mortgage term, the capital borrowed will be completely repaid.

Interest-only mortgage

Interest-only mortgages, as their name suggests, only pay interest on the loan - and nothing of the original amount borrowed. At the end of the mortgage term, the borrower will then have to repay the full loan amount. These mortgages are becoming much harder to obtain as lenders and regulators are worried about investors being left with a huge debt and no way of repaying it, particularly if the property does not increase in value as anticipated. The borrower will generally have to demonstrate a plan for how they will repay the original loan at the end of the mortgage term, such as by selling the property.

Hybrid mortgages

Hybrid mortgages are becoming more common. The most usual version of a hybrid mortgage is called an offset mortgage. These are now common in

Australia and New Zealand. The offset mortgage is a hybrid because it has elements of both repayment and interest-only mortgages.

Offset mortgages are linked to the borrower's savings account to reduce how much interest they are charged. Their savings are not used to pay off the mortgage; instead, they sit in a savings account that pays no interest. Lenders then deduct the amount in the savings account from the mortgage balance and only charge interest on the remaining amount when they calculate monthly payments. For example, if the borrower has a mortgage balance of £150,000 and £20,000 in their savings, they will only be charged interest on £130,000.

This type of mortgage allows borrowers to maintain their savings to use in the future without having to pay down the loan early.

How to use a mortgage

The use of debt is an interesting concept for investment, as on the one hand, debt is a valuable tool and can allow you to quickly expand your property portfolio. However, on the other hand, debt creates additional risk.

Generally, you will want to capitalise on using high levels of debt in the following situations:

- **Low rates:** When interest rates are low, at points in the market cycle when there is expansionary credit, you can lock in lower interest rates. In some scenarios, it may well be better for you to lock in at long-term rates even if they are at higher levels, if you have recognised a risk of rates climbing quickly throughout the fixed term.
- **Expanding portfolio:** If you are looking to expand your portfolio, debt is a useful tool. However, it will reduce your net income as your debt cost are higher. Hopefully, your property will increase in value and will amplify your capital appreciation.
- **Market Growth:** When the market is likely to grow in the early part of the market cycle, debt is a good tool to use to fund property purchases
- **Interest rates are tax-deductible:** When interest is deductable it can be a highly effective tool for investors because its cost can be used to reduce tax liabilities.

- **Amplify returns:** Returns can be amplified with debt because it is the cheapest form of capital, so it can help the investor to obtain a greater return from their equity.

An example of using a mortgage

Let's compare the potential return for an investor purchasing Plot 1 Kingsley Tower with and without a mortgage.

Let's assume that both investments grow by 5% p.a. after five years. In this case, the two alternatives will play out as follows:

Table 17.1: Plot 1 Kingsley Tower comparison of purchasing with or without a mortgage (£)

	Plot 1 Kingsley Tower (with mortgage)	Plot 1 Kingsley Tower (no mortgage)
Purchase Price	400,000	400,000
Initial Equity	100,000	400,000
Growth rate	5% p.a.	5% p.a.
Value after 5 years	486,203	486,203
Capital Appreciation on initial investment	86,203	86,203
Initial Investment	100,000	400,000
Return on Investment	86%	21%

Issues with being too highly leveraged

When appropriately used, leverage can be an effective tool for you to use to increase the return on your investment. The key is to avoid making decisions without proper consideration of your risk. Consider the following:

- **Counting on high levels of capital appreciation:** Many real estate investors assume that what has happened in the past will happen again. Just because property prices have rapidly increased in the past does not mean they will continue to do so in the future. If property prices have rapidly increased, it is unlikely that they will continue on the same trajectory. Hope for high levels of capital appreciation - but do not bank on them. When you plan out your leveraged real estate investments, look at three scenarios: best, worst, and most likely.

- **Ending up with too high a payment:** It can seem like a great investment to buy a property with a very low deposit payment. And it is easy to fall into the trap of looking at the numbers and seeing a high return on investment due to a very low cash outlay. The problem arises with the higher payments that come with higher leverage. For instance, if this is a mortgage, you can count on having to make monthly payments - and the more you borrowed, the higher the monthly payment. Suppose the market softens, or your properties experience higher-than-expected vacancies, or rents are not as high as you expected. In these cases, you could find yourself unable to maintain the higher mortgage payments. If you are unable to make the monthlies, your investment is in jeopardy.

- **Overpaying for a property because you can finance it:** Many investors overpay for a property just because they can afford to purchase a property with very little cash outlay. Do not fall into the trap of paying too much for a property simply because you can get a mortgage. Do your research, and look at the value of the property in the context of current and expected market trends. Paying too much could result in two future issues:
  - When it becomes time to complete, a valuer does not value the property as being worth what you paid. If this happens, you will have to make up the difference
  - Capital appreciation is minimal, or worse still, non-existent. If the market declines, you will be in serious trouble. Your overpriced property will be a significant drag, and you will not be able to sell it without accepting a loss

- **Cash flow is king:** Errors in calculating income or expenses will impact your cash flow. Cash flow is King! If you do not generate enough cash flow each month to pay your expenses, then you will have to top up the payments from your own money.

- **Debt capacity:** Debt capacity is something to which many people will not give a great deal of consideration, but it should be an important factor. Essentially, the more debt you have, the less additional debt you will be able to take on through future borrowing. Whilst loading up on debt may seem like a good idea, it will also mean that you will be restricted in what you can borrow in the future.

- **Increasing interest rates:** Interest rates go down, but they also go up! So, when looking at purchasing property with debt, particularly high levels of debt, you need to consider a situation where rates go up considerably. You need to assess how you can service debt in these situations, as when interest rates increase it is likely because the economy is overheating. So, do not count on putting the rent up or having a tenant.

CHAPTER 18

Currency Gains

Currency is a powerful tool that investors can use to increase their investment returns.

Below, I have set out the historic weekly currency rates for the AUD, GBP, and NZD to the USD between 31 January 1990 and 1 June 2020. You will notice that these currencies have fluctuated significantly throughout this period. Many investors who earn income in USD, or a USD-linked currency such as Asian investors, would have enhanced their return by currency appreciation.

Figure 18.1: Historic currency rates (versus USD)

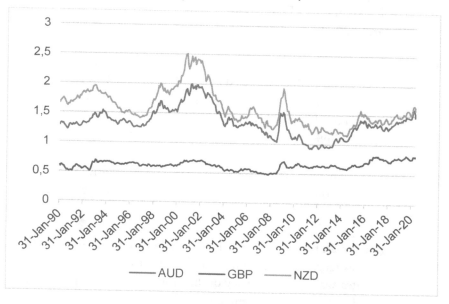

Source, OFX.com

Let me explain how this would work, by considering two different investors:

- Investor 1 - living in New Zealand, earning income in NZD
- Investor 2 - living in Hong Kong, earning HKD (pegged to USD)

For this example, I am assuming that:

- Both purchased the same property on 31 December for $NZD 500,000.
- Both purchased the property with cash.
- Over the same period, property prices grew by 5% p.a. over 12 years.
- On 31 December 2013, the investors sold the property for $NZD 897,000.

The returns achieved would not be the same. They would be as follows:

Investor 1
Purchase Price - $NZD 500,000
Sale Price - $NZD 897,000
Total Capital Gain - $NZD 397,000
Total Return – 79.4%

Investor 2
Purchase Price - $NZD 500,000 (USD 207,922, i.e., @ 1 USD = 2.404739)
Sale Price - $NZD 897,000 (USD 737,031, i.e., @ 1 USD = 1.217044)
Total Capital Gain = USD 529,109
Total Return – 254%

In this situation, the capital gains have been significantly magnified by currency appreciation. However, if investing offshore you need to consider the following:

- **Negative cash flow:** Costs can also be magnified if you need to top up the mortgage due to a rental shortfall. If the currency you earn depreciates against the currency of the property you have purchased, these differences will be magnified.

- **Currency depreciation:** Currencies can be very volatile, so losses can quickly be magnified. However, for patient investors this will be less of an issue, as any currency loss will only be realised at the time you sell. A paper currency loss is simply that.

CHAPTER 19

Ownership Structures

You need to consider the ownership structure for the property or properties you intend to buy.

The issue with property ownership is that if your position suddenly changes and for tax reasons it makes more sense to own the property in a company or trust rather than in your name, then the costs involved may simply mean that the change is not economically viable.

The use of companies and trust structures can be a highly effective way of managing income tax expenses, particularly for those taxed worldwide. For example, consider a scenario where a buyer living in the UK purchases a property in Australia. Because they are subject to income tax on their worldwide income, they would pay income tax on any income generated by their Australian property. However, what makes this situation worse is that because of the difference in the way which investment property is taxed in the UK (covered in Part 4A) they would only receive interest rate relief of 20% rather than being able to offset the full 100% interest which is allowed in Australia.

To avoid this unfair tax situation, they could purchase the property via a company. This would create a scenario whereby they were not generating any income each year. The income would be generated by the company, a separate legal entity. For as long as the income remained with the property, they would not create a personal income tax liability.

However, the use of companies and trusts is highly complex, and can create multiple consequences which you may not have fully considered. You will hopefully have gained a general view as to whether it makes sense to consider these structures from the information set out in this book. However, you will need to seek professional advice from a lawyer and accountant to ensure that everything has been considered.

Part 4B Recap

We have now made it through all the various elements of property investment 101. The final part has been how to drive investment performance.

To drive performance, you first need to understand how to measure it. You will need to master a general understanding of the balance sheet, cash flow, and income statement as they relate to you and your circumstances. Because every investor's objectives and personal circumstances are different, thinking through this really will be the best way for you to decide how to achieve your financial objectives and then track performance.

It is not enough to simply monitor performance; you need to understand how to drive it. There are only six things which will improve the financial performance of your investment:

- Cash Flow
- Tax Costs and Benefits
- Capital Appreciation
- Debt Reduction and Management
- Currency Gains
- Ownership Structure

It is your understanding of these and how you apply each to your investment that will determine your overall financial performance. As you develop your investment strategy, you will need to consider the interplay between these performance factors and your overall objectives, along with the time horizon you set to achieve them.

PART 5

Your Property Investment Strategy

It is now time to use this knowledge and work out your own investment strategy. You need to work out where your strengths are, understand them, and determine your best chance for success. To use the analogy of a cricket test match:

- Don't go after high-risk shots that won't work out. Look at lots of potential investment opportunities, and dismiss those that do not look like good investments.
- If opportunities come up that don't quite meet your objectives, take a good look at them, and if they won't work out, don't try to turn them into a scoring shot; just block them.
- If opportunities come up which are in the zone, go after them and score.

The key is only to go after opportunities where you know there is a high chance of success. The last thing you want to do is make an average opportunity try to work for you. Simply move on. **Only go after properties you know you can win on! Don't worry about letting a lot of investments go; I promise you that the world will not run out of real estate investment opportunities.**

So, how do you develop an investment strategy? Let's take the Six Investment Principles one step further. Given what we have learned, we know they fall into two specific parts:

- Planning & Investment Strategy
- Execution

Planning and investment strategy

You need a plan. The great thing about having a plan is that it does not have to be right or wrong. You simply need a plan to give yourself a starting point for where your investment journey will take you. There is no doubt that your plan and objectives will change over time.

There is one very good reason why you need a plan. If you do not have a plan, you will not understand where your strike zone is for the right type of property. Just like test cricket batsman, you want to make sure you hit the loose delivery and score off it. Buying property is the same: you need to go after the right opportunities because you want to score off them. Otherwise, just like in test cricket, you are likely to go after the wrong delivery and lose your shirt!

It is vital that you have a well-considered plan as to what your investment strategy is, how long you intend to hold property, and for what reason. It's vitally important to understand that your plan may involve multiple phases of growth where you sell and use the income generated to purchase larger assets, etc.

Objectives

What is it you are expecting to achieve? How long do you want it to take? My best advice is to work out where you want to end up, and you can work backwards from there.

Are you looking for a single investment property, or are you looking to build a property portfolio to fund your retirement? There is no right answer to this question. You simply need to give some serious thought to what your long-term objectives are.

Importantly, your objectives need to be realistic. I am sure you will be able to find a million books on property investment and investing which will tell you how to become a millionaire overnight by investing in property. I do not know how to tell you how to do that. In my experience, building a valuable property portfolio will take a lot of hard work, research, and investment of your time. In reality, if you want to build a property portfolio that you can rely on to deliver long-term income, it will take several years or even decades to do that.

Aspects to consider

What are your strengths?

The first part of developing your investment strategy is to determine what your strengths are as an investor. For example, ask yourself:

- Do you earn regular bonuses, which means that you can allocate specific amounts of money at given points in time?
- Are you particularly handy? If so, it may make sense for you to buy an existing property that you can renovate at a very low cost.
- Are you earning your income in a low tax environment?
- Do you have a currency advantage?

Everyone's situation is different. You simply have to determine where your specific skills, knowledge, and inputs to add value are.

The obvious scenario here is younger investors and/or lower-income earners who are trying to determine how they will ever get enough money to invest. For some, sadly, that may not be a reality - but for many, and even most, it will. Maybe you just need to think outside the box. And perhaps the journey might take longer than others. For lower-income earners, two paths might be:

- Club together with friends – you might not be able to afford to buy alone. However, you might be able to club your capital together with friends and be able to invest together.
- Buy in a lower cost market – for investors living in, say, London or Sydney, buying an investment property in their home location may simply not be feasible. However, lower-cost markets might be a great alternative.

Where to invest

Where are you going to invest? Part of this needs to be determined by your strengths, strategy, and how long-term your plan is.

In addition, your circumstances will significantly impact your tax liabilities which arise through the ownership of investment property. Consider the following:

- Australia - if you are an Australian resident (or citizen), you can purchase an investment property in Australia without additional stamp duty expenses. A non-Australian resident would have to pay an additional stamp duty of up to 8%.

- New Zealand - there is no stamp duty for either New Zealanders or foreign purchasers.
- UK - in the UK as a UK resident investor you will pay an additional stamp duty of 3%, and as a foreigner an additional stamp duty of 5%

How many locations you want to invest in will depend on your specific circumstances. My recommendation is that you track more than one market. I recommend that you look to track two different countries, and perhaps three locations in each of those markets.

Many people will feel uncomfortable with investing in other counties. However, there are several reasons why I think you should at the very least track other countries, even if you do not invest:

- Poor decision-making - it is not always a great time to buy in a market. However, you may be able to purchase a property elsewhere. It makes far more sense to invest offshore where there is greater upside potential, rather than simply trying to make a deal work or paying down debt on an existing investment.
- Diversification - it makes a lot of sense to diversify across countries. Different countries and cities move in different economic cycles. Having invested in more than one location provides a higher level of income and growth diversification.

Tax

Tax is an especially important consideration for investors. After your finance costs, it will likely be your largest cost, so you need to consider the tax impact.

For example, suppose you are living in the UK and plan on buying an investment property. In that case, the income generated by the rental income will be taxed as income, and you will not get a significant benefit from offsetting interest expenses. Whereas for an international investor, the income generated by buying in London will likely only pay 20% income tax on the net profit, and if you have a UK passport you will qualify for a £12,500 tax allowance.

An example strategy for those wanting to invest in the United Kingdom may be to focus on short to medium-term trading over periods of growth, rather than a long-term hold, due to the inability to depreciate the asset or recognise the full benefit of tax relief on all of your interest expense.

Length of time

You need to carefully consider the length of time you intend to own property.

In Australia, even though the stamp duty you will pay will be higher as a foreigner, you can depreciate the cost of the building and offset the full cost of the interest expense. However, the costs involved in selling are much higher from a capital gains tax perspective.

In contrast, in the UK the stamp duty will be lower and so will the capital gains tax be in the event of a sale. However, the tax benefits are not as appealing from a long-term ownership perspective as you cannot depreciate the asset or offset the full cost of the finance.

Company versus individual

You should consider the advantages and disadvantages of buying and holding real estate in a company or a trust. Whether or not it makes sense will depend on your circumstances and objectives. Some considerations are likely to include:

- Australia and New Zealand - there is little benefit from a tax perspective in these countries, as the corporate tax rates are 30% and 28% respectively.
- Double taxation - by owning property in a company, you will potentially have to pay more tax if significant profits are generated, as you may end up having to pay both corporate tax on the profit the company generates and income tax on the dividends or salaries the company pays. There are ways to minimise this issue; however, it should certainly be a consideration.

Real estate is cumbersome, and it is expensive to change the ownership of the property. For example, if you want to move from ownership from a company to an individual, you will create a tax liability.

Debt capacity

As you build your investment portfolio, one of the issues you will face as an investor is that of debt capacity. Regardless of the lender, the more property you own in a country, the more difficult it will become to borrow money.

Because banks do not work across multiple countries, the stress testing does not apply across multiple countries. You are likely to have to let banks know about the assets and property you own in other countries. However, in many situations, it will have little bearing on whether they will lend you money.

Currency benefits
Currency benefits can significantly magnify returns. They can also add an extra layer of complexity and risk. However, much of this risk can be mitigated through the fact that your tenants pay rent in the same currency.

What should you do next?
You now need to determine and write down what it is you are looking to achieve. I would suggest that for most people, this will be a certain level of income that they want to generate each year. So, if you are currently earning say USD 100,000 p.a. it may be to generate a net income of USD 100,000 p.a.

Next, you need to determine what property you will need to own to generate that level of income after all of the associated expenses. Because the property is such a good hedge for inflation you do not need to worry about growth rates because broadly speaking rents grow in line with inflation.

Next you need to determine a minimum of 3 markets that you want to focus on based upon the different taxation and ownership regimes. These will change for different people, I have given you a detailed overview of three markets Australia, New Zealand, and the United Kingdom you may want to focus on some cities in these countries or focus on other countries entirely.

Where you choose to focus is up to you. However, as a minimum I suggest you focus on countries for which you can easily determine and obtain the following:

- How property tenure works for domestic and international ownership
- Reliable market data
- Transparent information on taxation

Market information
Now that you have established your target markets, you need to develop your knowledge pool. Not only are you going to seek accurate market data, you will also need accurate information on tax and other regulatory information.

Quality of the information

You cannot make effective investment decisions without having the right information. If you make assumptions or decisions based on inaccurate or misleading information then you are setting yourself up for failure. That would be an expensive lesson in real estate investment!

Importantly, you will need to ensure that you are obtaining high-quality data. One of the biggest problems you will have is that there is a lot of information available. If you are serious about investing and building your knowledge base, you may well find you have to pay for market information. As an investor this is information which you should be willing to pay for; the reality is that collecting this data can be expensive but you should not be unwilling to pay for some of it. The cost of the information may be quite small relative to the impact it has.

When you are considering market data, consider the source. Sure, you can get research reports from agents for free, but how good are they? I can tell you from experience that the property agent market generally has two issues:

- **Transparency:** There is an unwritten rule in big agencies that the research teams do not report anything negative about the market. Therefore, they rarely write something which says the market will go down in value (or down in value significantly).
- **Bias:** As an agent, you know which part of the market you are focused on, i.e., prime, non-prime, etc. You also know where your supply of new instructions will come from. Where do you think your research will focus? And, will it be positive or negative about the area? It is easy to skew and spin research, as if the numbers do not look great then it is easy to talk about growth potential!

What market data to track?

So, what information do you need to track? Well, the reality is, the more the better. The key is not to get information overload, but to understand what the information is telling you. Just remember, you are only really trying to understand:

- What point in the cycle is the market in?
- What is the reality of pricing?
- How is the market changing?

I have set out below what I think is useful market information to keep your eye on.

Demographic and general economic information

Demographic and general economic information will help you to determine the point in the market cycle you are in. Changes in demographics are among the most influential factors in rental growth and property value growth. This information will include:

- **Location demographics:** Average age, income levels, local school quality and ratings, migration patterns, and population growth all have an impact on a real estate market's economic characteristics. Major demographic shifts can have a large impact on real estate trends for several decades.

- **Crime rate:** Safety is a key issue for all tenants. People want to live in a location that feels safe and secure, with low crime rates and strong levels of local policing. Criminality of whatever type will have a significant impact on tenant demand and rental growth.

- **Local economic growth:** Busy retail areas and high streets are good signs of active local economies. New employers are also great at improving growth expectations in a location. Economic growth tends to snowball, so the more growth that takes place, the more investment it will attract.

- **Local amenity:** What types of local amenities are in the area? Local retail, high streets, and commercial areas together with schools, banks, and local food and groceries shops are all important in underpinning local communities.

- **Population growth:** Typically, population growth is a result of other favourable factors, such as a low unemployment rate, an affordable cost of living, entrepreneurship, and access to a wide range of industries, to name but a few. If people are moving to an area, the number of potential buyers and tenants goes up.

- **The ratio of tenants to owners:** The ratio of rentals to owner-occupied homes is interesting to understand. Some areas just have more renters. If you are looking for income property, rental-oriented areas are naturally the best fit. However, if you are looking to trade property, you will want to consider locations that have high levels of home ownership.

Economic data

Numerous government agencies and private research groups produce economic data. While some of this information can be quite heavy going, you will want to follow high-level economic indicators. These provide a great high-level overview of the strength of national and local economies.

- **'Real' Gross Domestic Product (GDP):** The real GDP is the market value of all goods and services produced in a nation during a specific period. Real GDP measures a society's wealth by indicating how fast profits may grow and the expected return on capital. It is labelled "real" because each year's data is adjusted to account for changes in year-to-year prices. The real GDP is a comprehensive way to gauge the health and well-being of an economy.

- **Monetary policy:** Reserve banks use monetary policy to manage economic growth. Lower base rates will mean that the reserve bank is trying to stimulate the economy and generate economic growth, and higher rates will mean that the reserve bank is trying to cool down the economy. You need to monitor the interest rates set by reserve bank monetary policy in your target locations because they will impact mortgage rates, and therefore future values, and drive new developments and economic growth.

- **Consumer Price Index (CPI):** The CPI is a measure of the rate at which consumer goods are increasing (i.e., the inflation rate). It is calculated by tracking the price movements of a basket of goods and services used by an average household in the country. The CPI is a good measure of how much inflation is taking place in a given location, and a good indicator of general economic growth.

- **Consumer confidence survey:** Consumer confidence surveys survey random groups of individuals and ask them a series of questions about their general feelings on a range of broad economic measures, such as consumer spending and growth expectations. The basis of these surveys is that the more confident consumers feel about the current economic situation, the more they are likely to spend, and therefore the more the economy is likely to grow in the future.

- **Unemployment statistics:** The unemployment rate is a good indicator of the general health of the economy. It is assessed by government bodies and typically counts those people who are both not in work, and actively seeking employment. These measures can change between countries. Generally speaking, in most developed economies an unemployment rate at or around 5% is considered 'full' employment.

- **Retail sales figures:** Retail sales figures are data based on a random sampling of a series of retailers. Typically, larger items such as cars are not included in the measure. The measure is a good general indicator of economic confidence.

- **Manufacturing and trade inventories sales:** This data set is the primary source of information on the state of business inventories and business sales. Inventory rates often provide clues to the growth or contraction of the economy. Growth in business inventories may mean that sales are slow, and that the economy's rate of growth is also slowing. If sales are slowing, businesses may be forced to cut the production of goods, and that can eventually translate into inventory reductions.

- **Stock market:** The stock market is also a measure that can be used to gauge future economic performance. The premise is that more people will buy shares in a company if there is an expectation that prices are increasing. Increased demand will increase pricing. However, because some stock markets are broadly traded, such as the US and UK exchanges, they can also be significantly influenced by outside forces.

- **Household debt:** Household debt is defined as the combined debt of all the people in a household, including consumer debt and mortgages. A significant rise in debt has historically coincided with economic issues.

Housing data

As well as tracking demographic and economic data, you will also need to track housing data.

Macro housing data

Macro housing data is generally far easier to obtain than specific sales information, as large statistical groups generally publish it. It will include key housing metrics.

- **Housing requirements:** In most developed economies there is a shortage of housing in major cities. Many countries publish high-level statistics on what these are based on the overall level of supply and demand, together with expectations regarding new demand, including migration. There is good high-level data available in most countries about the volume of new housing that is required to meet demand every year.

- **Housing starts and completions:** These are also an important measure of future pricing and housing trends. How much housing is being built to meet future demand is a highly useful measure. If there is an undersupply of housing and no increase in new supply, then this indicates that pricing will likely stay the same or go up. Conversely, if there is an oversupply of housing and more supply is being delivered, then this will likely have a deflationary impact on house prices.

- **New planning applications and approvals:** There is a significant time lag between planning approval and the delivery of housing. So, new planning applications and approvals are a good leading indicator of supply constraints. However, just because planning approval is granted does not necessarily mean that the developer will build the property immediately.

- **Mortgage approvals:** The number of 'new' mortgage approvals (as opposed to re-mortgages) is an important indicator of housing activity, as it shows the general level of transactions.

- **Average house price to income ratio:** The average income to house price is calculated by dividing average house prices by gross average earnings. This measure is used to gauge the affordability of buying a home in various locations. The great thing about this measure is that it can be used in very specific locations, and can be used to compare different locations and changes over time. As the ratio gets higher fewer people will be able to afford to buy, and vice versa.

- **Mortgage payments as a % of income:** If mortgage payments are high, it is likely that house prices will not grow significantly without growth in real income or outside forces. However, this situation is also likely to indicate that rents may increase.

Pricing and market data

In addition to macro trends, you will want to access specific market data on the market you are looking at; this will include:

- Average Rents
- Average values
- Gross yields

What are these figures for your specific market(s) over a given time? Do not expect to outperform the market, so if you are considering a property wildly above these levels, it is probably not for you.

Taxation

Understanding the taxation systems for the property is important as well as the general trends in what is happening. As you have seen, tax can have a significant impact on your investment return. Tax changes can happen quickly, and can have a significant long-term impact on growth.

Regulatory information

You need to understand the regulatory environment. As a landlord, there will be obligations placed upon you, and you need to stay on top of them. Property managers will be able to assist; however, if you are self-managing your investment there is no excuse not to know - you have accepted that risk by not using an agent.

Breaches of landlord regulations can be very expensive, so one way or another make sure you have given some thought to information about future changes.

Building your network

Good investors have reliable networks that they can call upon to provide a sounding board for decision-making and share knowledge. You too should build your network. Unlike a social network where you mix with your friends, build an investment network where people know that you are connecting with them because you want their knowledge and advice. Likewise, they will want to connect with you too, as you will be a good potential client or referrer of new business.

There are multiple chat rooms and investment forums that you can get involved with to start developing your network. Importantly, do not forget the virtual parts of your network. Personal connections are great, but so too are virtual networks. In a post-COVID world, technology will continue to be of far greater importance than ever before in all manner of ways, including how we communicate with one another.

Below, I have set out some of the different resources you should consider in developing your network:

- **Property investment platforms:** It would be remiss of me not to promote my own business! There are many websites out there that provide access to high-quality real estate data, analysis, and investment tools. I think ours is the best, but you can decide for yourself. Visit our website at www.duvalglobal.com

- **Blog sites and chatrooms:** There are many good blog sites and chat rooms that talk about real estate and real estate investment. They are a great resource for you to use on your journey into property investment. There are many blog sites that you can join and subscribe to; I suggest you look around at what you are interested in. Again, follow our platform at **www.proptechpioneer.com**

- **News feeds:** Many news outlets have dedicated real estate news feeds which are worth looking at and reviewing. Likewise, there are other less well-known trade journals, such as the Estates Gazette or Property Week in the UK, or the Australian Property Investor. You may not want to pay for all of these, but most will send you their daily news feeds for free; even if you cannot access the stories, it is a great way to get a sense of property news.

- **Property portals:** Most countries have property portals where agents can promote property for sale.

- **Accountants:** You should know at least one accountant who can help you with preparing tax returns and give you some insight into the impact of various decisions. Tax is now a major consideration for those who want to be investors.

- **Lawyers:** A lawyer will be able to help you with the ins and outs of being able to purchase, and what is required. It would be great if the lawyer is familiar with the country you are looking to invest in. However, even if the lawyer is not familiar with the jurisdiction you are looking to invest in, they may be able to give you useful insights into how contracts work, and some avoidable issues.

- **Property manager:** You need to get to know a good property manager. You need to have someone who is dealing day-to-day with tenants, and who have their finger on the pulse. They will know what is required.

- **Agent:** You should have a network of property agents to talk to; all will be happy to meet and talk to you. You will find that you will be far better off talking to several agents rather than just one, to form your consensus. When you speak with agents, you need to remember that their impression of the market is limited to the buyers and sellers they come across, so the more of them you can speak with, the broader the view you will get. Do not just rely on one agent.

- **Other investors:** Of course, you will also benefit greatly from talking to other investors.

Execution

Now that you have planned your strategy, how do you execute it? You know what you want -execution is all about getting the right deal!

What is your risk?

You need to re-think the way you purchase property off-plan. The equation and thinking involved are not the same as buying a property in the secondary property market:

- **Second-hand:** There is a lot less risk involved in buying a second-hand property. Because of this, your risk-reward equation is completely different. Sure, you have the risk that something will go wrong with the building, or the rent does not work out to be what you expected. However, because the property already exists, there is an expectation that you have mitigated this risk and therefore will not be rewarded for the risk. Therefore, the only growth you should expect will simply be market return - which will be in line with the rest of the market.

- **New-build:** With a new-build, you are accepting a significant amount of both market risk and the construction risk of the developer as well as your own financial risk. There is absolutely nothing wrong with this. However, you need to consider how you are being rewarded for the risk you are taking. Risk should come with a reward, and you need to balance the advantages of buying a new-build against second-hand property.

We have already talked about the developer's risk in PART 1. But, what about your risk? The reality is you have several forms of risk to consider, which are:

- **Market Risk** - the market may change during the construction period, meaning you ultimately pay too much.

- **Mortgage Risk** - there is no guarantee you will get a mortgage, or get one on the terms you expected.

- **Construction Risk** - there is a risk that the construction may be delayed, or you might not get the property you bargained for.

- **Insolvency Risk** - there is a risk that the developer may go bankrupt, in which case you may or may not get all your money back.

In buying off-plan it is impossible to completely mitigate these risks, because the property you are buying simply does not yet exist. So, you need to accept that you are taking these risks.

Getting the best deal

What can you do to maximise your position in negotiations and get the best deal, and how can you drive portfolio performance?

Leveraging risk

You should accept that whatever happens, in buying off-plan you are taking a risk. How much is this risk worth? Well, it does not matter how much it is worth, it's about how you leverage it. You leverage risk by reducing the developer's risk and then seeking to be compensated for your own risk. How do you do this? By focusing on where their risk is.

- **Buying point in the sales cycle:** As an investor, your greatest advantage is that you can buy at any point in the sales cycle. And the developer's risk is highest at two specific points in the sales cycle:
  - At the very start of the sales campaign, when they need to sell the property to meet their pre-sales targets;
  - Post-completion if they still have apartments and they need to sell them.

These are the two points in the sales cycle when you have the greatest negotiating leverage, so you should target these points in time.

- **Developer type:** Think about who you are buying a property from, and where their pain points are. A smaller developer like the example we used may be constantly under pressure to sell, so you may always have a lot of negotiating leverage. In contrast, a larger developer may not be worried about further sales if they have met their pre-sales targets. Therefore, you will probably only be able to maximise your position at the end of financial quarters or the end of the financial year in the latter case.

Specification

See if you can reduce the specification so you can get a better deal. Most tenants are unlikely to pay more for a higher specification, so why shell out the cash for it if you don't have to?

Additionally, why buy a property if all the tenant amenities will add significant costs to the purchase price and your running costs?

Market access costs

You need to think about what *you* need to make a purchasing decision. How you need to consume information about a property will directly impact your additional costs in purchasing a property.

There is absolutely nothing wrong with buying a property via an exhibition or sales event. However, keep in mind that there is a cost involved in doing that. So, if you need to have a coffee table brochure, a full exhibition experience, and augmented reality to get your head around the property you will buy, there is a cost to that. As the consumer of that information, one way or another, you will need to pay for it.

An alternative way of thinking about it is this:

- Buy in a good market where there is a high level of protection for consumers
- Buy from a developer with a good track record of delivery
- Make sure the contract affords you enough flexibility.

A significant amount of cost is built into marketing budgets, so if you can find a way to digest and understand the property without all of the costs involved, you should share these savings with the developer.

Buying in Bulk

Do not underestimate the power of buying in bulk! Ideally, you should try to find ways to bring together groups of other buyers or friends to purchase with you. Bulk investors typically get discounts in the region of 10 - 20% off the market price.

Final thoughts

I want to leave you with a few final thoughts which you should consider as you hopefully build and develop a successful investment strategy.

Purchasing

As you start looking at opportunities and consider purchasing an investment for the first time or purchasing another property, give some thought to the following:

- **Only go after the right opportunities:** You can look at as many properties as you like, but just like my test cricket analogy, you should only swing at the ones you can score on. It does not matter if you do not buy a property you have considered. There will be many other opportunities in the future. Your return will be impacted forever by the decisions you make when you buy. So, if you cannot get the right deal, move on and find something else.

- **Focus on performance, not size:** There's no prize for just owning a lot of property - it's easy to buy property if you just pay more than anyone else. However, there is a difference between a well-performing property portfolio and one which is simply big. Buy, manage well, and drive performance.

- **Understand what motivates your seller:** If you have a large, listed developer, they are going to do a better deal when their risk is highest. Buy at quarter dates, before launch, or at the end of the financial year. Think about the buyer spectrum in terms of where you want to end up.

- **Develop a financial model where you can review your property purchase:** I have shown you how to track the financials, so either use a system that allows you to do this or build your own model in Excel.

- **Buy at the right point in the cycle:** If the market is at the top of the cycle, then the only way for things to go is down. If the timing is not right, either wait or look to other markets where the risk/reward profile is better.

- **Do not set a timeframe:** You cannot set a day and time to buy - simply have a plan, know your strike zone, and wait. Do not be too anxious to invest, as you will ultimately suffer from this approach.

- **Be realistic:** It will take several years to develop and implement your plan. People telling you that it can be done quickly are trying to sell you something!

- **Stress-test your purchase:** Things go wrong, so stress test assumptions in a financial model. Do not simply assume that everything will go right - things do not always go to plan.

- **Use your network:** If you have questions, ask your network and don't make decisions blind or be afraid to ask stupid questions.

Operating your portfolio

As you go through and build your portfolio, make sure you track and operate well:

- Record keeping - records are useful for tax, but also as a quick reference.
- Cost Management - keep one eye on costs, and do not make the fatal mistake of underestimating them.
- Track Performance - make sure you track your performance; it will help you understand what has worked and what has not, as you are not going to get everything right.

Thank you

Finally, thank you for purchasing a copy of my book. I hope that the information and insights in this book help you on your future investment journey. If you have any thoughts or feedback, I would love to hear from you at my blog **www.proptechpioneer.com**.

Best wishes
Ashley Osborne
Analyse, **Invest**, and **Prosper**.